90 0225261 8

KW-491-586

MODERN LEGAL STUDIES

FRONTIERS OF CRIMINALITY

v

AUSTRALIA
The Law Book Company
Brisbane • Sydney • Melbourne • Perth

CANADA
Ottawa • Toronto • Calgary • Montreal • Vancouver

AGENTS
Steimatzky's Agency Ltd., Tel Aviv;
N.M. Tripathi (Private) Ltd., Bombay;
Eastern Law House (Private) Ltd., Calcutta;
M.P.P. House, Bangalore;
Universal Book Traders, Delhi;
Aditya Books, Delhi;
MacMillan Shuppan KK, Tokyo;
Pakistan Law House, Karachi, Lahore

MODERN LEGAL STUDIES

FRONTIERS
OF
CRIMINALITY

edited by

IAN LOVELAND

*Professor of Law at
Brunel University*

LONDON
SWEET & MAXWELL
1995

Published by
Sweet & Maxwell Limited of
South Quay Plaza,
183 Marsh Wall,
London E14 9FT

Phototypeset by LBJ Enterprises Ltd of
Aldermaston and Chilcompton
Printed in England by Clays Ltd, St. Ives plc

A CIP catalogue record
for this book is available
from the British Library

ISBN 0 421 526300

No natural forests were destroyed to make this product:
only farmed timber was used and re-planted

ACKNOWLEDGMENTS

The chapters in this volume were initially presented as seminars in Queen Mary and Westfield College's 1993 Faculty Seminar Series. My roles as co-ordinator of the seminar series, and subsequently as editor of this collection, have been both enlightening and informative. My thanks are owed to all of the contributors, not simply for producing their own chapters, but also for attending other sessions in the series and thereby fostering a degree of corporate analysis which is perhaps often lacking in edited collections of this kind. I should at this juncture single out Niki Lacey for special thanks, both for her constant support for the project and for the unerring prescience and cogency of her advice and opinions.

I would also like to take the opportunity to express my gratitude to those of my colleagues at Queen Mary who lent their support to the series, especially Bill Swadling, Ian Yeats, Genevra Richardson, and not least Professor Hazel Genn, whose personal enthusiasm, and control of the Department's limited financial resources, made the project possible.

LIST OF CONTRIBUTORS

Lois Bibbings is a Lecturer in Law at the University of Bristol.

Alison Firth is a Senior Lecturer in Law at Queen Mary and Westfield College, London University.

Nicola Lacey is a Fellow of New College, Oxford.

Ian Loveland is a Lecturer in Law at Queen Mary and Westfield College, London University and Professor Elect of Law at Brunel University.

Wayne Morrison is a Lecturer in Law at Queen Mary and Westfield College, London University.

Tony Richardson is a Lecturer in Law at the University of Sheffield.

Colin Scott is a Lecturer in Law at the London School of Economics.

Peter Vincent-Jones is a Principal Lecturer in Law at Sheffield Hallam University.

Matthew Weait is a Lecturer in Law at Birbeck College, London University.

Celia Wells is a Reader in Law at Cardiff Law School, University of Wales.

PREFACE

by Ian Loveland

As Nicola Lacey suggests in her introductory chapter to this volume, "crime" is very much taken for granted as a concept in the teaching of criminal law. In many law schools, students' attention is directed almost exclusively to a series of technical rules within a bounded rationality which rarely pauses to ask why certain forms of behaviour should be subject to state imposed penalties. If such questions are posed, they are often dispatched in a desultory way, with reference to undefined and unexplored notions of "individual rights" or "the public interest". Alternatively, within the context of jurisprudential analyses of the legitimate extent of criminal sanctions, debate is located at a particularly rarified, cross-cultural, and hence very loosely contextualised level. The debate between Devlin and Hart on the inter-relationship between crime and societal moral values is perhaps the best example of this genre, in that it exemplifies the pursuit of generalised truths at the expense of practical explorations of the minutiae of empirical experience.

Frontiers of Criminality is designed to fill this particular gap in the criminal law syllabus by focusing attention at a detailed, empirical level on "the why and the how"—or as Lacey refers to it, the "contingency"—rather than "the what", of the criminal law. The book thus bears some resemblance to the series of essays in McLennan, Fitzgerald and Pawson's 1981 collection, *Crime and Society*. However, while that volume ranged over a wide historical and geographical terrain, most of the subjects chosen for this study have all been the subject of recent and often intense controversy. They are also all firmly linked by two thematic concerns, each of which is central to the questions that Nicola Lacey raises—why and how does behaviour become or stop being criminal?

The contributors to this volume are not exclusively criminal lawyers; some have been drawn towards an analysis of those particular aspects of the criminal law which play a significant role in their own individual specialisms. In her introductory chapter, Nicola Lacey employs the metaphor of the "lens" to illustrate the potentially multi-faceted nature of the ostensibly "given" character of crime. Far from being an "objective truth", the nature of crime varies profoundly according to the identity and viewpoint of the observer, and according to the "visual aids", be they political, economic or cultural in nature, which the observer willingly or unwittingly employs. Such a divergence of perception is to a degree built into the structure of this collection simply because notions of criminality are for many contributors a subsidiary or tangential element of their normal specialisation.

The essays are also shaped by an implicitly comparative perspective which is perhaps best labelled as emanating from a broadly defined notion of public law. In most western democracies, the existence of a supra-legislative constitution which delineates the fundamental principles of citizen-state relations lends an explicitly constituent character to many aspects of criminal law, in both the procedural and substantive dimensions. Debates as to the creation of new criminal laws, or the abolition of existing ones, are consequently joined simultaneously not simply at the level of efficiency or practicality, but also at the level of legitimacy. The constitution of the United States is perhaps the most obvious example. In the procedural sense, the search and seizure provisions of the Fourth Amendment, the rule against self-incrimination found in the Fifth Amendment, and the rights to counsel and trial by jury in criminal matters contained in the Sixth Amendment, are as familiar to constitutional as to criminal lawyers in the United States. In a substantive vein, the requirements of proportionality in punishment imposed by the Eighth Amendment, and the outright prohibition by the First Amendment of many efforts to criminalise certain forms of expression, demand a similar cross-fertilisation between the teaching and practice of criminal and constitutional law. The "constitutional" character of crime is far more opaque in this country as a result of Parliament's legislative sovereignty. However, this does not mean that character is absent, and the twin themes which pervade this book do much to draw it into the open.

The first theme focus on the role and nature of "the state" in criminalisation and decriminalisation processes. The second, often inter-related issue, is the variegated nature of the distinction between the "public" and "private" spheres of individual, group, and corporate behaviour. This concern embraces not simply whether behaviour should be regulated at all, but whether such regulation is best achieved through the ostensibly public mechanism of a criminal prosecution, or the apparently private vehicle of civil litigation, or through entirely informal processes of economic and social interaction.

It is a commonplace, but overly simplistic assumption that crime marks an unambiguous boundary of accepted behavioural standards, constructed and policed by a monolithic state which legitimises its action by presenting itself as the transmitter of pervasive societal values. This perception enjoys particular cogency in British political discourse because of our country's constitutional structure—in a unitary state with a sovereign legislature there is no obvious scope for intra-national variations in the definition of crime.

However, examination of particular activities suggests that the *state qua* definer and enforcer of the criminal law is often a highly fragmented structure; and as such the legitimacy of given definitions may be problematic. The United Kingdom's membership of the (now) European Union has lent an explicitly extra-territorial dimension to the substance and administration of many areas of criminal activity, as has, to a lesser extent, our accession to the European Convention on Human Rights. To a degree, therefore, criminality acquired an international character.

But even within the United Kingdom's borders, the notion of an homogeneous, pervasive criminal law is quite misleading. In one sense, fragmentation may arise because a formally unitary state has a long tradition of pluralism between different levels of government; thus local authorities might promote geographically specific bye-laws designating certain activities as petty crimes, or may apply different interpretations to the enforcement of criminal legislation defined in discretionary terms. Such variation is broadly perceived as legitimate. One says broadly here, not simply to acknowledge diffuse dissent within British society as a whole, but also in recognition of the distinctive legal and cultural tradition of the Scots nation towards matters of criminality. This is a tradition which, as several of the papers in this volume suggest, may lend both the procedural and substantive characteristics of the criminal law appreciably different forms north and south of the border.

Leaving aside, for the moment, the issue of Scots autonomy within Britain's constitutional order, the taken for granted legitimacy of the criminal law becomes more elusive as one considers increasingly expansive definitions of "The State". The efforts of the Thatcher and Major administrations to "privatise" many of the functions previously performed by explicitly governmental bodies clearly demands that any functionalist view of "government" now includes institutions whose public character would not have been self-evident even 20 years ago. As many of the contributions in this volume will suggest, such private agencies now play a substantial part in the governance of criminality. But it will also be suggested that definitions of "The State" can quite plausibly be extended further still into the ostensibly private sphere. Several chapters in this book advert to the role of pressure groups and the extra-governmental mobilisation of "public sentiment" through the mass media in influencing legislative or executive behaviour. Others find even more informal manifestations of "state action" in the ideological predispositions of small groups or even private individuals to impose sanctions on others as a result of the latter's presumed "criminality". In so doing, this collection makes a further contribution to the now substantial literature outlining the extraordinary complexity of the modern democratic state.

A striking illustration of *de jure* fragmentation within official state structures is provided by Richardson's study of the War Crimes Act, which explores notions of constitutionalism within the construction of criminality. The War Crimes Bill, which premises its claim to legitimacy on principles of international law, was twice rejected by the House of Lords even though it had attracted bipartisan support in the House of Commons. The Bill was therefore passed under the provisions of the Parliament Acts 1911 and 1949, a constitutional mechanism which had never been used (and arguably had never been intended to be used) to define criminal behaviour. The War Crimes Act also envisages an extension of the public sphere beyond hitherto accepted categories by targeting individuals who were neither British citizens nor within British territory when the supposed "crimes" were committed. In assessing criminal legislation which is both retrospective and extra-territorial, and thence constitutionally entirely unconventional, Richardson's paper raises a crucial question— are there no limits to the frontiers of criminality which may be staked out in a democratic society?

Richardson's critique is tellingly juxtaposed with Bibbings' analysis of the treatment meted out to conscientious objectors in the First and Second World Wars. In tandem, the two papers make it clear that our society apparently suffers no conceptual difficulty in attaching criminal sanctions both to an individual's excessive enthusiasm for war and her/his outright refusal to engage in it. Bibbings also highlights the sudden ruptures that political crisis can impose on traditionally accepted notions of the distinction betwen the "public" and "private". The introduction of conscription in 1916 was premised on the assumption that public morality compelled individuals to forego all control over their bodily autonomy—to place their lives at risk in defence of the "public interest"—and so accept that there were no inviolable spheres of private autonomy which lay beyond state regulation.

Bibbings also charts the myriad ways in which behaviour which Parliament has not formally designated as criminal may nevertheless attract sanctions, from both governmental and private sources, of an extremely severe and pervasive nature, which are effectively imposed without the procedural protections which the "accused" might expect from a criminal trial.

A less overt but similarly important fragmentation is frequently evident in the legislative process leading up to the classification or declassification of given behaviour as criminal. The capacity of pressure groups or corporate interests to shape policy formation within government is in itself, of course, indicative of a blurring between the public and private spheres. Wells' study of corporate manslaughter provides insight into the way in which powerful commercial interests have fought a successful defensive action, both in the courts and within the legislative process, to prevent a reform which would threaten business interests. This has been achieved despite persistent and vocal "public pressure" articulated in the mass media for a radical law reform, an outcome which might be thought to cast serious doubts on the legitimacy of state inaction, in so far as such legitimacy is assumed to derive from accurate reflection of popular sentiment. Wells also draws attention to the criminal law's evident incapacity to find the ingredients of "crime" in a multi-faceted, long term, process of corporate behaviour, even though the adverse consequences of such "risk taking" behaviour are both severe and entirely visible.

The sometimes perplexingly disparate impact of pressure group activity on the initial definition and subsequent enforcement of new forms of criminal liability is cogently revealed by Firth's chapter on the criminalisation of offences against intellectual property. In addition to exposing the limited capacity of traditional criminal law concepts to accommodate the rapidly changing nature of "property" in era of continuous and breathtaking technological advance, Firth also draws attention to the fluidity of the public-private divide by assessing the inter-relationship of the criminal and civil law in this field, and suggests that it is only when the latter becomes an inconvenient tool that property holders regard extension of the former as a desirable option.

Weait's analysis of the Serious Fraud Office uncovers a similar, but far more diffuse, process at work at a *de facto* rather than *de jure* level. Serious financial fraud was not only identified as a distinct form of crime in the early 1980s, it was also criminalised in an institutional sense, through the creation of a similarly distinct prosecuting agency supposedly equipped with sufficient expertise to secure convictions in this complex and esoteric area

of the law. In charting the Serious Fraud Office's evident failure
to achieve this objective. Weait finds common cause with Wells'
chapter in identifying the difficulties of attaching criminal status
to complex and continuing corporate processes. The case study
also suggests that substantive changes in the criminal law must be
accompanied by facilitative reforms to criminal law procedure.
Such reform is however problematic, for, albeit in a less draconian sense than the one adverted to by Richardson in respect of
the War Crimes Act, effective procedural reform in this area
raises substantial questions about the "accused's" entitlements to
due process.

Scott's chapter complements those of Weait and Wells by
assessing the role of powerful corporate interests in shaping the
scope and form of constraints on commercial autonomy in
relation to the law governing consumer protection. The pervasive
fragmentation problem is further complicated in this context by
the increasingly interventionist role played by European Community law in the consumer protection field. Scott also echoes
Firth's chapter by focusing on the question of the degree to which
crime is defined not by the intrinsic undesirability of given
behaviour, but by the extent to which such behaviour is being
adequately controlled through civil law mechanisms. The question of whether behaviour should be regulated through the
criminal or civil law is clearly a recurring manifestation of the
public/private divide. However, Scott suggests that this problematic issued is rendered more complex in consumer protection
issues by ongoing debates pertaining to the *de jure* construction
of a distinct category of regulatory malfeasance. Such behaviour
appears criminal in so far as "prosecution" is undertaken by state
authorities, but seems more akin to civil liability in terms of the
limited moral opprobrium attached to "conviction". In exploring
the implications that the emergence of regulatory crime has for
the clarity with which criminality is defined, Scott also returns to
the relationship between substance and procedure which is prominent in the chapters by Richardson and Weait.

The recent phenomenon of female victims of sexual crimes
employing private prosecutions following prosecuting agencies'
refusal to act lends a further dimension to arguments concerning
the respective rights and obligations of the citizen and the
government in imposing legal sanctions on proscribed behaviour.
Zedner pursues this theme by assessing recent changes in the law
of marital rape. The criminalisation of this action represents a
significant extension of the State's power to regulate the hitherto
"private" relationship of sex within marriage, an extension which

is in large part justified because it protects the private sphere of individual sexual autonomy. Marital rape again reveals the fragmentation of the State apparatus in defining the boundaries of criminality, in that reform was introduced through amendment to the common law rather than by statute, a process which (*pace* the War Crimes Act) has been portrayed as constitutionally illegitimate because of its *de facto* retrospective effect, and which is now (like the investigatory powers of the Serious Fraud Office) the subject of an action under the European Convention on Human Rights. Zedner's exploration of the shifting boundaries of criminality in sexual relationships also reprises the problems addressed in Bibbings' chapter raised by alterations in accepted notions of the State's right to regulate its citizens' bodily autonomy.

Similar issues of individual freedom and majoritarian morality are explored in Morrison's survey of governmental responses to drug usage. Morrison's chosen subject is perhaps unique among this collection in addressing behaviour about which there is little evidence of intra-state fragmentation as to its undesirability *per se*, although there is clear regional variation in the vigour of enforcement policies. The debate surrounding the criminalisation of drug use does however present an extremely complex cartography of the legitimate boundaries of public control of private autonomy. One can discern for example an apparently perverse respect for the drug user's private autonomy in the State's evident preference for addressing the "problem" by cutting off supply rather than attempting to reduce demand. But this co-exists with the constant refusal of state authorities to accord legitimacy to arguments that much drug use is a victimless activity indulged in by mentally competent adults which has no intrinsic adverse effects for non-users, a refusal which clearly elevates governmentally defined notions of the public interest far above considerations of individual choice.

The collection concludes with Vincent-Jones' critique of changes to the law on squatting in the post-war era. "Squatting" is a misleadingly uniform label for a particularly fragmented collection of criminal offences and civil wrongs. Squatting is undertaken by diverse individuals, for a variety of reasons, against a range of publicly, individually and corporately owned properties. Despite the mass media's periodic campaigns calling for pervasive criminalisation of unlawful occupation of property, the attachment of punitive sanctions to squatting remains a particularly haphazard activity, at the levels both of formal definition and practical enforcement.

As suggested above, the purpose of this series of essays is to disabuse law students and other readers of the notion that a

criminal lawyer's concern with crime should begin and end with
ascertaining whether a given state of mind and course of
behaviour fall within a defined boundary of proscribed conduct.
An informed understanding of the role played by the criminal law
in modern society demands that one considers not simply why
and how specific laws have been broken, but also why and how
they were initially constructed.

Nicola Lacey concludes her introduction by wondering if
criminal law might best be seen as an offshoot or perhaps even
sub-discipline of public law. As suggested earlier in this preface,
such a perspective would be an unremarkable observation to
criminal lawyers in the United States, where questions of criminal
process, punishment, and substantive offences themselves are
frequently addressed explicitly as matters of constitutional law.
While the House of Lords has latterly begun to look towards
American jurisprudence as a guide in assisting the development
of ambiguous areas of the common law, there is little immediate
prospect in this country of the kind of peaceful revolution which
will see the doctrine of Parliamentary Sovereignty replaced by a
supra-legislative constitutional framework in which the inter-
relationship between political liberty, private property and the
reach of the criminal law is made explicit. Nevertheless, the
increasing convergence of our domestic legal system with the
principles espoused by the European Union and the European
Convention on Human Rights suggest that the constitutional
rather than simply technical complexities of the criminal law will
become more apparent in future years. The modest ambition of
this collection of essays is to shed a little more light on this
particular feature of contemporary British society.

CONTENTS

TABLE OF CASES

TABLE OF STATUTES

TABLE OF EUROPEAN LEGISLATION

Chapter One

CONTINGENCY AND CRIMINALISATION
by Nicola Lacey[1]

Within undergraduate law courses, criminal law is often taught as a first year subject. The thinking behind this seems to be that criminal law has certain advantages in terms of both capturing students' interest and prompting their understanding. The supposed advantage consists in the familiarity of the ideas of crime and criminalisation. Students approach the subject with a sense that they already understand the basic nature of the enterprise. Indeed, the proscription of criminal behaviour forms, for many people, a stereotype of what law is all about. But, from the point of view of intelligent teaching and studying, the advantage all too often becomes a disadvantage. For the very common-sense familiarity of crime leads us to leave the notions of 'crime' or 'criminality', and in particular the ways in which the 'frontiers of criminality' are determined through practices of 'criminalisation', under-analysed.[2]

The tendency to take the idea of 'crime' for granted is probably exacerbated by the usual pattern of teaching criminal law in isolation from the sociology of deviance, which, in contrast to orthodox criminologies, reflects directly not only on patterns of offending behaviour but also on the social and political factors

---

[1] I should like to thank Liz Frazer, Ian Loveland, Andrew Sanders, Celia Wells and Lucia Zedner for their thoughtful comments on an earlier draft of this Chapter.

[2] The choice of terms in which to frame the arguments about 'criminalisation' is a difficult one. In particular, the terms 'crime' and 'criminality' are problematic. The idea of 'crime' resonates with an extra-legal notion of wrongdoing, sometimes evoked by criminal lawyers in the phrase *mala in se;* that of 'criminality' has been used within positivist and socially determinist criminologies which identify it with a natural, or socially produced but fixed, predisposition to break prevailing criminal norms. In the context of the present collection, the terms are used merely to refer to conduct which is interpreted as breaching socially constructed criminal laws. The questions raised by this usage will be subject to more detailed scrutiny as the argument proceeds. But in order to keep the constructionist assumptions which underlie my use of the term 'criminality' and the phrase 'frontiers of criminality' firmly in view, I shall continue to place them within single quotation marks.

which underpin them.[3] Furthermore, most criminal law courses pay scant attention to the broader criminal justice practices, such as policing, prosecution or sentencing, which are an integral part of how the 'frontiers of criminality' are constructed in any society. The idea that the 'frontiers of criminality' are interesting, or even problematic, is further obscured by the focus of most criminal law courses on a set of standard offences, which themselves confirm, rather than challenge, the familiar, stereotyped view of crime already referred to. The political and sociological questions raised by these offences are suppressed by their formulation in terms of legally, rather than socially, driven categories (for example, around particular pieces of legislation — the Theft Act rather than 'shoplifting' — or legal conceptions — 'murder' or 'manslaughter', rather than 'killing' or 'causing death'). The selection itself is rarely subjected to critical scrutiny, or even thought to call for explicit justification.

The argument of this chapter (as indeed of all the Chapters in this book) is premised on the belief that this under-analysis of the ways in which the boundaries of criminal law and criminal enforcement are constructed constitutes a serious intellectual weakness in contemporary pedagogic and scholarly treatment of criminal law. I take as my starting point the recognition that the 'frontiers of criminality' are contingent; that is, they might have been, and might be, other than they are. Given this contingency, any genuinely critical approach to crime and criminal law must include an attempt to confront and understand how their boundaries are constructed and managed — how they shift, who or what determines shifts or resistance to change. Criminal law scholarship, as much as criminology, needs to learn to escape its implicit reliance on the idea of crime as a 'given', and to subject references to 'crime', 'criminality', 'criminalisation' and even 'criminal law' to critical scrutiny. Only if it does so can it begin to address the question of whether there are any practical or normative limits to criminalisation in a moderately democratic polity such as Britain, and what the shape of these limits might be.

In this chapter, my principal aim is to raise and briefly discuss what I see as the main questions which have to be addressed by

---

[3] See, *e.g.* Cohen S. *Folk Devils and Moral Panics* (1972), Taylor I., Walton P., and Young J., (eds.), *Critical Criminology* (1975); Smart C., *Women, Crime and Criminology* (1976); Carlen P. and Collison M. (eds.) *Radical Issues in Criminology* (1980); Box S., *Deviance, Reality and Society* (1981); Gelsthorpe L. and Morris A. (eds.), *Feminist Perspectives in Criminology* (1990).

those of us who teach and study criminal law, if we are to confront the intellectual challenge posed by the contingency of crime and criminalisation. This discussion is intended to set the scene for the following Chapters, which deal with a range of concrete practices and hence provide varied contexts in which to consider some of the theoretical questions which I shall raise. However, I also want to make some general suggestions about the role of theory, explanatory and normative, in helping us to understand and come to terms with both the contingency of 'criminality' and the diversity which characterises actual practices of criminalisation. Contributions to criminological, sociological and criminal law scholarship which do address the contingency of criminalisation have often found themselves involved in something of a contradiction. On the one hand, a careful analysis of practices of criminalisation directs our attention to extraordinary diversity, complexity and fragmentation, at both substantive and procedural levels. This fragmentation seems to tell against the utility of any general normative theorising about the 'frontiers of criminality'. On the other hand, many scholars are also concerned to engage in political critique of the practices of criminalisation, and in particular to develop arguments about the over-extensiveness of criminal regulation, or the biases inherent in its conceptualisation or enforcement.

Clearly, the kinds of general normative theories exemplified by the famous debate between Hart[4] and Devlin,[5] or even the more detailed characterisations of a liberal theory developed by Feinberg[6] or Ashworth,[7] are of relatively limited use here. For they offer prescriptions which, whatever their recommendations in the areas to which they apply, operate at too high a level of abstraction to get a firm critical foothold with respect to a wide range of pressing practical issues. Even more importantly, they simply fail to address themselves to a large number of issues of both substantive regulation and style and means of enforcement. Yet empirical research suggests we should consider these broader issues as of direct relevance to the social practice of criminalisation; hence they must be encompassed by our political critique. Do the lessons of actual diversity and fragmentation recommend a postmodernist stance, which rejects the search for coherence

[4] Hart H.L.A., *Law, Liberty and Morality* (1963).
[5] Devlin P., *The Enforcement of Morals* (1968).
[6] Feinberg J., *The Moral Limits of Criminal Law: Harm to Others; Offence to Others; Harm to Self; Harmless Wrongdoing* (1984–1988).
[7] Ashworth A., *Principles of Criminal Law* (1991) Chaps. 2–4.

and a grand, universalising, normative or explanatory theory[8]? If so, what kind of theory, if any, do we need?

How are the Boundaries of 'Criminality' Managed? Who or What Engages in this Management?

To speak, as I have, of 'criminalisation' or of the 'frontiers of criminality' appears to presuppose that something or someone is, or has, been 'doing' the criminalising or 'constructing' the frontiers. Here we confront an ambiguity which is central to the idea of 'crime' in contemporary Britain. One culturally endorsed way of looking at crime is as something which is not primarily a legal, but rather a moral, category and hence, on one influential view, as outside the ambit of deliberate legislative change.[9] Hence the role of criminal law is basically to reflect and articulate a pre-existing conception of wrongdoing. Yet from another culturally endorsed point of view, criminal law-making actually creates rather than reproduces categories of 'crime'. The relevance of both perspectives have sometimes been expressed in terms of the ideas of *mala in se* and *mala prohibita,* and reconciled, somewhat uncomfortably, on the basis that they refer to different areas of criminal law.[10]

I shall return below to consider the significance of this ambiguity in the idea of crime. What I want to emphasise here is that central to each of these dominant social understandings of crime is the image of the state as playing the key articulating or defining role. From either point of view, it seems appropriate to think of criminalisation as the concern of the state, acting in pursuit of the 'public interest', to protect the rights and interests of all members of the community by upholding certain fundamentally important shared standards, and in some sense (literally or symbolically) to protect society itself. Yet even the briefest consideration reveals that the idea that either the state, or indeed any other identifiable

---

[8] Smart C., *Feminism and the Power of Law* (1989), Chaps. 1, 4, and 8 "Feminist Approaches to Criminology: Postmodern Woman Meets Atavistic Man", in Gelsthorpe L. and Morris A. (eds.), *Feminist Perspectives in Criminology* (1990); "Law's Truth, Women's Experience", in Graycar R. (ed.), *Dissenting Opinions* (1991); Carty A. (ed.), *Postmodern Law: Enlightenment Revolution and the Death of Man* (1990); Douzinas C., Warrington R. with McVeigh S., *Postmodern Jurisprudence: The Law of Text in the Texts of Law* (1991).

[9] Hart H.L.A., *The Concept of Law,* (1961) Chap. 8.

[10] cf. P. C. Smith J. and Hogan B., *Criminal Law* (7th ed., 1992), pp. 15–18; Ashworth A., *Principles of Criminal Law* (1991), pp 19–27.

agency or process, is in control here is wildly inaccurate. A number of separate problems can be identified and call for consideration. In the first place, even to the extent that it is legitimate to identify a special role for the state in the construction and management of the 'frontiers of criminality', the state itself is fragmented and its boundaries far from easy to identify. Of course, we can point to central cases such as the enactment of criminal statutes, the formulation of judicial precedents and the pronouncement of convictions in criminal cases, the exercise of executive powers in the criminal justice area on the part of government ministers, the police, penal authorities and so on. Already we can see the diversity of political and professional groups embraced within the conception of 'the state'. To this list we need to add local authorities, who make bye-laws and influence regional enforcement practice, and, with increasing relevance, the European Court, Commission and Parliament. Given the diversity of their structure, political orientation, responsibilities, professional training and culture, the idea that the relevant activities of even these 'core' state institutions add up to a coherent process or unitary agency, managing the boundaries of criminal liability, is absurd.

Furthermore, a wide number of groups which are not clearly 'state' or even directly 'state-sponsored' agencies have an important influence on decisions about, and practices of, criminalisation. For example, pressure groups of various kinds affect the legislative process and enforcement practices[11]; the mass media affect legislative, judicial and enforcement processes and have enormous influence in constructing and legitimating particular conceptions of 'real' crime and shaping moral panics about particular forms of offending behaviour[12]; lawyers play a part in preparing cases for court and, particularly, in advising clients whether to plead guilty and to what charge. Victims of, and witnesses to (what might be officially defined as) crime, play an important role in shaping officially recorded crime: if they do not recognise what has happened as 'criminal', or have reasons for avoiding contact with formal criminal justice agencies, particular areas or instances of potentially criminal behaviour will go unrecorded. There is every reason to think that these 'failures to

[11] See Harlow C. and Rawlings R., *Pressure Through Law* (1992), Chap. 5.
[12] Box S., *Power, Crime and Mystification* (1983); Cohen S., *op. cit.;* Cohen S. and Young J., *The Manufacture of News* (1973); Ericson R., Baranek P. and Chan J., *Visualising Deviance* (1987); Sparks R., *Television and the Drama of Crime* (1992).

criminalise' form distinctive patterns along a number of lines. Even those who are subject to criminal regulation often shape the norms and practices which are applied to them through strategies of 'creative compliance'.[13]

More directly, a wide range of 'private' agencies are involved in the execution of what might be regarded as state or public functions in the area of criminal justice. Notable instances include private surveillance and policing bodies, businesses involved in the management of prisons and other criminal justice institutions, and lay and voluntary bodies involved in penal practices, or processes of diversion, of 'offenders' from the formal criminal process.[14] If we are to begin to understand how the boundaries of criminalisation are constructed in our society, all of these groups and practices will have to be taken into account.

A second issue raised by the apparently simple question of who manages the frontiers of criminal liability is that, as our discussion has already implied, the frontiers of crime are not determined by specific, identifiable acts of law-creation, or even of authoritative legal interpretation. The boundaries of what we might call 'practical criminality' have as much to do with enforcement and application practices as with crime-defining, law-creating acts — what we might call 'formal criminality'. Indeed, the separation between law creation and law enforcement all but disappears when one reflects upon the complicated social processes which transmute articulated criminal proscriptions into criminal justice enforcement.[15]

I want to leave aside for a moment the relevant jurisprudential questions about the determinacy of legal rules or other standards, and to make a simple assumption that, wherever law-creating acts or decisions can be identified, they set some limit upon what can legitimately be proceeded against as a crime. Even on the basis of this assumption, it is perfectly clear that the putative area within those legal 'frontiers' bears only a tangential relation to the social practice of criminalisation. Most obviously, certain enacted criminal laws are enforced to a far greater extent than others. For

---

[13] See McBarnet D. and Whelan C., "The Elusive Spirit of the Law's Formalism and the Struggle for Legal Control" (1991) M.L.R. 848.

[14] See Johnston L., *The Rebirth of Private Policing* (1992); Matthews R., (ed.) *Privatising Criminal Justice* (1987).

[15] See the discussion in the pieces by Scott and Weait in this volume. See also McBarnet D., *Conviction: Law, the State and the Construction of Justice* (1981); McConville M., Sanders A. and Leng R., *The Case for the Prosecution: Police Suspects and the Construction of Criminality* (1992).

example, the so-called regulatory offences are enforced to a relatively very small extent: indeed, as the term 'regulatory' suggests, they are not even thought of as unambiguously 'criminal'. This is just one illustration of the fact that, of all the activities which might plausibly be argued to come within existing offence definitions, some kinds are more likely to be reported and/or formally proceeded against than others. These boundaries themselves shift according to factors such as media preoccupations; prevailing popular or political perceptions of social problems, risk and danger; availability of resources; bureaucratic and other constraints on police and prosecution.

Less obviously, but equally importantly, some activities which clearly do, or can plausibly be argued to, lie outside the 'frontiers' of legal proscription may in fact be proceeded against as if they fell within them. For example, the police may harass and arrest young black men on the streets as if their mere presence constituted an actual or threatened offence. The replacement of the old 'Sus' laws with the power to stop and search under the Police and Criminal Evidence Act 1984 appears to have made little difference to the way in which some groups of people are systematically drawn within the boundaries of criminality despite having changed their formal qualification in this respect. The Prevention of Terrorism Acts constitute a particularly vivid example of racially targeted means of criminalisation which all too often draw in people who are properly outside the 'frontiers of criminality'.[16]

Indeed, assumptions about the predispositions and 'legality' of the behaviour of many groups — gay men, Irish people, women who earn their living from prostitution — affect public, police, prosecution or judicial attitudes towards them. When combined with the tractability of offence definitions and failures, or abuses of procedural safeguards, these lay and official attitudes may engender conduct which has the result that many members of those groups are drawn within the boundaries of actual criminalisation even though their behaviour does not, formally, justify this. This aspect of criminalisation resonates, interestingly, with the pre-occupation of much nineteenth and early twentieth century criminology with criminal types, rather than with forms of behaviour.

This is not merely a question of a difference in the extent of enforcement. Indeed, as the last example began to indicate, in its

[16] See Hillyard P., *Suspect Community: People's Experience of the Prevention of Terrorism Acts in Britain*, (1993) Chaps. 4–5.

reference to actions which can be seen as both within and without criminalisation, the two-dimensional spatial metaphor of 'frontiers' or 'boundaries' is inapt to capture what is at stake. For what we are dealing with is a complex and dynamic process of categorisation and discrimination rather than a static practice of deductive reasoning from premises set by a legal definition. Moreover, it is a process which is transformative rather than merely selective. How are we to understand this process? We could adapt the metaphor by starting out not from the idea of a determined terrain of 'criminality' but from that of an area of conduct to which, given prevailing interpretive conventions, formal criminal proscriptions might plausibly be applied. On this basis, we might think of decisions made by social actors within the relevant social processes as a set of lenses, of varying shapes and sizes and colours. The shape, colour and size of the lenses might be seen as an infusion of values, expectations and assumptions which not only cut out of sight parts of the behaviour potentially under scrutiny but also affect the appearance of what is let through. Of any particular instance of human behaviour, a relevant actor or decisionmaker (this might be an ordinary citizen, a police officer, a member of the prosecution service, a news reporter, a judge) might not see it (as potentially criminal) at all; might see it as technically criminal but not worth proceeding against; might see it as too problematic to address; might see it in many different ways, with clear and concrete implications for his or her own subsequent responsive behaviour.

The metaphor of the lens attempts to capture the idea that, notwithstanding our references to 'behaviour' as if it were something which unproblematically exists outside of our selves, what is at stake here is in fact something rather different. What we are concerned with is not 'behaviour' in the raw sense of physical actions accompanied by states of mind, as represented in orthodox criminal legal conceptualisations of *actus reus* and *mens rea*. Rather, we are concerned with the interpretation of human conduct. Indeed, contrary to our usual ways of talking about criminal law, what we are really focusing on here is not primarily the 'behaviour' of those who are found to have committed offences and hence are *criminalised* but rather the human practices which *criminalise*. This focus on criminalisation as an interpretive human practice leads us back to our original puzzle about who or what, if not a unitary conception of the state, is doing the criminalising. It also entails that the metaphor of the lens, whilst an improvement upon the spatial metaphor of frontiers around a terrain, has its own drawbacks. For the metaphor still suggests an idea of the interpreter as passive — as merely receiving the image through the lens — and as separate from the lens. It poses, but does not help us to answer, the question of what the nature of these lenses is, and how they relate to human consciousness and interpretive practice. I shall return to this question in the next section.

Furthermore, the notion of criminalisation as an interpretive activity takes us back to the jurisprudential question which I bracketed earlier; that of the status and determinacy of formally articulated legal standards. For it suggests that these legal standards too may be understood as lenses — as interpretive frameworks — which shape and predispose, rather than determine, interpretive practices, and whose effects are contingent upon how, when, and by whom they are used. It is important to see that the legal interpretive frameworks do set up some constraints. For if we give up this idea, we also abandon one important foothold for a critique of the abuse of criminalising power. Yet these formal constraints are partial and their strength, crucially, depends on the interpretive conventions which constrain executive and judicial power at all stages of the criminalising process.

Our analysis so far, then, shows that in attempting to understand the 'frontiers of criminality' in any society, a multiplicity of actors and processes and of interpretive and enforcement as well as overtly law-creating practices, will have to be taken on board. It undermines the very idea that straightforwardly law-creating or crime-defining legal practices mark out a terrain over which criminal enforcement then operates.

Agency, Discourse and Practice in the Construction of 'Criminality'

Underlying this discussion of the social practices contributing to the construction of the 'frontiers of criminality' are some basic questions of social theory. Individual decisions and deliberate human agency are clearly involved at a number of the relevant stages. Yet, equally clearly, these individual decisions are influenced and constrained by a number of social factors, evoked in the previous section by the metaphor of lenses. It is necessary to develop an understanding of these relevant social factors if we are to make sense of criminalisation. I am going to refer to these lenses as discourses and practices. By using these terms, I mean to evoke any relatively systematic set of values, understandings, expectations or conventions expressed or realised within a relatively structured field of linguistic or other conduct. This usage, of course, implies the inaptitude of the metaphor of the lens; as we noted above, the problem with the metaphor is that it assumes a separation between lens and agent, whereas it is the actions and attitudes of agents which, in a significant sense, constitute practices and discourses. Yet the utility of the notions of discourse and practice lies precisely in the fact that, whilst they are not separate from human behaviour, they are not wholly reducible to (even collections of) individual human actions — otherwise they would not be able to influence behaviour, or play the role that they do in helping us to make sense of the world.

A little more needs to be said about these conceptual tools before we proceed to apply them to the question at issue. As I have defined them, the notion of "practice" incorporates, but is not exhausted by, that of "discourse". Examples of practices relevant to understanding criminalisation would be policing (in all its forms); the activities of defence and prosecution lawyers; legislation; adjudication; pressure group lobbying; 'creative compliance'.[17] These and other practices are often played out in the context of relatively stable institutions such as the legal system, the legal profession, news media, the police, the Crown Prosecution Service and interest groups. Within such areas, more or less distinctive forms of practical knowledge develop around specific activities — arrest, sifting through possible cases for prosecution, advising clients, reporting events and so on.

By the term "discourse", I mean to evoke systems of values, expectations, explanatory frameworks (such as stories) which take a distinctively linguistic form. Defined in this way, discourses overlap with what many criminal justice scholars call "ideologies". My preference for the term "discourse" lies in its focus on the salience of linguistic frameworks in the practice of criminalisation, and hence its importance in our attempts to understand that practice.[18] If we are to understand practices of criminalisation, we have to understand how the behaviour of individuals, agencies, interest groups and other collectivities relates to prevailing cultural discourses relevant to their particular activities and to criminal justice as a social issue. For, whilst those possessing and acting upon the 'practical knowledges' I have referred to may not be able (or willing) to articulate them, discursive knowledge is nonetheless implicit in practices, and is

---

[17] See n.13, above.

[18] I continue to use the term 'ideology' where the linguistic is not my central focus and where I am referring to the legitimating functions of sets of ideas about crime and criminal justice at a general level.

susceptible of articulation by, and interpretive debate among, those not engaged in the practice even if not always by those who are. Hence the relationship between discourse and practice is an intimate one. To engage in adequate critical scrutiny of criminalisation we have to attend (and so give linguistic articulation) to, for example, the professional culture and 'operational ideology' of the police[19]; to the level and kind of attention paid to 'crime' generally, and to particular sorts of crime in the mass media and popular culture[20]; to the role of law and order in prevailing political debate and policy[21]; to the assumptions about individual responsibility and human agency which are implicit in the conceptual framework of criminal laws.[22]

Notwithstanding the salience of the linguistic in the practice of criminalisation, however, it is important not to collapse the notion of practice entirely into that of discourse. The practices of legislating and of sentencing, for example, whilst they have irreducibly discursive aspects, also have (all too) material implications, and the material effects of the power deployed within the discourses in terms of which criminalisation is realised must remain at the centre of an adequate critical analysis. Furthermore, as I noted in my discussion of discourse, it is possible to be engaged in practices — to have the necessary practical knowledge — without having discursive knowledge. The fact that a particular police officer might not recognise a sociologist's discursive reconstruction of the conventions and assumptions which underlie his or her policing behaviour neither undermines the status of that behaviour as a meaningful social practice, nor calls into question the competence of the police officer as an actor within the practice.

Some social theorists have conceived institutions such as the police, the legal profession, news media, and even the relatively stable practices which operate around them and the discourses in which they are expressed, as social *structures*. Certainly, thinking of the legal system, or the professional culture of the police, as structures can be valuable in capturing the social power and reality of what might otherwise be seen as intangible ideas. However, it also has disadvantages, most obviously in that it

<hr />

[19] *cf.* Manning P., *Police Work* (1987): Sanders A., "Personal Violence and Public Order"(1988); *International Journal of the Sociology of Law* 359.

[20] See references at n.12, above.

[21] Brake M. and Hale C., *Public Order and Private Lives* (1992); Waddington D., *Contemporary Issues in Public Disorder* (1992).

[22] See Lacey N., Wells C. and Meure D., *Reconstructing Criminal Law,* (1990) Chap. 1; Norrie A., *Crime, Reason and History,* (1993).

tends to construct them as unitary or monolithic and, to some degree, insulated from the effects of human agency. Indeed, it sets up an intractable opposition between human agency and social structure as rival conceptual frameworks for understanding the social world. One great advantage of the concepts of practice and discourse as tools of social theory is that they mediate this opposition: human practices and discourses are real and effective, but they are neither intractable nor static. Since human life is lived across, and in terms of, a multiplicity of practices and discourses, these interpretive frameworks in terms of which we attempt to make sense of the world are open and constantly shifting. For example, the practice of public policing is not (entirely!) impervious to liberal political discourse, and nor is the practice of conviction and appeal entirely impervious to the oppositional discourse of injustice and the practice of pressure groups.

This last point leads us to a second advantage which the conceptual framework of discourse and practice enjoys as com-pared with that of agency and social structure. This is that it allows us to be open to the ways in which practices and discourses are themselves fragmented and even contradictory. The discourse and practice of criminalisation, for example, embraces the views of both Devlin and Hart; it reflects not only instrumental efforts at crime control but also, and simultaneously, preoccupations with due process.[23] Whereas the idea of criminalising institutions as constituting social structures teaches us to expect coherence and unity, the framework of discourse and practice allows us to take on board the contested and fragmented nature of crimi-nalisation as well as its important unifying threads. Nonetheless, it is useful to employ the notion of social structures as constella-tions of relatively fluid practices and discourses; for example, one might describe gender, class or race as social structures in this specific sense, so as to underline their power. I do not want to rule out this kind of usage in the debate on criminalisation, although I do want to resist the suggestion of unity and fixity which the common-sense idea of structure carries with it.

A wide variety of discourses and practices such as those mentioned in the previous paragraphs are of importance in understanding the operation of the overall social practice of criminalisation. This is the case even where we are dealing with

---

[23] Hence Packer's famous models of the criminal process are better seen as aspects of one complicated set of practices rather than as alternative types of system: Packer H., *The Limits of the Criminal Sanction* (1968).

what appear to be clear cases of deliberate and innovative strategies of criminalisation or decriminalisation. The importance of these various contributions to the overall practice of criminalisation may best be illustrated by introducing another conceptual tool; the idea of *power*. In being cautious about the language of social structure, I do not want to lose sight of the real power of criminalisation; indeed, I want to show how discourses and practices enable criminalising power to operate in society. In much legal and political theory, power is conceived as something akin to a form of property: as something which, flowing from status, wealth, political position or any other source, can be exercised, and which can be won or lost.[24] In recent social theory, however, Foucault has questioned the adequacy of this 'property' conception of power, and has pointed out the ways in which power subsists, less tangibly but no less influentially, in a wide array of discourses and practices spreading throughout the social body.[25] In this sense, power is not owned or wielded by any one agent or institution: rather, it has productive *effects* via the operation of practices and discourses.

I would argue that it is important to draw on both 'property' and 'practice' conceptions of power in understanding processes of criminalisation. Certainly (pace Foucault), it is helpful to think of significant actors in criminal justice practices as wielding property type power, which they can be accorded or deprived of by legal and political change. A good example would be a power to arrest or imprison, notwithstanding their discursive aspects. Yet property type power is not always effective, for in areas beyond those of brute force its exploitation depends on the deployment of discourses and practices which enshrine their own powerful directions and constraints. For example, as several of the Chapters in this volume record, legislative and executive attempts to render corporations criminally liable for a range of fraudulent dealings, like prosecution strategies designed to render corporations liable for manslaughter, often founder. This is not so much because of concrete procedural or substantive barriers but rather because of discursive resistance exemplified in the practices of relevant decision-making agencies — courts, witnesses, lawyers,

[24] See Lukes S. (ed.), *Power* (1986).
[25] Foucault M., *Power/Knowledge: Selected Writings and Interviews* (1980); *Discipline and Punish* (1977). For further discussion of the relationship between the 'property' and 'practice' conceptions of power and their role in applied social theory, see Frazer E., and Lacey N., *The Politics of Community*, (1993) Chaps. 1 and 6.

the police. In other words, if corporate accountability or ideas of corporate blameworthiness find no place or only a marginal place in broader social understandings, it may be difficult or impossible to impose criminal liability. The same could be said for the criminalisation of behaviour envisaged by regulatory offences. Thus even where a deliberate attempt to exercise power on the part of an identifiable agency is involved, the boundaries of 'criminality' depend on the operation of broader social practices and understandings.

These insights underline the importance of looking beyond the material or instrumental to attend to what are sometimes called the symbolic aspects of criminalisation or decriminalisation policies. Indeed, the recognition of what we might call the 'materiality of discourse' shows that we must be careful not to draw a strong dichotomy between the instrumental and the symbolic. For broader cultural understandings of crime affect particular policies, and are capable of subverting the intended meaning of legal or executive change, or indeed of supplying an astute decision-maker with possibilities of pursuing more than one political end by means of any one reform strategy. For example, observe how government decisions to criminalise or decriminalise by legislation can score political points by exploiting the ambiguity in the notion of crime identified above. On the one hand, government is constructing law and order problems as *political* issues, to which it is responding; formal legislation thus offers government the opportunity to represent itself as instrumentally effective. At the same time, it can draw on a prevailing discourse of crime as in some sense *pre-political* — that is, as wickedness or mere lawlessness or even pathology — as something from which we — that is, any 'good citizen' — would distance him or herself.[26] In this sense, formal criminalisation is exploited as an occasion for the evocation of an underlying, symbolic consensus, appeal to which may be a significant mode of governmental self-legitimation. In such instances, government's legislative shifting of the boundaries of liability itself depends upon and expresses the contingency of crime, yet simultaneously deploys a powerful social discourse which constructs crime as 'given'. The purpose of the legislation is to make criminal that which is not already criminal, yet its rationale is that that behaviour is in another sense already criminal. Conversely, a decision to decriminalise can enjoy a similar dual legitimation; government's liberal cre-

---

[26] For discussion of this kind of strategy in the area of public disorder, see Lacey, Wells, and Meure, *op. cit.*, at Chap. 2.

dentials are fostered in that it gets credit for actually drawing back the boundaries of 'criminality'; yet its action is justified in part by the implication that the conduct in question was never really criminal in the first place.

It is also important to recognise that deliberate legislative or judicial shifts (perhaps we should say 'attempted shifts') in the frontiers of criminal liability often have symbolic effects which are less obviously envisaged or welcome. For example, the formal criminalisation of a kind of conduct, the practical proscription of which proves for one reason or another to be impossible or very difficult to enforce, may be counterproductive. This counter-productiveness may consist in the proscription's being seen as implicitly legitimating that form of behaviour. Incitement to racial hatred would be a good example here[27]; its virtual non-enforcement is seen by many as implying covert approval of the behaviour formally proscribed. It may also consist in undermining the images of instrumental effectiveness, universality and evenhandedness, which persist even in the face of the general selectiveness and patterning of enforcement practices, and which are central to criminal law's perceived legitimacy (examples here might include those of gaming laws and a variety of offences concerning sexual 'morality').

Finally, the discussion in this section confirms the need to question the prevailing view of formal criminalisation via legislation as in some sense a real or direct shift in the 'frontiers of criminality' and hence as an effective move in the 'fight against crime'. Yet we also need to recognise the importance of this prevailing view in shaping the role of criminalisation as a mode of social governance. For it opens up the potential for political gains by government even where the changes in question in fact add (or subtract) nothing of substance to (or from) the existing array of criminal prohibitions. The recent adoption of an offence of prison mutiny — the government's principal response to the critical analysis of the Woolf Report[28] — is a good example. Here, most clearly, the discursive simply *is* the material.

To sum up: in this section I have used certain conceptual social-theoretical tools to probe a little more deeply into the shape and significance of the ideas of 'crime' and 'criminalisation'. What the discussion has shown is that, even to the extent

[27] Public Order Act 1986 (s. 18); see Lacey, Wells, and Meure, *op. cit.*, pp. 118–120: Fitzpatrick P., "Racism and the Innocence of Law" (1987), in Fitzpatrick P. and Hunt A., (eds.) *Critical Legal Studies*.
[28] *Prison Disturbances April 1990*, Cm. 1456 (1991).

that we focus on what are conventionally understood as instances
of state-initiated law creation — planned and apparently powerful manipulations of the 'frontiers of criminality' — we cannot
assume that the formally articulated changes correspond straightforwardly with any real change in our interpretive social processes of criminalisation. In a number of direct and indirect ways,
broader social understandings and institutions — what I have
called discourses and practices — are relevant to the nature and
significance of the ensuing change. Making something an offence
does not always serve the same functions or have similar effects
on behaviour or attitudes; precisely the same can be said for
removing something from the ambit of formal criminal proscription. Moreover, the choice among modes of criminalisation, and
the degree of decriminalisation, can be highly significant. This
means that to understand the 'frontiers of criminality', we always
have to look beyond the articulated, and even the covert, aims of
the identifiable agencies involved. We have to take on board not
only the interaction of the decisions and policies of the different
agencies involved, but also the shifts in meaning and effect which
are produced by the discourses and practices which subsist within
and beyond the obvious contours of the criminal process, and
which cut across the obvious institutional divisions which mark
that process.

Can we think of 'Criminal Law' and 'Criminalisation' as Unitary Categories?

The next theoretical issue to which we need to attend is the
presupposition, implicit in reference to the 'frontiers of criminality', that 'crime', 'criminality' or 'criminalisation' are indeed
unitary categories, however fragmented their management may
be. As our discussion so far has suggested, the very use of these
terms is fraught with difficulty.[29] For example, when we refer to
crime as 'behaviour which breaches criminal laws', do we mean
all that behaviour which might be proceeded against as criminal,
or do we mean that behaviour which in fact comes to the notice
of criminal justice agencies? With the first sense, we seem to rely
on a dubious assumption about the potential determinacy of legal
categories. Whilst formal legal proscription is certainly one
important index of how a society draws the 'boundaries of
criminality', it cannot be regarded as anything more than a

[29] See above, n.2.

preliminary and highly flexible interpretive move in a long and complex set of social processes. With the second sense of 'crime', we confront an even more baffling set of questions of demarcation: should we include all those instances reported to the police, or known of, or suspected; or should we confine ourselves to those cautioned or prosecuted, or even to those resulting in formal conviction? (The last is clearly an unduly narrow test, but we should bear in mind that it is the one which sits most happily with the idea of a presumption of innocence). The very subject matter of criminal law and criminology appears to slip through our fingers, as 'criminalisation' is revealed as consisting of a number of interlocking social practices whose operations leave the boundaries of 'criminality' anything but precise.

There could hardly be a better testimony to the impossibility of finding any unifying thread in terms of the content of criminal laws, or the scope of actual criminalisation, than the Chapters in this volume. Quite apart from their broad scope and diversity of subject matter, the local shifts of 'criminal frontier' which many of them trace illustrate the utter contingency of the scope and content of criminal liability. Yet, significantly, at the level of much popular and political discourse and in legal practice, doctrine and education, the notion of crime continues to be regarded as some kind of unity. Certainly, in political discourse the idea of crime as an infraction which threatens both society and all its members is of fundamental importance to the perceived legitimacy of criminal punishment, and of other aspects of state or state-sponsored coercion via criminal justice practices. Similarly, in legal education, the specificity and legitimacy of criminal law are explained in terms of its distinctive response to urgent threats to certain interests, widely recognised as fundamentally important to human lives, where the authors of those threats exhibit a threshold level of responsibility and hence culpability for their actions. In the face of the actual diversity of the subject matter of formal criminal proscription, we need to ask ourselves how this image of unity is maintained. In both spheres, the answer has to do with the focus of debate on a very limited area of the terrain of 'criminality'. In political debate, new instances of criminalisation, such as disorderly conduct or insider dealing are introduced in the context of debate about general evils such as 'serious public disorder' or 'corporate fraud' which command consensus as core instances of criminality. Debate about regulatory offences, or the shifting of boundaries at the lower levels of criminal culpability, rarely enjoys parliamentary discussion or commands media attention. Furthermore, the impact of enforcement on the actual practice of criminalisation is almost always kept out of view. Hence, it is no accident that one of the more critical and well informed newspapers could introduce a discussion of the official criminal statistics with the observation that 'Recorded crime increased by 79 per cent. during Mrs. Thatcher's premiership *in spite of* consistent real growth in the law and order budget and the recruitment of 15 per cent. more police officers' (my emphasis).[30]

In a significant sense, of course, government's practice of criminalisation is a gigantic, and very effective, confidence trick. At one level, political discourse about crime presupposes it as 'objective' or 'given', and purports to direct policy to reduction of the real crime rate. Similar assumptions underlie the criminological idea of the 'dark figure of unrecorded crime'. This phrase is useful in reminding us that debates about crime generally focus on a highly selective sample of all that which might have been included. Yet we should not overlook its dissonance with a discursively central feature of the legal notion of criminal procedure — the presumption of innocence. In one sense, no behaviour should be regarded as criminal until proven beyond reasonable doubt to be so, and we should guard against the risk that an assumption that something is clearly or already criminal may encourage procedural laxity and the kind of blatant bias which leads to miscarriages of justice. At another level (which certainly includes policy discussion in the Home Office) it has to be acknowledged that enforcement is highly selective and that the financial costs of increasing its level are certain and massive, whilst its social and political returns are uncertain and even negative. All this entails, of course, that too much emphasis on its criminalisation and law and order credentials is a dangerous strategy for government. For, as the headline quoted above implies, in putting its criminal enforcement money where its law and order mouth is, government may well engender an apparent worsening of 'the crime problem'.

In legal education, criminal law courses focus on a core of traditional offences organised in terms of the most widely recognised interests — offences against person, property, state, public order. The basic issue of how crime is socially constructed is generally not addressed, criminal laws themselves being presented as descriptive labels for, or equivalents of, 'real crimes'. Apart from a brief treatment of the more serious road traffic

[30] *The Guardian*, March 28, 1991.

offences, criminal law courses rarely stray into terrain in which either the Devlinian social cohesion argument, or the liberal harms argument adapted by Hart from Mill, would begin to look strained or implausible. In particular, the so-called 'regulatory' offences make only the briefest appearance. This appearance is generally in the context of a discussion of strict liability. The function of this discussion is usually to confirm the centrality of the presumption that offences include a *mens rea* requirement, by underlining the exceptional nature of its rebuttal. This is, of course, an effect which can only be secured by maintaining the bias in substantive focus already mentioned and by keeping criminal law teaching pure of anything approaching an empirical assessment of the frequency of different kinds of offences. The selectivity of criminal law books and courses, it should therefore be noted, serves a distinct ideological function in underpinning the image of crime and criminal law as unified and coherent social practices.

It could be objected, however, that most criminal law commentators explicate the unity of criminal law not in terms of subject matter but rather in terms of its distinctive procedure. Similarly, political institutions tend to invoke criminal legislation where distinctive forms of state reaction — criminal punishments — are seen as an appropriate or expedient social response. Criminal laws, it is said (relatively accurately if somewhat unilluminatingly), are those whose enforcement attracts certain distinctive forms of procedural safeguard and mode of proof — and, it might be added, attract the enforcement powers and activities of a distinctive constellation of state and state-sponsored agencies.[31] Can criminalisation, then, be seen as a unitary practice at least at this formal, procedural level, or in terms of the distinctiveness of the sanction imposed in response to criminal conviction?

Here too, a moment's consideration, and a perusal of the chapters in this book, reveals fragmentation and diversity rather than uniformity and coherence. To start with, we must note the vast range of penal measures with which, in more or less devastating ways, our society marks those ultimately convicted of offences. At one end of the spectrum, we have penal practices such as imprisonment, which physically separate, and physically and psychologically mark, their subjects with stigmatising and other effects which, for many prisoners, last all their lives. At this

---

[31] See Smith and Hogan, *op. cit.,* pp. 18–20; Williams G., *A Textbook of Criminal Law* (1983), pp. 27–29.

end of the spectrum, the criminal process genuinely punishes in a sense which might be thought appropriate to the moralistic discourse of culpability and blame which characterises one popular stereotype of crime.[32] At the other end, criminal sanctions include diversionary measures such as cautions and discharges, and penalties such as fines and other deprivations which, in many formally criminal cases, constitute little more than taxing or licensing practices in terms of both their meaning for the offender and their broader social meaning. Indeed, in some of these areas the image of the offender as the passive recipient of a penalty, as opposed to an active participant in negotiating the shape of the enforcement process, may be misplaced. The very idea of punishment, then, is deeply fragmented, and the idea that criminalisation inevitably represents a practice of moralistic penalisation and blaming is certainly not sustainable.

A consideration of procedural practices which may lead up to conviction reveals an equally bewildering diversity. Even among cases brought to court, procedures are far from uniform: only a tiny proportion of defendants receive trial by jury in the crown court — the mode of trial widely taken to exemplify 'criminal procedure'. (It is significant in this respect how surprised criminal law students, among others, are when they discover the proportion of cases heard by lay magistrates and the proportion of guilty pleas.) In cases heard before either crown courts or lay or stipendiary magistrates, the procedure will vary according to whether or not the defendant has pleaded guilty, and the operation of formal standards and burdens of proof in this process in turn depends on the quality of legal advice available and the subjective situation of the defendant (in terms of how much pressure he or she feels to plead guilty). An initial report to the police, particularly if it involves an alleged property offence or what the police see as a non-serious offence against the person, may well simply be stamped 'No Further Action' or even 'No Crime'. If it does result in any further action, this may consist not in investigation and reference to the Crown Prosecution Service but rather in a formal or informal caution or, in

---

[32] In teaching criminal justice, I am constantly struck by the high proportion of (even liberal) students who regard imprisonment as the only real kind of punishment, and by the extent to which (despite my efforts to the contrary) our class discussions tend to reflect the idea of imprisonment as the paradigm criminal sanction. The difficulty of escaping this framework assumption is, I think, evidence of the power of this particular feature of the prevailing discursive construction of criminalisation and penality in contemporary Britain.

some areas, the initiation of a process of mediation with the alleged victim. No unified set of principles constrains the range of discretionary powers which determine the course of a defendant's progress through this ideologically central path of criminal procedure.

So far I have been concentrating on a narrow selection of criminalising practices and institutions. In fact, criminal processes are very much more diverse than those represented by police, the CPS and the courts. In a number of areas, distinctive regulatory bodies, and even self-regulatory bodies, wield what are either the formal or the functional equivalent of criminal enforcement powers (significantly, it is sometimes difficult to tell the difference between the two). In areas as diverse as city fraud, health and safety at work regulation, environmental pollution regulation, and many forms of licensing, regulatory agencies are vested with both investigative and enforcement powers which generally pre-empt those of the police and criminal courts.[33] Military authorities have their own policing processes and criminal courts. Vast numbers of private agencies, or agencies which have been invested in more or less overt ways with public powers, are involved in surveillance, policing, enforcement functions — in shopping malls, at airports, in workplaces. If anything, this tendency to the diversification of criminal and quasi-criminal enforcement is on the increase: as our social and political institutions resort to criminal enforcement in response to a greater and greater diversity of social problems, so the procedural means of enforcement are developing and diversifying apace. In the face of this diversity it is impossible to identify a unified practice of criminalisation in terms of distinctive procedural approaches. Indeed, it is increasingly difficult to be certain where the boundaries between criminal and non-criminal (administrative, civil, regulatory) enforcement can be said to lie.[34]

Criminalisation in Relation to Other Practices of Social Ordering: Resistance and Openness

Must we conclude from what has been said so far that any meaningful discussion of criminalisation or criminal justice prac-

---

[33] See, for example, Hawkins K., *Environment and Enforcement* (1983).
[34] An interesting example of this is provided by a report in the *Financial Times*, March 23, 1993. p. 14, in which the author, assessing the relative efficacy of the U.S. approach to regulation of 'white-collar crime' via the Securities and Exchange Commission, refers throughout to market 'offences' and 'offenders' in single inverted commas.

tices is impossible? This would, I think, be a *reductio ad absurdum*. For one thing, a culturally dominant set of ideas about crime and criminal justice exists, both in the sense of having concrete effects on consciousness and practice, and in the sense that we can identify core instances of the imposition of criminalising power. The point of reflecting on the diversity of criminalising practices and their blurred frontiers is better to understand their social meaning, rather than to analyse them out of existence. But a recognition of both the contingency and the diversity of 'criminality' does raise one final theoretical question to which we need to advert before drawing together the threads of this discussion. For once we come to see criminalisation as just one (itself complex) set of practices among many powerful practices involved in constructing and maintaining social order, the question arises as to how this particular set of practices and discourses relates to others operating over the same terrains of human behaviour.

Many of the chapters in this book consider particular political decisions to criminalise, rather than to rely on civil or adminstrative enforcement, or examine the relation between these different legal regulative modes in particular contexts. Several of them look beyond these other legal modes to the relative influence of social practices such as education, popular debate in the media, conventional morality, the use of brute force, religion, the imperatives of commerce. The question of the relation between criminalising and other ordering practices would seem to be an excellent example of something which is inapt for general theorisation, since it is highly sensitive to the specificities of both explicit legislative and regulatory/enforcement context. Nonetheless, some general points emerge from the chapters in this book, as well as from broader evidence, about the factors which militate in favour of or against formal or actual criminalisation in particular areas. For political or structural reasons, it appears to be difficult to impose effective criminal regulation in certain areas: corporate crime of many kinds provides the clearest example here. Conversely, certain forms of behaviour — notable examples include male homosexual conduct and female prostitution — retain an informal criminal status even in the absence of direct criminal controls or following formal decriminalisation.[35]

Most obviously, the political and economic strength of particular interest groups can be a potent source of resistance to formal

---

[35] Smart, *op. cit.*, (1976), Chap. 4; Edwards S., *Women on Trial*, Chap. 2; Power H., "Gay Rights and Entrapment" (1993) New L.J. 47.

criminalisation or to effective criminal enforcement.[36] The tardy and partial actual criminalisation of white collar crime is perhaps the most spectacular example here, although interesting converse questions arise about why some attempt at criminalisation was made in the 1980s. One possible explanation — that it was a symbolically effective way of legitimating a more generally deregulatory policy with respect to financial institutions — once again reminds us of the interaction between criminalising and other social ordering practices. Another important source of resistance, reflected in Chapter 5, is a cultural understanding hostile to, or inconsistent with, the criminal responsibility of particular agents in particular spheres: the idea, for example, that responsible behaviour emanates from individuals rather than groups, and that only individuals rather than collectivities are genuinely blameworthy — an idea which finds expression both in technical doctrinal *mens rea* requirements and in enforcement practices on the part of police, coroners and courts.[37] Technical difficulties of proof (which may themselves be produced or exacerbated by exercises of economic power or by adverse cultural understandings) are another source of resistance to criminalisation, as is scarcity of enforcement resources (again note the interaction between this and other factors).

Each of these sources of resistance may well engender a predisposition to less hard-edged, typically punitive or formal means of regulation. They may indeed inhibit the very recognition of something as the kind of social problem or harmful behaviour for which any attribution of responsibility is apposite. On the other side of the coin, factors which lend currency to criminalising interpretations of conduct include cultural shifts of the kind described in chapter five, moral panics, political expediencies (flowing for example from electoral gains to be had from exploiting 'law and order issues'), economic pressures and the political imperatives which flow from them (reflected for example in the general correlation between levels of imprisonment and those of unemployment.)[38] We should also remember in this

---

[36] See McBarnet and Whelan, *op. cit.*
[37] *cf.* Wells C., *Corporations and Criminal Responsibility* (1993).
[38] See Melossi D., "Gazette of Morality and Social Whip: Punishment, Hegemony and the Case of the US, 1970–1992", 2 (1993), *Social and Legal Studies* 259–273; Box S., *Recession, Crime and Punishment* (1987). The drop in the prison population in 1992 in this country (now in the process of dramatic reversal) appears to mark an exception to this general tendency, which is probably to be explained in relation to rather distinctive circumstances impinging on police morale and incentives to divert less serious cases from the formal criminal process.

context that it can be useful for government to diffuse political responsibility for certain perceived social problems by promoting their construction as a matter of individual wickedness rather than as failures of collective commitment or social policy. This diffusion is a politically attractive aspect of the strategy of criminalisation in certain contexts, since it allows government to exploit the sense in which the discourse of criminal blaming is in some sense apolitical (because it responds to a 'pre-political' conception of 'real crime'). I would argue that this is a constantly relevant factor in understanding local shifts in practices of criminalisation.

Conclusion: Is there any place for General Theorising about the 'Frontiers of Criminality'?

We return, in conclusion, to the question of where the high degree of diversity, fragmentation and contingency to which I have been alluding leaves the general project of theorising about the 'frontiers of criminality'. In the light of our analysis, how should we assess the potential contributions of Devlin's vision of criminal laws as justified by their maintenance of a seamless web of common morality and by their necessity to social order, or Hart's development of Mill's principle that the coercive power of the State should be invoked only to prevent harm to others or on strictly circumscribed paternalist grounds? Clearly, each of these has an important place among the dominant cultural discourses and practices of criminality and criminalisation, these discourses and practices themselves being fragmented, contested and often contradictory. However, even assessed as normative sketches of an *ideal* criminal process, neither operates at a sufficiently concrete level to generate critical principles which could address themselves to all, or even most, of the institutions and norms encompassed within the practices of criminalisation as they currently exist. One important limitation of Hart's theory, which addresses itself directly to the question of the proper boundaries of criminalisation, is that it only concerns itself with state power. Yet, as we have seen, contemporary criminalisation spans a range of state and extra-state practices, and deploys forms of power ignored by most traditional political theory and hence outwith its analysis of legitimation.

Nonetheless, the question of how ethically, as well as prac-tically, to set limits to the practice of criminalisation remains an urgent one. It seems unduly defeatist to abandon the search for some general critical principles simply because of the complexity of the world. Rather, I would suggest that we need to reconceive the theoretical project here in less ambitious but more concrete terms. Certainly, we may acknowledge the importance of reflection on what kinds of personal and collective needs and interests should be regarded as of the greatest importance and hence as subjects for a range of social and political efforts at recognition and protection. Yet we should not expect such normative reflection to generate concrete critical limiting principles in themselves. Indeed, a genuine commitment to democracy would suggest that the role of such reflection is to inform democratic debate rather than to foreclose it. Once we have conceived criminalisation as a complex set of social practices which both exercise and deploy a range of kinds of power — the 'property' type of power wielded by state institutions or wealthy corporate bodies, but also the 'practice' type of power which infuses a wide range of social discourses and disciplines — we may begin to address the question not just of how to limit, but also of how to legitimate, criminalising power within a democratic polity. One concrete way of doing this may be to reconceive criminal law as a form of public law, both in the sense that it is involved in rendering certain kinds of publicly relevant behaviour accountable, and also in the sense that criminalising practices generate and deploy a wide range of public powers, in both formally public and private bodies and officials. These powers themselves raise important questions of legitimation, which might be resolved in terms of criteria such as accountability, openness and democratic mandate.

In other words, we have to find a central place for criminalisation in our critical theory of governance, and to begin to think about the democratisation of all aspects of criminalisation practices. The normative theories of Hart, Devlin, Feinberg and, to a lesser extent, Ashworth focus primarily on the *creation* of criminal norms: what kinds of criminal laws is it legitimate for the state to enact? Yet, as we saw above, in the social practice of criminalisation, creation, interpretation and enforcement cannot be separated. Hence the democratic legitimation — through consent, consultation, representation, participation or otherwise[39] — of the whole range of practices involved in criminalisation, is the most pressing normative and practical question facing the contemporary criminal process. Indeed, this has been acknowledged by some of the most influential pressure group and other

---

[39] See Beetham D., *The Legitimation of Power*, (1991).

public assessments of the criminal and penal process in recent years.[40] It remains, however, a question far from the reform agenda in contemporary Britain.

The reconstruction of criminalising practices in accordance with principles of democratic governance is not, however, the only way in which general social and political theory is relevant to the study of contemporary criminal justice. For the complicated facts of criminalisation revealed by studies such as those in this book also raise a different kind of general, social-theoretical question. This is the question of what these practices tell us about our society, about its modes of governance, about its conception of citizenship, about its idea of and degree of regard for the people who make it up. Echoing the questions posed by Braithwaite,[41] we might ask about the extent to which these studies reveal disintegrative, excluding, them-and-us, stigmatising modes of criminalisation, or reintegrative, inclusive criminalisation strategies. And we might ask whether there is any general pattern to this or whether the approach differs across local areas of criminalisation. We might then draw some conclusions from these studies about the nature of the society we live in. These conclusions would, of course, be more interesting wherever they could be considered in the light of similar research in other countries, within a framework which considered the general shape and contribution of criminalisation practices, relative to other less coercive practices, to the generation and construction of social orderin different kinds of societies. Once again, we are moving into the area of very general questions of, and hypotheses within, social theory — yet theoretical questions which reveal the strong continuity between theoretical insight and the analysis of concrete practices. Theory, then, can usefully work in at least two directions across the 'frontiers of criminality': as a framework (no more) for critique of current practices; and, in eliciting general conclusions from concrete analysis, as a framework for understanding how social order is produced in different contexts.

The real challenge confronting any attempt to understand the 'frontiers of criminality' therefore lies in reconciling sensitivity to the complexity and diversity of the social practice of criminalisation with theoretical frameworks which inevitably operate at some level of generality. In my view, it is possible to adopt a methodology which accepts the necessity — indeed inevitability — of theoretical frameworks for both explanatory and critical

[40] See, for example, the Woolf Report, *op. cit.*, n.28.
[41] Braithwaite J., *Crime, Shame and Reintegration*, (1989).

purposes, but which escapes the monolithic model of crime or criminality as givens, or of criminalisation as a substantively coherent and procedurally unitary state-directed practice. A properly theorised, critical approach to the 'frontiers' of criminal liability is necessary if commentators are to expose the abuses of power which all too often characterise practices of criminalisation. Only within such a framework can we begin to address the question of how such abuses may be avoided or, at least, minimised — not least by rolling back the 'frontiers of criminality' in favour of less typically coercive modes of social ordering.

Chapter Two

CRIMES WITHOUT FRONTIERS?
THE WAR CRIMES ACT 1991.
by Tony Richardson

The War Crimes Act 1991 empowered prosecuting authorities in the United Kingdom to bring proceedings for murder, manslaughter, or culpable homicide in respect of actions violating the laws and customs of war, committed in Germany or territory under German occupation between September 1, 1939 and June 5, 1945. The Act extends to individuals who were not British citizens when the offences were carried out but who were, on March 8, 1990 (or thereafter), citizens of, or residents in, the United Kingdom, Isle of Man, or Channel Islands. The Act was Parliament's response to the Report, published in July 1989, of an Inquiry chaired by Sir Thomas Hetherington and William Chalmers.[1]

The Government had established the Inquiry following the emergence of evidence that many alleged Nazi war criminals had obtained citizenship and/or residence rights in Britain since 1945. The Report recommended that the jurisdiction of United Kingdom courts should be extended to encompass trials for acts of manslaughter and murder which amounted to war crimes.

In November 1992, the Lord Chancellor indicated in the House of Lords that the special unit of the Metropolitan Police set up to investigate allegations made to the Hetherington/Chalmers Inquiry, was considering "some 99 allegations involving persons said to range from 63 to 85 years of age".[2] The Lord Chancellor would not comment on the likelihood of any prosecutions. However, continuing press speculation that prosecutions were pending was heightened following the libel case in Scotland between Anton Gecas and Scottish Television.[3] It is also clear that the opposition to the Act continues unabated both in

---

[1] *Report of the War Crimes Inquiry*, (Cm. 744 (1989)).
[2] *HL Written Answers*, November 23, 1992, No. 59.
[3] *The Independent*, July 18, 1992 suggested that four cases were being considered for trial.

Parliament and in the country at large.[4] Given the unlimited legal sovereignty of the United Kingdom Parliament in respect of non-E.C. matters, the legality of the War Crimes Act is beyond question. However, opposition to the legislation on the grounds of its alleged illegitimacy or unconstitutionality has been intensive, pervasive and sustained.

This chapter begins by analysing the precise nature of the objections to the Act. It continues by suggesting that such criticisms rest upon a particular reading of history and a limited conceptualisation of the role and purposes of the criminal law in a modern western society. The chapter concludes by outlining a reconceptualisation of the basic issues raised by the Act, foremost among which is the political necessity for a legislative response to the on-going challenge of the Holocaust.

For purposes of presentation as much as analytical rigour, opposition to the Act may be characterised under four headings. First, one can discern a 'substantive constitutional' dimension, concerned primarily with the legislation's alleged retrospectivity. Secondly, the Act is said to violate due process norms inherent in traditional British understandings of the rule of law, in so far as the mechanisms through which it is envisaged that guilt will be proven preclude the holding of a fair trial. A third strand of criticism focuses on such pragmatic factors as the cost of investigation and trial. Finally, one may identify a more amorphous category of objections: these might be termed moral or political, and they raise wider questions pertaining to the way in which our contemporary democratic society should respond to the historical legacy of the Holocaust.

Substantive Constitutionality — Retrospectivity

That the Bill's passage involved resort to the Parliament Acts 1911–49 for only the fourth time in their history indicates the Acts' controversial nature, as does the fact that it was the subject

---

[4] See for example, Richardson T., "War Crimes Act" (1992) M.L.R. 73–87: Ganz G., "The War Crimes Act 1991 — Why No Constitutional Crisis?" (1992) M.L.R. 87–95, p. 87; Cunningham A., "To the Uttermost Ends of the Earth" (1991) *Legal Studies* 281–303: Steiner E., "Prosecuting War Criminals in England and France" [1991] Crim.L.R. 180–188: McMurtrie S. (1992) "The Constitutionality of the War Crimes Act 1991" [1992] Stat. L.R. 128–149; Cottrell R., "The War Crimes Act and Procedural Protection" [1992] Crim.L.R. 173–175. The most comprehensive account of the background to and campaign for the Act is from the historian David Cesarani, *Justice Delayed: How Britain became a Refuge for Nazi War Criminals* (1992).

of a free vote in the Commons.[5] Resistance to the Bill in the Lords was premised largely on the argument that it was unconstitutional because of its alleged retrospectivity. The infrequency with which the Parliament Acts have been invoked makes it difficult to identify conventional rules which would justify the House of Lords exercising its delaying powers under the Acts, although one commentator has suggested retrospective criminal legislation is a suffficiently grave departure from orthodox governmental practice to merit such intransigence in the Upper House.[6]

The opposition case was succinctly expressed by Lord Hailsham:

"I pass shortly through the question of retrospectivity. I answer the question perfectly simply. If legislation is necessary to render these trials lawful, then there is retrospectivity whatever anyone may say. If there is no retrospectivity, then we do not need to legislate at all".[7]

Since retrospective legislation is not *per se* unconstitutional in the narrow legal sense in the United Kingdom, the objections expressed by Lord Hailsham and other peers hinge upon what may best be described as elements of a substantive notion of the rule of law; namely the maxims *nullum crimen sine lege* and *nulla poena sine lege*,[8] which suggest that it is unjust that acts which were legal when done should subsequently be held criminal and punished.

At a superficial level, such slogans provide a plausible foundation on which the Act's opponents might build. However, as Ashworth suggests,[9] these maxims are not absolute truths. Rather they are merely two of many, often competing, values which constitute the ideology of the criminal law in a liberal democratic society. Recasting the debate in these terms indicates that the question of the constitutionality of retrospective law has a dual aspect: it embraces the issues both of fairness to citizens who may have relied upon the pre-existing law, and of the overall public interest served by the subsequent legislation. The rather more firmly grounded opposition to the Bill in Parliament suggested

---

[5] See Ganz, *op. cit.*
[6] McMurtrie, *op. cit.*
[7] *HLD*, December 4, 1989, col. 630.
[8] Hall J., "Nullum Crimen Sine Lege" (1937) Yale L.R. 165–193. For a cogent modern discussion relating the maxim to the limits of the criminal law see, Ashworth A., *Principles of Criminal Law* (1991).
[9] *ibid.*, pp. 52–57.

that the War Crimes Act would fail on both counts by working grave unfairness on individuals without conferring any substantial benefit on society at large.

The issue of fairness arose in several forms. One line of argument, vigorously pursued in the Lords, questioned whether the Act altered settled government policy, and therefore infringed the constitutional convention that the decisions of a previous administration should not be questioned. Lord Mayhew (a junior government minister in the first Attlee government) was particularly concerned to establish that a firm decision had been taken in 1948 to cease all war crimes' trials. Mayhew maintained that, in the words of Winston Churchill, Atlee's cabinet had decided 'to draw a sponge across the crimes and horrors of the past'. In this respect it was suggested that the onus was firmly upon the Bill's proponents to show that a change of fact or substance had occurred since 1948 so as to justify a change of policy.

Whether Parliament should consider itself bound to respect such a convention is a large question. However, this aspect of the opposition case seemed empirically ill-founded. The Hetherington/Chalmers Inquiry had conducted research to address this anticipated objection. The Inquiry concluded that "it cannot be argued that the British Government took a positive decision not to prosecute war criminals in this country".[10]   The nub of the objection was, therefore, whether mere inaction by past governments could amount to constructive notice to former Nazis that if they entered the United Kingdom they would never be prosecuted for alleged war crimes. Fairness is obviously an extremely amorphous concept in this context, but it presumably extends to individuals as well as to government. Given that the only way alleged war criminals could legally have entered this country would have been by directly concealing their involvement with genocidal activities, fairness hardly seems to demand that they then be given a subsequent immunity from prosecution.

Nor did the Bill's opponents unambiguously address the question of the public interest that might be served by 'retrospective' legislation. It is clear, as one peer put it, that "reasons of politics rather than justice led to the decision in 1948".[11] The real issue was whether it was contemplated that no one in "Britain accused of the mass murder of Jewish prisoners . . . should be tried". That, rather than the political reputations of Ministers, was —

[10] At para. 9.6.
[11] Lord Annan, *HLD,* April 30, 1991, col. 690.

and remains — the key issue. In this light, the public interest served by enacting the measure is put into stark relief. It is contended here that the opponents of the Act signally fail to answer this charge. This question deserves further discussion, but this is best reserved until the section below dealing with the impact of the Act on the fundamental values of the criminal justice system.

At this point, it is apposite to outline and analyse the arguments preferred by the Hetherington/Chalmers Inquiry on the related issues of jurisdiction and retrospectivity.[12] As the Inquiry indicated, British criminal law is "essentially territorial in nature", albeit with a few exceptions.[13] Thus, a statute which seemingly claims jurisdiction over actions committed during the course of the Second World War, by people who were not British subjects, and regardless of where the acts occurred, immediately raises the charge of retrospectivity.

The core of the Inquiry's argument against this contention involved defining the essence of retrospectivity broadly as "(a law) is retrospective if it applies to or affects actions in the past". The specific exemplification of this is encompassed within the twin maxims of *nullum crimen sine lege* and *nulla poena sine lege, i.e.,* no state may enact legislation deeming an act criminal or rendering it punishable by law if it was not considered to be a crime when committed. Accordingly, the argument's next step was to consider whether or not the acts or omissions adumbrated by the Act might be said to be criminal at the time of their commission. The Inquiry suggested that such a conclusion was entirely defensible, since, in accordance with the principles of international law, 'violations of the laws and customs of war' were, by 1939, recognised as crimes by the international community. The relevant principles were codified in the Hague Conventions of 1899 and 1907 (to which all the belligerent parties in the Second World War were signatories). The Inquiry also saw a strong case for arguing that the Conventions merely restated what was by then international customary law. Thus, Article 1 of the Preamble to the Hague Convention No. IV attested to governing norms which flowed from "the principles of the law of nations, derived from the usages established among civilised peoples, from the laws of humanity and from the dictates of the public conscience". Similarly, the International Military Tribunal at Nuremberg stressed that the Law of the Charter was:

---

[12] Paras. 6.35–6.44.

[13] For example, the offences recognised in the Geneva Conventions Act 1957 and the Genocide Act 1969.

"(not) an arbitrary exercise of power on the part of the victorious nations, but in the view of the tribunal, as will be shown, it is the expression of international law existing at the time of its creation; and to that extent is itself a contribution to international law."[14]

Consequently, the War Crimes Act offences constituted breaches of the (customary) law of war in 1939. Therefore, the Inquiry felt able to claim that no new substantive criminal offence would be created by extending the jurisdiction of U.K. criminal courts to the perpetrators of such crimes.

This conclusion nevertheless left open the jurisdictional objection to the Act. The Inquiry addressed this criticism by seeking to draw a clear distinction between what has been termed substantive and what has been termed procedural, retrospectivity.[15] The former entails the criminalisation of previously legal behaviour; the latter merely empowers domestic courts to try behaviour which was criminal, but beyond the domestic jurisdiction, when committed.

The Inquiry's argument turned to a speech made in 1942[16] by the then Lord Chancellor, Lord Simon, to support the contention that enacting procedurally retrospective legislation was a legitimate, if rarely exercised, Parliamentary power. Lord Simon had argued that "national Courts . . . are equally entitled to exercise whatever criminal jurisdiction would be conceded them by International Law . . .".[17] Similarly, Lauterpacht, writing in 1944,[18] maintained that to extend the criminal jurisdiction of the domestic courts to war crimes committed by aliens abroad "would involve no question of retroactivity, contrary to justice and established principles of law". Thus, since the murder of civilians in the course of belligerent occupancy contravened international law, and so constituted a war crime over which international law would allow the courts of other belligerent states to claim jurisdiction, it was permissible for Parliament to legislate accordingly.

However, the Inquiry did not advance any convincing reasons for making a distinction between substantive and procedural

[14] *Judgment of the International Military Tribunal for the Trial of Major War Criminals*, p. 38, in n.4., Cmnd. 6964 (1946).
[15] Steiner, *op. cit.*
[16] 1942 being the year when the Allies began to formulate a policy for dealing with war crimes; see Richardson, *op. cit.*, (1992).
[17] *HLD*, October 7, 1942, col. 579.
[18] Lauterpacht, "The Law of Nations and the Punishment of War Crimes" (1944) *British Yearbook of International Law*, 58–95.

retrospectivity. The key paragraph (6.44) merely restates the familiar form of the argument. No independent reasons are developed, although the Inquiry actually suggests that legislation confined to extending jurisdiction "would not be retrospective". As will be seen below, it is possible to construct an adequate justificatory argument for the substantive/procedural distinction, but this is merely hinted at in the Inquiry's report. This lacuna in the Inquiry's case for the legislation was mirrored by similar omissions in the opposition's arguments. Objectors simply assumed that retrospection was bad *per se,* whatever form it took. They thus conferred an absolute status upon what is, in effect, only one (albeit important) guiding principle of the criminal law.[19]

A recent commentator has suggested a more satisfactory basis for the extension of jurisdiction by exploring the distinction between the terms "retroactive" and "retrospective". The former means that a statute changes the legal status of an action at the time it was committed. The latter merely means that the provision "facilitates conferring a different legal status on acts from that date".[20] The basic nature of the action remains unaltered, but now the courts can exercise jurisdiction over such acts.

Given that the Inquiry had itself refused to extend jurisdiction to cover crimes against humanity, precisely on the grounds that their legal status under international law was unclear in the 1939–1945 period, it would seem to have covered the substance of this point itself. However, McMurtrie finds this argument unsatisfactory, citing case law which both supports a strong presumption against retrospective legislation, and, more specifically, against the argument that extending jurisdiction in the proposed way does not amount to retrospectivity.[21]

Consistency with judicial authority is no doubt an important element in the analyses of constitutional legitimacy of retrospective legislation, but it is overly simplistic to assume that such factors cannot be overridden by other public interest considerations. This point is dealt with in the final section of this chapter. However, the British legislation is not a unique initiative. Several Commonwealth countries have enacted similar measures, and it

---

[19] Ashworth, *op. cit.,* Chap. 3.
[20] McMurtrie, *op. cit.,* pp. 144–145.
[21] McMurtrie, *op. cit.,* pp. 141, 145, quoting Lord Reid in *Waddington v. Miah* [1974] 2 All E.R. 377 at 379; and Lord Brightman in *Yew Bon v. Kenderaan Bas Mara* [1982] 3 All E.R. 833 at 836, where it is clearly stated; "a statute is retrospective if . . . it attributes a new disability, in respect of events already past".

is helpful to consider how they have broached the issues of constitutionality and retrospectivity.

Australian and Canadian Experience

The 1988 amendments to Australia's original War Crimes Act of 1945 followed the recommendations of the Menzies Report,[22] which barely touched upon the issue of retrospectivity. The matter was regarded as one of merely extending the jurisdiction of the courts, an initiative which it implicitly distinguished from substantive retrospection. Menzies concluded that the new Act could "reasonably be defended as not offending either the International Covenant [on Civil and Political Rights] or any rule against retrospectivity although it would be a very unusual step that would arouse controversy".[23]

The first action brought under the legislation, *Polyukhovich v. Australia*,[24] immediately vindicated this judgment. Polyukovich challenged the War Crimes Amendment Act 1989 on the grounds of its retrospectivity. The majority of the judges found that there was no legislative disability regarding the power to pass retro-spective legislation *per se*. For the majority, retrospection clearly meant the *ex post facto* criminalisation of previously lawful conduct. In the absence of a specific constitutional provision prohibiting the exercise of such a legislative power, the only grounds upon which the plaintiff could rely in the instant case was the argument that the particular form assumed by the retrospectivity alleged to be characteristic of the Act was that it infringed the separation of powers by amounting to trial by legislature. A minority of the judges accepted this contention. However, the majority rejected this argument, holding that the court was substantially involved in both the application of the facts to a legal rule and to a substantive determination of guilt or innocence.[25]

This variation on the separation of powers theme was also aired in the House of Lords by opponents of the United Kingdom's Bill, some of whom characterised the measure as a "modern form of a Bill of Attainder'.[26] This argument seems ill

---

[22] Menzies R., *Report on the Review of the Material Relating to the Entry of Suspected War Criminals into Australia*, (1987) .

[23] *ibid.*, paras. 17.12–17.18.

[24] *Polyukhovich v. Australia* (1991) 172 C.L.R. 501.

[25] *per* Mason C.J. at 536; Dawson J. at 647.

[26] McMurtrie, *op. cit.*, pp. 146–147.

founded. The Act does not select either a named individual or specific group of persons for punishment, nor make any determination of fact nor pre-judgment of guilt. All these matters are reserved for the courts. Litigation in Canada also reinforces the contention that the United Kingdom's Act was an entirely legitimate initiative. After a hard fought campaign,[27] the Canadian government set up a committee of inquiry, the Deschenes Commission, which reported in 1986.[28] The Commission concluded that there were alleged Nazi war criminals resident in Canada, and that the existing War Crimes Act 1946 did not provide an appropriate means to prosecute them. Accordingly, Deschenes recommended that the criminal code be amended so that war crimes would be offences under Canadian law whether or not Canada had participated in the specific war in which it was alleged the crimes had been committed. Deschenes also suggested that Canada should assume jurisdiction over crimes against humanity whenever, and wherever, committed.

The Canadian Charter of Rights and Freedoms in the Constitution Act 1982 provided several potential obstacles to enactment of the Deschenes recommendations. Section 7 of the Charter specifically guarantees the right of every individual not to be deprived of the right to life, liberty, and security of the person except "in accordance with the principles of fundamental justice", and also prohibits retrospective legislation.

In one of the first cases brought under the new provision — that of Imre Finta[29] — the retrospectivity issue was immediately raised. However, the court interpreted the Charter as reserving the legislature's right to enact retrospective legislation. The court distinguished a retroactive statute — which takes "an act or omission that was not previously criminal, and retrospectively deems that act or omission to be criminal as at a later date", from a retrospective statute, which did not create any new offence, but merely retrospectively gave Canadian courts jurisdiction over criminal offences committed outside Canada.

The court's reasoning, echoing the discussion in the Deschenes report,[30] seemed to accept that war criminals constituted a distinct category of offenders, against whom wider concerns of public

---

[27] Matas D. and Charendoff S., *Justice Delayed: Nazi War Criminals in Canada* (1987).
[28] Deschenes, The Hon. Jules (1986) *Canadian Commission on Inquiry on War Crimes* (Ottawa: Ministry of Justice).
[29] *R. v. Finta* (1989) 61 D.L.R. (4th) 85.
[30] *ibid.*

interest justified some erosion of the Charter's presumption against retrospection. Indeed, the judgment suggested that a fundamental injustice would occur if jurisdiction were refused in such cases on the grounds of retrospection; such a refusal would be tantamount to concluding that the killing of unarmed non-combatant Jewish civilians in occupied territory was not a crime under the general principles of law recognised by the community of nations.

The Rule of Law: A Denial of Due Process?

Opposition to the War Crimes Act also fastened on arguments deriving from the due process elements of western notions of the rule of law.[31] Many lawyers taking part in Parliamentary debates on the Bill argued that its terms made a fair trial impossible.[32] Objections included unreasonable delay, the evidential regime, and the unequal resources available to the prosecution and defence.

The Hetherington/Chalmers Inquiry itself had been aware of the problems posed by attempts to prosecute alleged Nazi war criminals some 45 years after the event,[33] and had cited Article 6 of the European Convention on Human Rights as a benchmark. The right to a fair trial is, of course, a key aspect of the rule of law viewed as a set of juristic principles.[34] The Bill clearly satisfied some elements of the "fair trial" concept; hearings were to be public, and before the ordinary courts. However, the Bill's critics clearly thought that it endangered what they regarded as fundamental aspects of procedural fairness directed to the protection of individual rights.

Thus, the substantive delay was said to amount to an abuse of process of the court, and acted to the prejudice of the accused. The changes in the law of evidence relied upon by the Inquiry[35] introduced a risk of bias creeping into the proceedings, and the unequal resources of the prosecution and defence prevented any prospect of fairness in a public trial. Such criticisms go far beyond

---

[31] See Jowell J., "The Rule of Law Today", in Jowell J. and Oliver D., (eds.), *The Changing Constitution* (1985); Allen T., "Legislative Supremacy and the Rule of Law" (1983) 44 Cam.L.J. 111–143.
[32] For example, Lord Irvine, *HLD*, December 4, 1989 col. 673: Lord Hailsham, *HLD*, June 4, 1990 col. 1174.
[33] Paras. 9.32–9.34.
[34] See Allen, *op. cit.*
[35] Paras. 9.31–9.43.

the tentative defence offered by the Inquiry, and demand independent rebuttal.

Delay and the Rules of Evidence

It was common cause amongst many of the Bill's opponents that the question of delay was fatal to any possibility of a fair trial. There was general resort to the aphorism that "Justice delayed is justice denied" — said to originate in the Magna Carta.[36] Recent cases[37] have firmly established that the concept of abuse of process of the court is a residual common law power which enables a court to discontinue vexatious or prejudicial proceedings against the accused. The purpose of the concept is to limit the prosecution power by resort to an implicit standard of fairness. In other words, the constitutional dimension emerges once again, in that an implicit function of the concept is to protect the court (and indirectly the accused) against an unfair encroachment by the executive. This reasoning was clearly expressed by Lord Devlin in *Connelly v. DPP*[38];

> "Are the courts to rely on the Executive to protect their process from abuse? Have they not themselves an inescapable duty to secure fair treatment for those who come or who are brought before them? To questions of this sort there is only one possible answer. The courts cannot contemplate for a moment the transference to the Executive of the responsibility for seeing that the process of law is not abused.

Opponents relied upon a wider, implicit meaning of delay. There is of course no limitation period for murder, but the Bill's opponents argued that initiating any prosecution some 50 years after the alleged crime offends underlying principles of fairness and decency. Yet, the examples given, fail to sustain this case, or if more charitably interpreted, are equally compatible with a narrower meaning of abuse of process; namely that of delay prejudicial to the accused, but where the prosecution power is

---

[36] Lord Irvine, *HLD*, December 4, 1989 col. 673.
[37] See *D.P.P. v. Humphrys* [1977] A.C. 1, H.L.: *R. v. Derby Justices, ex p. Brookes* (1985) 80 Cr.App.Rep. 164; *R. v. Sunderland Magistrates Court, ex p. Choudhoury* (Unreported, July 29, 1988): *R. v. Grob* (Unreported, July 29, 1988); *Bell v. D.P.P.* (1985) A.C. 937 (P.C.); *R. v. Central Criminal Court, ex p. Randle and Another, The Times,* November 20, 1990.
[38] [1964] A.C. 1254 at 1354.

valid.[39] Thus, the key objections cited included the problems of identification,[40] and the difficulty of establishing an alibi.[41]

Neither matter is unique to Nazi war crimes. In cases laying down the guidelines to be followed where the evidence consists wholly or mainly of visual identification, the courts have refused to develop an exclusive inadmissibility rule, but instead leave it to the judge to rule upon the weight of the evidence. Where the evidence consists wholly or mainly of identification, and the quality of that evidence is poor, then in the absence of other evidence, the judge may withdraw the case from the jury and direct an acquittal. The overriding interest safeguarded by such power is maintenance of the integrity of the entire judicial process. Consequently, unless it can be shown that the proceedings represent, for example, an attempt to deprive the accused of the right to conduct an adequate defence, it would seem that the issue of specific prejudice, whether in respect of war crimes or any other offence, is most appropriately dealt with by the trial judge at the conclusion of the prosecution case.

Despite the fears of Lord Bridge that the Bill would leave no room for the judge's common law power to stay proceedings, the Government clearly stated to the contrary.[42] The Bill also contains two further safeguards against the possibility of an abuse of process; section one requires the consent of the Attorney-General for all prosecutions; and the accused may apply for dismissal of the case on the grounds of insufficient evidence.

The objections on the grounds of the difficulty in establishing an alibi defence cover two aspects of alleged prejudice. First, the difficulty of actually proving an alibi at a distance of 50 years. This criticism touches upon the presumption of innocence, the claim being that the passage of time hinders attempts to make a full answer to the charges. Secondly, the objection raises the separate issue of the likely resources available to the defence, who, it is claimed, will not have the financial and other means necessary to collect evidence, trace witnesses and so on. The critics also raised the associated issue of the likely bias to be experienced by an accused seeking co-operation from, for example, the (then) Soviet authorities, which may have regarded the

[39] See *Amato v. R.* (1982) 140 D.L.R. 405 at 442.
[40] Lord Ackner, *HLD*, June 4, 1990 col. 1121. Several speakers referred to the difficulties surrounding identification and events in the trial of John Demjanjuk in Israel to indicate some of the potential problems.
[41] *ibid.*, col. 1186.
[42] *HLD*, April 30, 1991 col. 738.

accused as a Nazi collaborator or a traitor.[43] However, this would again seem a matter most appropriately raised at the trial. Subject to the defence having full access to all the materials of the Crown, and the opportunity to cross examine all the Crown's witnesses, it is difficult to prejudge the issue in the way suggested by the Bill's opponents. Moreover, the defence could still raise the issue that a presumptive delay of the scale likely to be experienced in such a trial so seriously prejudices the defence case that it constitutes an abuse of process. The authorities also suggest that the onus would lie upon the prosecution to rebut the inference of prejudice arising from delay.[44] However, it remains the case that the likely form of defence objections arising from delay refer to specific prejudice affecting the defence case, such as the death of key witnesses, the loss of documentary evidence, and so forth.

Given the nature of the issues addressed in this section, it is also worthy of mention that an additional implicit factor seems to permeate the doctrine of abuse of process — that of the public interest in prosecuting serious criminal offences. In the Australian case of *Jago v. District Court of New South Wales*,[45] Kirby P. specifically referred to this condition as a factor relevant to the court's evaluation of the issues. As one Canadian commentator suggests:

> . . . human rights, like all rights of law, must have a co-existing system of enforcement to be effective . . . (there) are also human rights inherent in the due process system itself, such that trials of persons accused of monstrous crimes . . . are nevertheless carried out objectively, dispassionately, and according to the rule of law."[46]

This theme is more appropriately discussed later, in the section dealing with the representation of the issues. But even without further comment, it is obvious that the Bill's opponents premise their objections on a concept of fairness centred exclusively on protecting the individual rights of the accused, a perspective which may place unduly narrow limits on the legitimate frontiers of criminal liability.

The opposition case also maintained that defendants would be denied the right of confrontation and cross examination of his/her

---

[43] *HLD*, June 4, 1990 col. 1090.
[44] *Bell v. D.P.P.* [1985] A.C. 937.
[45] (1989) 87 A.L.R. 537 at 577.
[46] Fradkin L. "Holocaust and Human Rights Law" (1986) 12 *Boston College Third World Law Review* 44–58.

accusers in open court, and that this would greatly prejudice the defence case. Given the differences between the law of evidence in England and Scotland, and given the highly controversial, indirect method adopted by the Government to reform the Scots laws of evidence in respect of war crimes, the two jurisdictions merit separate treatment.[47]

The Inquiry was well aware of the procedural points, in particular the right to obtain the attendance, examination, and cross examination of witnesses provided by Article 6(3) of the European Convention on Human Rights. The Inquiry also admitted that it was desirable for witnesses to appear in person, "so that their evidence could be challenged . . . and the credibility . . . assessed". However, since many witnesses lived abroad, were old and frail, and unlikely to travel to the United Kingdom, other means of gathering their evidence had to be considered. The key proposals focused upon obtaining evidence via live television link, or by letters of request and evidence on commission — in both instances preferably video recorded. These proposals owed much to the recommendations of the Roskill Commission dealing with complex fraud cases,[48] subsequently enacted in section 32 of the Criminal Justice Act 1988.

It seems difficult to sustain the objection that the rules of evidence were deliberately altered to sustain prosecutions under the Act: the changes in the 1988 legislation were couched in general terms. However, the substance of the objection is that the changes mean that key witnesses may not appear in person, so depriving the court and the jury of the opportunity to observe a direct challenge to the credibility of their evidence. However, unless one concludes that all such evidence is always to be inadmissible, the issue is essentially one of the adequacy of the safeguards deployed to minimise the risk of compromising a fair trial.

Safeguards

Leave of the court is required before evidence obtained by live television link can be admitted.[49] Apart from the technical problems and its considerable cost factor, live television allows both the accused and the jury to see the witness give evidence,

---

[47] See below, pp. 43–44.
[48] The Roskill Commission's recommendations are considered in more depth in Weait's chapter in this volume.
[49] Criminal Justice Act 1988, s.32.

and permits cross examination. The trial judge also has the discretion to exclude evidence obtained by letter of request "in the interests of justice".[50] The relevant considerations here include whether any possibility of a challenge by cross examination arises, and whether the local law allowed the parties to be legally represented. The clear implication is that where there is no opportunity for cross examination, the trial judge can exclude the evidence.

Finally, there is the possibility of evidence taken on commission. Although the Inquiry did not see any particular advantage in this method over that of letter of request, commission is not an apposite method in Scotland, where the case law strictly circumscribes such evidence on the grounds of its potential unfairness to the accused. The objection to such evidence is framed in terms of the absence of the opportunity for oral cross examination before the judge or jury. This objection will not necessarily hold, since the Commissioner can be the trial judge.[51]

Procedural Fairness — the Scots Dimension

In effect, the debate on the changes in procedure affecting Scotland became a highly controversial issue because of the differences between Scots and English evidentiary rules, and because of the method adopted by the Government to amend Scots law. Prior to 1980, evidence in Scots criminal trials had to be given personally in court. It was not until the passage of the Criminal Justice (Scotland) Act 1980 (s.32) that provision was made for taking evidence on commission or by letter of request. However, the weight accorded by Scots courts, of the right to personal confrontation, is such that case law interpreting the Criminal Justice (Scotland) Act has restricted such evidence to purely formal matters, on the grounds that to do otherwise would unfairly deprive the accused of the opportunity for oral cross examination.[52] This entrenched presumption of personal appearances by witnesses in Scotland triggered great controversy over the Government's attempt to introduce an equivalent pro-

---

[50] *ibid.*, s.29.

[51] In the recent libel case brought by Anton Gecas against Scottish Television over an alleged libel contained in the programme "Crimes of War", the trial judge, Lord Millington, opened the trial in Vilnius, the capital of Lithuania, taking evidence on commission. In this case contact with the court in Edinburgh was maintained by telephone; *The Independent*, February 12, 1992.

[52] *Muirhead v. HM Advocate* [1983] SCCR 133.

vision to section 32(1)(a) of the Criminal Justice Act 1988. The Government's efforts to introduce the change, ahead of the War Crimes Bill, fuelled suspicion that the evidentiary reform was motivated entirely by that Bill's anticipated needs. The appropriate clause in the Law Reform (Miscellaneous Provisions) (Scotland) Bill was successfully ambushed by opponents of war crimes legislation in the Lords. The Government reintroduced the clause in the Prisoners and Criminal Proceedings (Scotland) Bill; once again, the proposal encountered determined, albeit ultimately unsuccessful opposition in the Lords, in what amounted to a re-run of the substantive debates on the War Crimes Act.

The case against changing the law of evidence focused upon the nature of the adversarial process. Under that form of trial, to quote Lord Wilberforce:

"[A] man has a right to be tried in the presence of his accusers and of his witnesses . . . the right to have his witnesses there and to confront them; the right for the jury to be confronted with them and for them to be confronted with the jury."[53]

In other words, a fair trial could not be guaranteed without the personal appearance of all the major players. Opponents in the Lords were not satisfied with the safeguards in the clause.[54] In addition, the trial judge's residual power to comment on the competency of the evidence remained undisturbed. This suggests that, once again, the basis of the critics' case was the absolute prioritisation of individual rights.

Procedural Fairness: the Canadian experience

As an aid to evaluating the competing arguments here, it might be apposite to refer briefly to the Canadian experience. Canada has already conducted four war crimes trials.[55] The Deschenes

[53] *HLD*, May 1, 1990 col. 948.
[54] The safeguards included the proviso that the judge to whom application is made is satisfied that:
　　a) the evidence is necessary for the proper adjudication of the trial, and;
　　b) the granting of the application is in the interests of justice, and;
　　c) the court is satisfied as to the arrangements for giving evidence in this manner.
　　In case the "justice" test is thought to be too wide the judge must be satisfied as to the fairness to the defendant of granting such a request, *i.e.* there is an overall fairness test protecting the defendant.
[55] *R. v. Finta* (1989) 61 D.L.R. (4th) 85: *R. v. Pawlaski* (1990) 293 SCO; *R. v. Reistetter* (1990) 321 (SCO); *Secretary of State v. Jacob Luitjens* (1989) 2 FCR (Vancouver).

Commission had stressed that any prosecution required the co-
operation of foreign governments in granting access to witnesses
and relevant archival material. The Deschenes Commission took
pains to suggest measures which would ensure such evidence met
the standards of Canadian justice. It laid down[56] the following six
conditions: strict confidentiality; independent interpreters; access
to original documents; access to witnesses' previous statements;
examination of witnesses in accordance with Canadian rules of
evidence; and videotaping of evidence taken abroad which was
then filed with the court.

The Federal Government's response to this cautionary advice
accepted that any person residing in Canada and accused of a
crime committed abroad, was entitled to be tried in a manner
consistent with Canadian standards of law and evidence, including the Canadian Charter of Human Rights and Freedoms.[57] This
commitment led the judge, in *Pawlawski*[58] to rule, at first
instance, that a fair trial was not possible if premised solely on
commission evidence videotaped in the (former) Soviet Union. In
Reistetter,[59] the death of a key witness and another's unwillingness
to testify led to all charges being dropped.

Finally, in *Finta*, one ground for the preliminary constitutional
challenge was the possibility of bias said to result from the
collection of evidence from governments not considered "free
and democratic". After a thorough review of the Deschenes
Commission findings, the Court concluded that there were no
grounds to support automatic inadmissibility; it was for the trier
of fact to assess the weight of such evidence. In reviewing the
relevant jurisprudence, the court cited the case of *United States v.
Trucis*,[60] which raised the issue of the inherent untrustworthiness
of evidence from the (former) Soviet Union:

"In any event, devices familiar to the American legal system and
available with respect (to the projected dispositions) . . . such as
cross-examination; videotaping itself; and also the opportunity prior
and/or at trial to adduce testimony as the setting within which the

---

[56] At pp. 890–891.
[57] S.ll(g) of which states: "Any person charged with an offence has the right not to
be found guilty on account of any act or omission unless, at the time of the act
or omission, it constituted an offence under Canadian or international law or
was criminal according to the general principles of law recognised by the
community of nations".
[58] See n.55, *supra*.
[59] *ibid*.
[60] (1989) 89 F.R.D. 671 at 674.

depositions are taken — all offer significant assurance that credibility issues can be fully explored before the fact finder . . .."

This reasoning seems no less apposite to litigation conducted in Britain. In view of the Act's various safeguards, combined with the residual discretion of the judge to evaluate the weight and credibility of the evidence, it is difficult to sustain the charge that the War Crimes Act creates special procedures which amount to unjustifiable interference with basic mechanisms of the adversarial process.

A Level Playing Field? Disparities in Resources

Critics extended their objections as to the Bill's alleged inherent unfairness to the likely inequality of resources between the prosecution and the defence. The objections suggested that the Inquiry was prosecution minded,[61] and ignored the near impossible burden that preparing a successful defence would impose. The implication is that such an imbalance would threaten the integrity of the entire criminal justice system, because, to quote Lord Donaldson, "a fair trial assumes an equal opportunity to disprove as well as prove. It assumes a level playing field".[62] Of course this objection applies across the field of criminal justice, and indeed to the legal system as a whole. However, with regard to criminal proceedings, disparity in resources has sometimes been cited as one reason why the principles of fairness to the accused should be given priority.[63] In the Bill's Committee stage, the Government sought to reassure the critics by pointing to the experience of serious fraud cases.[64] However, former defendants in serious fraud cases have highlighted the problems facing the defence as a result of the prosecution's greater manpower and financial resources.[65] Nevertheless, Canadian war crimes have yet to provide any evidence to suggest that the defence has been prejudiced by financial constraints.

Pragmatic Objections: The 'Costs' of Conviction

Since the enactment of the Bill, its opponents have directed their energy towards arguing against its enforcement. One strand of

[61] per Lord Shawcross, HLD, April 30, 1991 col. 644.
[62] HLD, June 4, 1990 col. 1174.
[63] Ashworth, op. cit., p. 77.
[64] Richardson, op. cit., p. 82.
[65] See The Independent, January 5, 1993. The issue is explored further in Matthew Weait's chapter in this volume.

this argument focuses on the apparently pragmatic objection of the prohibitive cost of mounting a prosecution. In both Houses of Parliament there has been a series of questions querying the Act's on-going costs,[66] implying that such expense represents a waste of resources and a false set of priorities. In Australia, the issue of financial costs has also figured prominently in debates over implementation of the legislation. The June 1992 decision to close down the Special Investigations Unit for War Crimes was said to be primarily on the grounds of exorbitant expense.[67] The net result of such a decision, ostensibly taken on purely financial grounds, effectively sabotages any further action against alleged Nazi war criminals, and may be seen as subverting the legislation.

Clearly, the cost of implementing war crimes trials in purely financial terms is considerable. However, to accept such expense as a sufficient justification for non-enforcement of legislation compromises an issue of fundamental justice by reference to a narrow criterion of economic rationality. "Cost" may also bear a wider meaning, and may extend to include such matters as the moral cost to the system of justice as a whole, of not giving such legislation practical effect. A consideration of such costs is therefore our next subject of enquiry.

Moral and Political Objections

This section embraces a cluster of ostensibly disparate arguments which, on closer examination, reveal a common leitmotif. The weight attaching to the arguments here is considerable, particularly as the preceding pages have suggested that opposition to the legislation is rooted in concerns about retrospectivity, procedural due process, and the financial costs of enforcement can be readily undermined.

It thus follows that if the Act's opponents are to sustain the case against it, they must do so on the basis of arguments within this fourth category. Ultimately this category is also the broadest in that it operates not so much at the intra-legal level, but at the level of the integrity of the criminal justice system as a whole. In other words, one must reject the interpretation of the rule of law as a set of juristic precepts, and regard it instead as the embodiment of society's political ideals.[68] In its starkest form, the

---

[66] *HLD*, July 7, 1992 col. 105–106; July 9, 1992 col. 707.
[67] "Prosecuting WWII Persecutors", in Boston College, *op. cit.*, n.46, above.
[68] Allen, *op. cit.*

argument asserts that the legislation contravenes the fundamental purpose and rationale of the criminal law, and so constitutes an illegitimate extension of state-power.[69]

That the Bills' opponents characterised it as "a denial of British Justice" was not merely a rhetorical device. In part, use of this powerful label was employed to encapsulate the argument that the Bill is simply a quest for vengeance.[70] The question of the legitimate boundaries of criminal liability was thereby transformed into a debate about the justification for, and scope of, punishment.[71] This, in turn, tended to be reduced to the classic dichotomy between retributivism and consequentialism.[72] By then asserting that retribution collapsed into revenge, the Act's opponents assumed that the case against prosecution was conclusively demonstrated.

Since not even the Bill's most implacable opponents could seriously assert that it is beyond the legitimate bounds of the criminal law to take action against mass murderers, on what grounds is it asserted that it is not legitimate to prosecute Nazi war criminals? It is by posing this question that the analytical continuum between the more extreme political opponents of the Bill, which, in effect, is a form of conspiracy theory, and the more temperate opposition can be seen.

The underlying premise is an assumption that time and distance render action unnecessary and unjustifiable. Temporal and geographical distance combine with an eclectic mish-mash of views ranging over such disparate issues as the Christian virtues of forgiveness and mercy, to the demands of European reconciliation, safely to consign the issue to the sanctuary of history. The characterisation of the legislation as a product of an essentially Jewish lobby (*i.e.* that it is extra-territorial in terms of source as well as jurisdictional reach) underscores the belief that by some alchemy, particularistic interests are being foisted upon the criminal justice system to the overall detriment of British Justice. Few of the Bill's opponents went so far as Lady Saltoun, who inquired:

> "was it decent and fitting that we should take such a step in order to enable aliens to be revenged on other aliens for something done in a foreign country nearly half a century ago?"[73]

[69] See Lord Shawcross, *HLD*, April 30, 1991 col. 644.
[70] *HLD*, June 4, 1990 col. 1138 and 1179.
[71] *HLD*, June 4, 1990 cols. 1098–1099.
[72] Richardson, *op. cit.*, pp. 78–80.
[73] *HLD*, December 4, 1989 col. 644.

Her views were not however unique. The Commons was also
informed that, "We all know how this began — with one of the
biggest lobbies in history, in California. It was highly financed in
order to bring not justice, but revenge and retribution. That is
how it all started".[74]

Such viewpoints rest on a parochial view of history which, in
effect, neutralises the impact and consequences of the Holocaust.
Moreover, their evident marginalisation of a minority group, the
denial of that groups' history, and its designation as 'alien', fits
poorly with the presumption that modern Britain is an avowedly
pluralistic society.

This denial of history is, however, a necessary stage in any
argument which seeks seriously to claim that prosecuting Nazi
war criminals would contravene fundamental standards of justice.
The case for prosecuting Nazi war criminals invokes such basic
values of liberal democratic society as the sanctity and dignity of
human life, and the protection of physical integrity; values which
the late Professor Hart referred to as the "minimum conditions of
natural law".[75] These are not marginal or particularistic claims.
Rather they are elements of what have been referred to as
'foundational values'[76] within liberal democratic society. Such
values embrace both individualistic concerns of freedom and
autonomy and the protection of the system itself which guarantees such values. In fostering individual rights, government must
both respect them itself and safeguard them against breach by
others. If the criminal justice system singularly fails to act against
those who have allegedly breached the rights of countless other
human beings, it is difficult to envisage in what sense that system
can claim to act in a manner consistent with its own fundamental,
justificatory values. In short, as Rosenbaum claims, "the integrity
of a system of rights invariably hinges upon whether and how it
administers legal justice in fulfilment of its obligation to do so".[77]

If this argument can be sustained, the criticism that the Act
contravenes basic principles of justice by illegitimately extending
state power through the agency of the criminal law falls down.
However, the case for the legislation can also be made on
positive grounds; to this end it is necessary to relocate the Act
within a wider context of morality, history, and law.

[74] *HCD*, December 12, 1991 col. 43.
[75] Hart H., *The Concept of Law* (1964), pp. 188–189.
[76] Lacey N., *State Punishment: Political Principles and Community Values* (1988)
pp. 98–99.
[77] Rosenbaum A., "On the Issue of Prosecuting Nazi War Criminals", in Bauer
Y. (ed.) *Remembering the Future*, (1988) vol. 11, p. 1284.

Conclusion

This final section suggests that if one places the Act in its wider moral, historical, and legal context, one reveals not that its passage and enforcement threaten traditional notions of justice, but rather that a failure to prosecute alleged Nazi war criminals would itself amount to a denial of justice. Whilst the legislation raises far-reaching issues concerning the role and scope of the criminal law, these implications in no way breach the legitimate role of the criminal law in a liberal democratic political system. In contrast, reference to the basic values of such a system suggests that the Act is a necessity.

The Moral Dimension

At this level of abstraction, it is assumed that the criminal justice system expresses an underlying moral theory. Lacey describes this moral framework as operating at the "first level of generality".[78] It covers fundamental issues such as the links between a criminal justice system and the "preservation and protection of the most important values in any given society". In liberal theory, it is incumbent upon the legal order to recognise and protect meta-legal (moral) rights through the agency of the criminal law. Thus, if one accepts that the right to life and the protection of physical integrity are of a 'minimum content of natural law', the protection of such values through the criminal law is a prerequisite for the preservation of society.

Any reference to such constitutive or fundamental rights immediately raises questions as to their origin, justification and content. These questions are far beyond the reach of this chapter.[79] However, whichever view is adopted on such questions, the resolution of any tension between individualistic and systemic considerations presents a moral issue which must be addressed with reference to an overriding moral principle.[80] In the case of the War Crimes Act, the moral issue presents a clash between the need to enact and enforce the legislation in order to protect the system's fundamental values, and the need to uphold constraints within the system geared to limiting the form which

---

[78] *op. cit.*, pp. 98–105.
[79] See, for example, Gewirth A., "The Basis and Content of Human Rights" (1981) in Pennock R. (ed.) *Human Rights*.
[80] *ibid.*

such prosecution can take. The opposition case asserts that the legislation exceeds the legitimate bounds of the criminal law because it cannot meet these limiting standards. More controversially, their viewpoint implies that the legislation is not necessary to protect such values in the first place.

Faced with the monstrous reality of the offences, it is difficult to support this argument. To fail to prosecute such crimes, thereby allowing their perpetrators to go free, suggests an implicit condonation of the behaviour concerned. To deny the possibility of prosecution — with appropriate safeguards — thus imputes the integrity of the system as a whole. In the face of mass murder — the denial of the most elementary and basic right, that of the victims' right to life and physical integrity — to fail to prosecute, seriously compromises the morality of the legal order.

The Historical Dimension

In effect this section might be subtitled "The Challenge of the Holocaust — the Systematic Destruction of European Jewry", for it was from such a context that the crimes which the Act confronts emerged. A link with the previous section can be seen if the events constituting the Holocaust are seen as the total negation of morality through the agency of state-sponsored violence.[81]

The opposition case presupposes either neutralising the significance of the Holocaust, or remaining silent about it. The net result of this position is to consign the Holocaust to history — to the past. In contrast, the Act's supporters presuppose the continuing significance of the Holocaust even at this late stage. The Act's opponents adopted a variety of different positions regarding their understanding and characterisation of the Holocaust. All these positions were directed, however, to showing that the legislation was an unwarranted extension of the criminal law, whose objective could be realised only at too high a price. Thus, Lord Longford declared that the Holocaust was unique and incomprehensible to anyone other than its victims; all that society could do was to commiserate and forgive.[82] In contrast, others, while acknowledging the dreadful crimes committed, considered the Nuremberg trials as the only effective response. It was also suggested that future concerns about promoting European inte-

---

[81] See Bauman Z., *The Holocaust and Modernity* (1989), Chap. 7.
[82] *HLD*, April 30, 1991 col. 663.

gration made it unwise for anyone to attempt to disinter such a past.[83]

An alternative opposition perspective argued strongly that the Holocaust was far from unique; rather it was "comparable to many other equally horrible but equally unpunished crimes".[84] This position again raised the issue of selectivity; why were these atrocities being singled out for special attention? To some, the answer was that the Act was a result of "one of the biggest lobbies in history",[85] which again suggested that the legislative process was in some way being subverted by alien forces.

The net effect of these characterisations reveals a common ground which, at best, neutralises the Holocaust or demeans, trivialises or ignores it. In the present day context of Holocaust denial, the resurgence of anti-Semitism and racism, such approaches come dangerously close to contributing to the process of historical revisionism.[86] Such arguments suggest that the Holocaust has no lessons of relevance to the contemporary world, and embody the common message that any legislative response in the form of criminal sanction is totally unjustified. However, it is possible to contextualise the Holocaust in history in a way that holds out crucial lessons for contemporary society. Bauman argues that:

> "[T]he Holocaust was not simply a Jewish problem, and not an event in Jewish history alone. The Holocaust was born and executed in our modern rational society, at the high stage of our civilisation and at the peak of human cultural achievement, and for this reason it is a problem of that society, civilisation and culture."[87]

Consequently, Bauman suggests, to consign the Holocaust to history is more than neglect; it is "a dangerous and potentially suicidal blindness".[88]

Bauman identifies several crucial factors within modernity which contributed to the "unique" encounter leading to the Holocaust: the modern state's monopoly of coercion and violence; the accompanying form of modern rational administration and organisation — bureaucracy; and the generalisation of instrumental rationality, which resulted in the de-coupling of

---

[83] Edward Heath, *HCD*, December 12, 1989 col. 897.
[84] *HLD*, December 4, 1989 col. 653.
[85] Edward Heath, *HCD*, December 12, 1989 col. 43.
[86] See, for example, Seidel G., *The Holocaust Denial* (1984).
[87] *op. cit.*, p. x.
[88] *ibid.*

rationality from morality, (and, in the form of positivist legal theory, of law from morality). In this situation the issue of the moral-ethical limits of the modern state evaporates. There is no action that such a state cannot aspire to, even to the extent of legislating for genocide. Thus, there would be no grounds upon which it would be possible to prosecute war criminals, who could claim merely to be acting in accordance both with morality and (positive) law.

A legal response to the Holocaust calling for prosecution of Nazi war criminals rejects such arguments, and re-affirms the fundamental moral values underpinning liberal-democratic society. Such legislation is a vindication of the rule of law in the ideal sense, and also serves a number of important, but subordinate functions. Trials of suspected Nazi war criminals put on the record the appalling atrocities committed during the Holocaust, whilst showing that individuals were responsible for such acts — not abstractions such as the SS or the Einsatzgruppen. Added to this purpose of exposure, the law's denunciatory value cannot be underestimated. Use of the criminal law is clear notice that such acts will neither be condoned nor tolerated, regardless of the effluxion of time, or the cost and inconvenience of prosecution. Added to these functions are the educative effects on the second or, indeed, third post-war generations, who need the insight into the roots of racism, hatred, prejudice and the effects of state-sponsored violence, which a trial provides.

That factors such as exposure, denunciation, and education play a legitimate role in the development of the criminal law has been questioned by many of the Bill's opponents.[89] But, since the criminal law is society's strongest form of official condemnation, drawing what are perceived as serious social harms within its embrace performs symbolic and educational functions. Given that it is possible to argue consistently for the legislation at the level of fundamental moral principle, symbolic and educative factors can be seen as perfectly legitimate, albeit subordinate, influences on the law's scope and reach.

The Legal Dimension

In 1957, a Home Office Minister introduced the Geneva Conventions Bill to the Commons with the following words:

> "[T]he Bill marks a considerable departure in our criminal law . . . it makes liable to the criminal jurisdiction of our domestic courts . . .

[89] *HLD*, April 30, 1991 col. 680.

offences wherever the breaches are committed and regardless of the nationality of the accused. . . . There is very limited precedent for such a provision . . . but we believe that this departure is necessary if we are to honour certain new types of international obligation now recognised as morally binding."[90]

These international obligations derived from the (four) Geneva Conventions of 1949. At no point in the Parliamentary debate was exception taken to this extension of criminal jurisdiction. The Geneva Conventions Act 1957 was seen as a necessary response to the demands of international law, and it is with respect to such law that any wider evaluation of the War Crimes Act must deal. For the 1991 Act's opponents, the 1957 legislation was an irrelevance, since it applied only prospectively. Yet the relevance of international law cannot be dismissed so lightly. Indeed, the Inquiry itself pointed out that, in 1939, the Hague Conventions of 1899 and 1907 were "accepted by the civilised world as part of the international law governing the laws and customs of warfare"[91] when it proposed to extend the courts' jurisdiction. Given that war crimes, which included the murder of civilian populations, were regarded as international crimes by 1939, the key issue thus resolves itself into one of the jurisdictional bases upon which states might claim authority to act against alleged war criminals. Under international law a series of principles for determining jurisdiction have evolved.[92] These include universal jurisdiction, under which a state may claim jurisdiction over certain acts — generally regarded as being universal crimes[93] — even though the usual links between the prosecuting state, the alleged offender and the victim, are lacking. The rationale for such a jurisdictional claim ultimately flows from the universal nature and effect of the criminal act itself: such acts are classified as *delicta juris gentium* (grave offences against the law of nations itself). Obviously the Hetherington/Chalmers Inquiry concluded that it was permissible to claim jurisdiction.

The problem also received judicial analysis in the recent Australian case of *Polyukhovich*, where Toohey J.'s reasoning is particularly apposite. After pointing to the conceptual distinction

---

[90] *HCD*, July 12, 1957 col. 716.
[91] Para. 5.42.
[92] Akehurst M., "Jurisdiction in International Law" (1973) *British Yearbook of International Law* 145–257; Randall K., "Universal Jurisdiction under International Law" (1988) Texas L.R. 785–841.
[93] Such as piracy and the slave trade; see Randall, *op. cit.*

between whether a crime exists and the scope of the jurisdiction to prosecute, he indicated that the two issues;

> "are also inextricably linked. . . . Where conduct, because of its magnitude, affects the moral interests of humanity and thus assumes the status of a crime in international law, the principle of universality must almost inevitably, prevail."[94]

Having suggested that international law enables states to assume universal jurisdiction over war crimes, the question arises whether so adapting domestic jurisdiction overextends the criminal law. The normal basis of criminal jurisdiction is territorial. But this principle is not absolute. In exceptional cases such as piracy, British court have affirmed that:[95]

> "With regard to crimes as defined by international law, that law has no means of trying or punishing them. The recognition of them as constituting crimes, and the trial and punishment of the criminals are left to the municipal law of each country. But whereas according to international law the criminal jurisdiction of municipal law is ordinarily restricted to crimes committed on its terra firma or territorial waters or its own ships, and to crimes by its own nationals wherever committed, it is also recognised as extending to piracy committed on the high seas by any national on any ship, because a person guilty of such piracy has placed himself beyond the protection of any State. He is no longer a national, but 'hostis humani generis' and as such he is justiciable by any State anywhere."

Since war crimes fell within the category of international crimes in 1939, the question of whether international law constitutes part of English law without express Parliamentary adoption is irrelevant; international law confers a right to exercise such jurisdiction, and this right should be exercised. To reject this view is both parochial, and unduly restrictive of the development of an international perception of the fundamental tenets of the rule of law.

War crimes constitute an exceptional category of crimes; it is this character which justifies assumption of jurisdiction. Jurisprudentially, the development of the law of war was historically distinct from that of human rights law. Factors such as military necessity and the need for (humanitarian and other) restraints led to the central emphasis upon reciprocity,[96] and a consequential

---

[94] At p. 663 (1991) 172 C.L.R. 501 at 663.
[95] In re Piracy Jure Gentium [1934] A.C. 586 at 589.
[96] Draper G., "Human Rights Law and the Laws of War" (1971) Virginia Jo. Int. L., 326–342.

concern with protection of narrowly defined groups of persons. Nevertheless, this limited humanitarian component played an increasingly important role within the development of the law of war, and this element, allied to the purpose of the law, clearly points to an increasing convergence with an evolving human rights law. The restrictions imposed upon state and individual conduct by the laws of war, reflect a tempering of the central concern of national sovereignty by vestigial humanitarian concerns. In the face of state-sponsored genocide such as the Holocaust, the need for a human rights law is paramount. It is therefore possible to begin to relocate the laws of war on a continuum of laws protecting human rights. As Toohey J. observed in *Polyukhovich*:

> "Fundamental values and the laws of wars themselves, being rules limiting the means of aggression not rules permitting violence, arise from a desire to preserve humanity and humanness in relations between all people. They are themselves, in this sense, humanitarian norms."[97]

Extending domestic jurisdiction to allow prosecution of Nazi war criminals contributes to this evolving human rights law. The basic values it aims to protect are those of humanity itself, respect for human life, and human dignity. Such values are constitutive of the moral infrastructure of liberal democratic society. Failing to adopt such a jurisdiction therefore undermines the rule of law in both the domestic and international arena. States do not exist in an international vacuum; the reality of the Holocaust demands that limits are placed upon the unrestricted exercise of sovereignty in order to protect the interests of humanity and human rights. In this sense, the legitimate frontiers of the criminal law are determined by the fundamental moral norms upon which civilisation depends. Refusal to condone such crimes against humanity, and to prosecute their perpetrators, is of continuing significance and urgency. Failure to act decisively — even at this late stage — both denies justice to the countless victims of the Holocaust, and sets a negative precedent for the future. Far from being an illegitimate extension of jurisdiction and an arbitrary exercise of state power, the War Crimes Act is a pre-requisite if justice is to be done. To quote the words of David Cesarani, "Justice delayed may not be justice denied, after all; but history denied will never lead to justice".[98]

---

[97] (1991) 172 C.L.R. 501 at 675.
[98] *op. cit.*, p. 267.

Chapter Three

STATE REACTION TO CONSCIENTIOUS OBJECTION
by Lois Bibbings

This chapter explores the various governmental, corporate and individual responses to the issue of conscientious objection during the First and Second World Wars. Attention is directed both to the formal content and implementation of the conscription legislation, and also to other governmental and social practices which affected the treatment of objectors. Conscientious objection is not an issue which has always had obvious, formal connections with British criminal law. However, this chapter argues that those purporting to be objectors were often subject to more severe treatment, from both governmental and non-governmental sources, than others who either refused to obey, or violated "traditional" criminal law provisions.

The First World War

The Military Service Acts 1916–1918 introduced compulsory military service for able men in certain specified age groups.[1] The Acts reversed a century old tradition of military reliance upon volunteer and professional forces.[2] In requiring citizens to serve in the armed forces, the Acts represented a substantial invasion of individual liberty. Those targeted by the Acts were compelled, not simply to surrender their freedom of movement, but also to place their lives and physical well-being at considerable risk, and to accept that they would be called upon to kill or maim other human beings.

The Parliamentary debate over the 1916 Bill reproduced, in a rather different form, the tension between individualistic conceptions of liberty and a wider "public interest" which Richardson identified in chapter 2 as central to the issue of the legitimacy of

---

[1] The first Military Service Act 1916 provided for the compulsory enlistment of all single male British subjects aged 18–41; s.1(1)(a). Subsequent measures extended this group to include all able-bodied men within prescribed age limits.
[2] See Hearnshaw F. "Compulsory Military Service in England", (1916) *Quarterly Review*, April 416–437 and Fortesque J., *The British Army, 1783–1801* (1905).

the War Crimes Act 1991. The public interest at stake was, clearly, the need for Britain and its allies to triumph in the war in which they were engaged.[3] For Prime Minister Asquith, subjecting men to conscription simply; "deemed in law . . . what everyone recognised to be their duty as a matter of moral and national obligation in the time of greatest stress in all our history".[4] The realm's long term survival was not, however, regarded as sufficient justification by many M.P.'s for so draconian an intrusion upon private autonomy. Nor were moral imperatives invariably viewed as being so clearly cut. Sir John Simon, the Home Secretary, was the most prominent of a number of Liberals who opposed compulsion. Simon's distaste for the measure was sufficient to cause him to resign from the Government.[5] His opposition to the Bill rested on various grounds. He suggested that Prime Minister Asquith had not honoured a commitment that conscription would not be introduced until the Government had accurately ascertained how many able, single men would decline to serve voluntarily. He also considered that the opposition which compulsion would raise in the country at large would handicap the war effort to a greater extent than the extra military personnel, thereby procured, would assist it. Fundamentally, Simon's resignation was prompted by a question of moral, or perhaps constitutional, principle: "[T]he real issue is whether we are to begin an immense change in the fundamental structure of our society".[6] That change was to encompass a sacrifice of individual liberty to a majoritarian perception of the public good. The principle of voluntary enlistment was part of the "birthright" of the English people.[7] Consequently, supporters of the Bill were "infecting themselves with a false doctrine"[8], namely the belief that:

"This country would greatly gain if we could not only in this connection [conscription], but in fiscal matters, social matters, any other matters, carry the organisation of this country, not up to the point to which it is now carried by voluntary effort, but carry it

---

[3] The debate as to the desirability of compulsory military service had rather longer roots, however; see Adams R. and Poirier P. *The Conscription Controversy in Great Britain 1900–1917* (1987), Chap. 2.

[4] *HCD*, January 5, 1916, col. 961.

[5] See Simon's resignation speech: HCD January 5, 1916 col. 962–978 and Simon J., *Viscount Simon, Retrospective* (1952), p. 107.

[6] *HCD*, January 5, 1916 col. 963.

[7] *HCD*, January 5, 1916 col. 974.

[8] *HCD*, January 12, 1916 col. 1657.

further, even for military purposes by force, and even at the expense of substituting a great deal of State machinery for a great deal that is voluntary and self-sacrificing."[9]

The "real truth", which the Bill's advocates had forgotten or cast aside, was that "military organisation by force is the very system which this country united to destroy".[10]

Simon's position attracted only minority support in the Commons. However, at least initially, opposition outside Parliament to the introduction of conscription had seemed widespread. For example, in 1915 Beatrice Webb recorded a pervasive "feeling against conscription amongst thoughtful working men".[11] The No-Conscription Fellowship (NCF) was at the forefront of campaigning,[12] whilst both the Independent Labour Party and the trade union movement generally opposed compulsion prior to 1915[13]: in September of that year, the then equivalent of the Trades Union Congress had rejected the principle of military conscription by an overwhelming majority.[14] Even in 1916, *The Labour Leader* went so far as to warn of the possibility of revolution if the measure was enacted.[15] However, the Labour Party officially altered its stance, and union resistance lessened following a series of compromises within the Cabinet and Parliament. The voluntary system of recruitment was reopened,[16] hence allowing men, who had not already attested their willingness to serve, avoid the humiliation of being a conscript. Assurances were also given that industrial conscription would not follow.[17] Thus, in early 1916, the emergency measure was passed amid a growing concern that the length and severity of the conflict necessitated more recruits and greater sacrifices. However, the Military Service Act 1916 included a clause which decreased the universality of its provisions.

[9] *ibid.*
[10] *ibid.*
[11] B. Webb to B. Balfour, October 28, 1915, Passfield Papers, II.4.g.f.45. (British Library of Political and Economic Science).
[12] The work of the N.C.F. is described by Kennedy T., *The Hound of Conscience* (1918).
[13] See Thomis M., *The Labour Movement in Great Britain and Compulsory Military Service 1914–1916* (1966), (Unpublished MA thesis: London University).
[14] *HCD*, January 12, 1916 col. 1650.
[15] January 13, 1916.
[16] CAB 37/140/17; *HCD*, January 5, 1916 col. 961.
[17] Cole D., *A History of the Labour Party From 1914* (1984), pp. 27–28.

Conscientious Objection — the Substantive Law

For the first time, "conscientious objectors" to military service were granted statutory recognition.[18] The "conscience clause" had been a late and hastily drafted addition to the Bill.[19] Sir John Simon suggested that one body of M.P.'s had seen it as "a laughing matter".[20] The clause was a compromise aimed at pacifying both the pro-conscriptionists, such as Joyson-Hicks M.P. (Conservative), who generally opposed it,[21] and those liberals like Reginald McKenna, Chancellor of the Exchequer, and Walter Runciman, President of the Board of Trade, who had grave objections to compulsion.[22] Thus, the inclusion of this provision ensured the enactment of the Bill with a large majority whilst also symbolising that, in a purportedly democratic state, some respect for individual scruples remained. However, the result of these compromises was a provision which was ambiguous in both substantive and procedural terms.

Section 2(1)(d) of the Military Service Act 1916 (MSA 1916) listed "conscientious objection to the undertaking of combatant service" as a ground upon which an individual could apply for exemption. However, the Act did not specify the foundations upon which a valid objection could be based. Further uncertainty existed regarding the level of exemption available to genuine objectors. If an applicant was recognised as possessing an objection he could be granted partial exemption (from combatant service only); conditional exemption (exemption provided he undertook work of national importance); or absolute exemption from the terms of the Act,[23] although there was some doubt whether this last option was available to objectors.[24]

There had been no Parliamentary consideration of the option of explicitly making refusal to be conscripted a criminal offence.

---

[18] There had already been a degree of recognition for those who objected to oath taking, religious instruction in schools, compulsory vaccination, and to a limited extent, military service. See Braithwaite C., "Legal Problems of Conscientious Objection to Various Forms of Compulsion under British Law" (1968), *Journal of the Friends Historical Society* pp. 3–18.

[19] John Rae estimates that the decision to insert such a provision could not have been made prior to January 1, 1916; *Conscience and Politics: The British Government and the Conscientious Objector to Military Service 1916–1919* (1970), p. 27.

[20] *HCD,* January 12, 1916 col. 1648.

[21] See, for example, Joyson-Hicks' speech at *HCD*, January 19, 1916 c. 422–427.

[22] See CAB 37/139/58, December 28, 1916.

[23] MSA 1916 s.2(3).

[24] See below pp. 66–67.

Instead, such men were deemed to have enlisted and were placed under military control.[25] This may have been a result of the speed with which the "conscience clause" was drafted, and an assumption that those who were genuine would acquire adequate recognition, whilst those who were not would be forced to admit their lack of honesty once faced with military discipline and punishment. In addition, those who considered that non-compliance should attract punishment could not complain of the liberal nature of the military system of penalties which an uncooperative individual would face.

Due Process of Law?

The exemption claims were processed by a three-tiered civil tribunal system.[26] Applications were to be made to local tribunals whose members were not required to possess any legal experience or training. Dissatisfied applicants could appeal as of right to an area appeal tribunal and then, if the appeal body consented, to the Central Tribunal. Both of the appellate tribunals included legally qualified members.[27]

Neither the Act, nor its implementing regulations, made comprehensive provision concerning the procedures that the tribunals should follow. The Military Service Regulations ((Amendment) Orders SR&I) 1916 No. 53 specified that hearings should generally be in public, that objectors might be represented by any person of their choosing, and that objectors were to be allowed to question witnesses, or the Military Representative who was contesting the application for exemption. However, there was certainly no suggestion that objection should be construed as a crime in the sense of requiring tribunals to adhere to criminal law standards of due process. Nor, at this stage, was the matter discussed at any length in Parliament.

The courts were also reluctant to use public law doctrines to place tight controls on the tribunals' procedural autonomy. In *R. v. Central Tribunal, ex parte Parton*,[28] the High Court rejected arguments that tribunals should conform to due process standards

---

[25] MSA 1916 s.1(1)(b).

[26] See MSA 1916 s.2(7), Scheds. 2–3.

[27] Unfortunately, a comprehensive assessment of the tribunals' work is not possible because of the lack of full official documentation; the Ministry of Health, which gained responsibility for these records after the war, decided in 1921 that the majority of tribunal papers should be destroyed. PRO MH 47/3.

[28] [1916] 3 T.L.R. 476.

comparable to those used in its own hearings. *Parton* held that the adequacy of tribunal procedures should be measured, not against the model of a criminal trial, but against the newly emerging adminstrative law doctrine of "fairness". The court made specific reference to the House of Lords' decision in *Local Government Board v. Arlidge*.[29] *Arlidge* had expressly rejected the contention that "fairness" required governmental bodies to adopt judicial procedures, since such standards might "seriously impair administrative efficiency".[30] *Arlidge* suggested that tribunals and other goverment bodies should enjoy considerable autonomy to devise their own procedures, with the scope of that autonomy being decided on a case by case basis. *Parton* saw no need to lay down procedural guidelines for the conscientious objection tribunals to follow, beyond confirming that the Central Tribunal need not grant applicants an oral hearing. The laxity of this framework meant that it would, in formal terms, be difficult for tribunals to abuse procedural constraints on their autonomy. Empirical evidence suggests, however, that even these lax controls were frequently breached, and that, in terms of the rather more abstract issue of the hearings' conformity with due process notions of the rule of law, tribunal behaviour was systemically indefensible. The conduct of hearings, and the decisions reached, were widely criticised; indeed the tribunals have often been blamed for the non-recognition of genuine objectors. Thus, many of those who applied for exemption experienced abuse and condemnation from the tribunals and either failed to gain any form of exemption, or were granted a level which they could not accept. Whilst some of these failures could be attributed to ambiguities within the legislation, the use of lay members and the fundamental impossibility of assessing a person's beliefs, there were clearly other factors which caused many tribunals to treat objectors unfavourably.

There were many instances when tribunals would treat applicants on conscience grounds with evident scorn. The NCF's organ, *The Tribunal*, commented upon the "Scandalous maladministration of the Act", and reported a tendency for tribunals to rebut, bully and condemn objectors. Those who claimed that their objection was based upon political or moral rather than religious, grounds faired particularly badly.[31] Similarly, Philip

---

[29] [1915] A.C. 120.
[30] *per* Lord Shaw at 130.
[31] March 8, 1916. Not all objectors were treated equally; Quakers' applications were most likely to be accepted by tribunals, whilst political objectors faired worst.

Snowden M.P. (Independent Labour Party) noted that; "a great many of the tribunals seem to take delight in heaping scorn and insults upon the applicants who appeal before them for exemption on this ground [conscientious objection]".[32]

There were frequent reports of tribunal members who, with blatant disregard for their impartial role, denounced pacifism and conscientious objection. Tribunal members called objectors blackguards, shirkers, cowards, criminals and, perhaps most significantly, traitors. The Chairman of Nairn City Tribunal told one applicant on conscience grounds: "You [conscientious objectors] are the most unlawful pack who ever walked this earth" and condemned him for colluding with the German Emperor.[33] In a similar vein, a member of Oldbury Tribunal accused an objector of cowardice and insolence.[34]

The liberal and radical press, particularly *The Tribunal* and *The Labour Leader*, exposed weekly the irregular and unjudicial behaviour of some tribunals. Criticism also appeared in less likely places; in *The Times* the Bishops of Oxford and Lincoln called for more respectful treatment for applicants.[35] The Local Government Board, which was responsible for the constitution and procedure of the tribunals,[36] was also aware of these allegations of prejudice and harsh treatment. The Board's President, Walter Long, responded in March 1916. He issued a circular to the local tribunals which noted that: "Some tribunals are alleged to have subjected applicants to somewhat harsh cross examination with respect to the grounds of their objection" and called for an end to such practices.[37] The circular was not binding upon the tribunals, and complaints continued.

Some applicants found that they were effectively denied a full hearing. For example H. E. Stanton recorded that his appearance on March 8, 1916 at Luton Local Tribunal took less than three minutes.[38] Whilst this could in part have been a reaction to Local Government Board guidance to avoid delays,[39] it appears from surviving records that it was those claiming to be objectors who were most likely to receive a brief or superficial hearing.

[32] *British Prussianism: the Scandal of the Tribunals* (1916), p. 8 (Manchester: National Labour Press).

[33] *The Tribunal*, March 8, 1916.

[34] Snowden, *op. cit.*, p. 8.

[35] *The Times,* March 14, 1916. Also, see The *Daily Chronicle*, March 29, 1916 and The *London Star*, March 1, 1916.

[36] See MSA. 1916, Sched.2, Pt.6 and Military Service (No. 2) Act 1916, s.4(4).

[37] R.70, March 23, 1916, PRO MH 47/142.

[38] Stanton H. *Diaries,* Vol. I, p. 9 (manuscript — privately owned).

[39] R. 36, February 3, 1916, PRO MSS MH 47/142.

The behaviour of the Military Representative often exhibited a sufficiently distinct bias against objectors to compromise the fairness of the tribunal proceedings. The Representative was a party to the hearing and presented the military stance where there was an official objection to exemption being granted.[40] However, a number of Representatives often adopted, and were allowed to adopt, the role of a prosecutor in a criminal trial. They would bully and insult objectors and bombard them with accusations and threats. The Representative at Fulham Local Tribunal was said to interrogate applicants[41] and Captain Bax of Middlesex Appeal Tribunal was particularly criticised for his rough treatment of objectors.[42] The result in some extreme instances was that both the tribunal members and the Representative joined together in attacking applicants and then proceeded to refuse exemption. In a few tribunals this problem was compounded as some of the local bodies permitted the Representative to act as an adviser to the members or even as an extra member of the panel.[43] The Representative at Hyde in Cheshire even retired with the members when they considered their decision.[44] Such practices became so widely publicised that the War Office directed Representatives to alter their behaviour.[45]

The somewhat cavalier nature of the procedures adopted by some tribunals was, on occasion, matched by their substantive decisions. Several tribunals refused to grant absolute exemption, or even conditional exemption, from military service to those applying on conscience grounds, often relying upon the ambiguous phraseology of the exemption provision to justify their actions. The Middlesex Appeal Tribunal decided that the Military Service Act, 1916 allowed successful applicants on conscience grounds only to be exempted from combatant duties.[46] Other tribunals interpreted the exemption provision to mean that absolute exemption was not available to objectors. This was challenged in the King's Bench Division. The court ruled that the tribunals had no statutory power to grant absolute exemption.[47]

[40] SR&O 1916, No. 53, Pt.1, 16(c).
[41] See Snowden, *op. cit.*, p. 5.
[42] *The Sentinel*, July 28, 1916.
[43] See *Western Daily Press*, February 19, 1916 on the Bristol Tribunal and Colonel Burges.
[44] Snowden *op. cit.*, p. 7.
[45] See *The Recruiting Code* (1918), s.187 (London: Ministry of National Service).
[46] Minutes of the Middlesex Appeal Tribunal, March 23 and 29, 1916, PRO MH 47/144.
[47] *R. v. Central Tribunal, ex p. Parton* [1916] 3 T.L.R. 476.

This decision triggered a prompt legislative response. Section 4(3) of the Military Service Act (Session 2) 1916 stated unequivocally that all statutory forms of exemption could be granted to objectors. Nevertheless, some tribunals still failed to grant absolute exemption arguing that exemption from combatant duties was appropriate as section 2(1)(d) specified that this was the only form of objection which was legally recognised.[48] The Middlesex Appeal Tribunal granted no certificates of absolute exemption during the period of conscription[49] and the Central Tribunal decided that absolute exemption should only be available in exceptional circumstances.[50] A more extreme example of substantive irregularity is provided by the case of Harold Bing. Mr Bing's application was dismissed once the tribunals realised that he was only 18 years old and thus, they concluded, too young to possess a conscience![51]

Such examples of tribunal practice would suggest that hearings often operated as a denunciatory rather than investigatory process. As such, they provided an 'official' source of legitimation for, and encouragement of, a more pervasive and informal mistreatment of conscientious objectors.[52] The State and its institutions also perpetuated such sentiments through other means. Wartime propaganda, by implication, encouraged such attitudes. Alfred Leate's famous Kitchener poster demanded that men do their patriotic duty; those who obeyed were praised as heroes, those who resisted or refused to cooperate were, at best, unconventional.[53]

The deviance of conscientious objection was frequently identified by non-governmental sources as a threat to the war-effort. Refusals to fight, if too widespread, could mean that there were too few recruits to ensure victory. In consequence, claiming to be an objector, or defending this stance, was frequently branded as deviant behaviour even before the introduction of conscription.[54]

---

[48] See Snowden, *op. cit.*, pp. 9–11, 17.

[49] PRO MH 47/143.

[50] Minutes of the Central Tribunal, July 6, 1916, PRO MH 47/1.

[51] Harold Bing audio tape, 358, Reel 2 and p. 7, Oral History Recordings, Department of Social Records, Imperial War Museum.

[52] This presumably symbiotic relationship between state action and public opinion provides an interesting illustration of a Durkheimian analysis of the relationship between legal form, social structure, and popular sentiment; see the chapter by Celia Wells in this volume at pp. 116–118.

[53] See, generally, Haste C., *Keep The Home Fires Burning; Propaganda in Britain in the First World War* (1977).

[54] For example, from the early days of the war, patriotic women were handing out white feathers to those who refused to enlist. See Wiltshire A., *Most Dangerous Women: Feminist Peace Campaigners of the Great War* (1985), p. 1.

From 1916–1918 objectors were stigmatised, taunted, and hounded in society. A soldier returning from the war described the existence of a "general loathing for conscientious objectors" and their "social ostracism".[55] Anti-objector sentiments were encouraged and heightened by various commentators. "Conchies" were publicly condemned by prominent members of the clergy,[56] in schools, in the press and within the home.[57] Objectors were stereotypically portrayed as being enemy agents, unpatriotic, cowards, or shirkers. Much of the press expressed similar opinions to those of the most prejudiced tribunal members. The *Daily Express* described objectors as traitors who were helping to stab the army in the back and were effectively "fighting for Germany".[58] In contrast The *Daily Sketch* chose to ridicule objectors by following the progress of one such man in the Forces.[59]

The role of the press over this issue seems to provide an obvious example of what Cohen subsequently termed 'deviancy amplification' in respect of so-called 'moral panics'. The process begins when media attention fastens on unconventional forms of behaviour. The behaviour concerned is then intensively and intemperately attacked, condemned, and exaggerated by the press and various prominent members of society,[60] until public opinion becomes seized (temporarily) with the fear that the country is facing a profound threat to its dominant values and interests.[61] Whether one would be correct in attaching the moral panic label to popular perceptions of conscientous objection in 1916–1918 is a question that defies easy answer. It does, however, seem clear that the framework of moral stigmatisation within which objectors were placed had a significant influence in determining the nature of the official and unofficial 'punishments' to which they were exposed.

---

[55] Gill E., "The Soldier and the Conscientious Objector", p. 19, in Brockway F. (ed.) *The No-Conscription Fellowship: A Souvenir of its work during the years 1914–1919* (1919).

[56] D. Boulton notes that nine out of ten pulpits had been turned into "high-pressure recruiting platforms", *Objection Overruled* (1967), p. 96.

[57] For an account of these phenomena, see Reader W., *At Duty's Call: A Study in Obsolete Patriotism* (1988), Chap. 5.

[58] *Daily Express*, September 11, 1914.

[59] *Daily Sketch*, April 15, 1916.

[60] See *ibid.*, and Cohen S., "Mods, Rockers and the Rest: Community Reactions to Juvenile Delinquency", (1967), 12 *Howard Journal*, pp. 121–130.

[61] Cohen S., *Folk Devils and Moral Panics* (1972), p. 9.

The Consequences of Non-Compliance

Those who claimed to be objectors and were refused exemption by the tribunal, or themselves refused to accept the level of exemption which the tribunal granted, would become eligible for military service. If they failed to respond to call-up papers they were liable to be arrested by the police and charged as deserters. A Magistrates' Court would fine them and place them in military custody.[62] This brought them within the criminal justice system for a brief transition phase. For some this experience was a direct result of the tribunals' reluctance to recognise objectors.[63] At least one magistrates' court acknowledged this and purported to remedy what the Bench perceived as an injustice. Henry Smith had not been granted any form of exemption by the tribunal system; nevertheless, the Magistrates, when considering whether to hand him over to the military authorities, decided that he was a bona fide objector and consequently declined to make an order transferring him to military control.[64]

At the beginning of the period of conscription, the magistrates' court appearance was the end of the objector's involvement with the criminal justice system. These men were now subject to military rules. Disobedience would constitute offences under military law. Thus, they became subject to a different, more substantively rigorous form of "quasi-criminal" law. Subsequent instances of disobedience could result in disciplinary action, trial by court-martial and harsh forms of military punishment.

Within the bounded rationality of the military justice system, to which the due process norms associated with the civilian criminal justice process had limited applicability, offenders were on occasion treated far worse than ordinary criminals in the outside world. Objectors were particularly vulnerable to unoffical forms of summary punishment. Some were simply sent to France, in defiance of War Office instructions.[65] One of the most common punishments which objectors experienced was known as "crucifixion", a technique which involved the use of painful physical restraints. The Manchester *Guardian* recorded the more unusual experiences of one man who was placed into solitary confinement in a hastily dug, water-logged pit in the ground.[66] *The Tribunal*

---

[62] For procedure, see (1916) *Registration and Recruiting* pp. 13–15 (London: HMSO). See p. 67, n.54.
[63] This was an opinion which was held by the NCF; *The Tribunal*, April 20, 1916.
[64] *The Tribunal*, July 13, 1916.
[65] Rae, *op. cit.*, p. 144.
[66] June 20, 1916.

reported the case of Private John Gray who had been stripped naked and repeatedly immersed in a pond.[67] Evidence as to the treatment of objectors by military authorities is, however, mixed. Existing alongside such instances of brutality as those mentioned above, is testimony both from individual detainees and the organisations representing their views as to the courtesy, consideration and fairness of individual military officers.[68]

Objectors were also liable to the full range of offical military punishments. These included the death sentence for offences of cowardice and desertion. Asquith had issued a Directive to the commander-in-chief in May 1916 which stated that no such sentences were to be carried out on objectors without Cabinet consent.[69] As a result, all such sentences imposed upon conscripted objectors were commuted. In contrast, some 266 soldiers who had not claimed to be conscientious objectors prior to joining the military were shot for cowardice during the First World War.[70] Reports of harsh treatment of objectors by the military led the Government to provide for the transfer of such men to serve court-martial sentences in civilian prisons.[71] This change of policy perhaps owed less to a desire to protect objectors, than to a realisation that their presence in the armed forces was both an embarrassment and a waste of military time. Although objection was not formally a crime, objectors were not treated as detainees being held as a result of a breach of the civil law. Nor were they granted the same beneficial regime as had been extended to Sufragettes.[72] This further example of the *de facto* criminalisation of conscientious objectors is perhaps of limited significance. The largest categories of civil law prisoners, debtors, were, by 1914, subject to the same regime as first or second class misdemeanants; they were compelled to work, and were no longer allowed to receive food from outside sources.[73]

In being classified as 'ordinary criminals' for the purposes of their detention, objectors faced solitary confinement, hard

[67] July 12, 1917.
[68] Rae, *op. cit.*, pp. 138–145.
[69] See G. Murray to J. Graham, G. Murray Papers, Bodleian Library Oxford, December 28, 1920.
[70] Dutfield M., "Executing Orders" (1992) *New Statesman and Society* October 23, p. 22.
[71] Army Order X, AO 179, 1916.
[72] Rae, *op. cit.*, pp. 201–204.
[73] Radzinowicz L. and Hood R., *The Emergence of Penal Policy in Victorian and Edwardian England* (1990), pp. 581–582.

labour, poor accommodation, and the hated silence rule.[74] Indeed, a number of objectors experienced these aspects of imprisonment on repeated occasions through the "cat and mouse" system; once a sentence was served the individual would be returned to the military, where continued disobedience could result in further punishment.[75] The plight of these men produced a second government concession which represented a more overt recognition of the failure of the tribunal system; nevertheless, it still fell far short of unconditional release. The Home Office allowed those objectors in prison, who were willing to cooperate, to be reassessed by the Central Tribunal. Provided the Tribunal found them to be sincere, they could join the Home Office (work) Scheme.[76] About 3,700 men accepted this offer, although 985 'Absolutists' consistently refused to cooperate in any way.[77] The scheme was little better than imprisonment; those who accepted it found themselves undertaking hard labour often in even more severe conditions. Instead of being in the military or in prison, they were performing physical labour in exposed areas of the British countryside. Some found that they were working on military related tasks, or were assisting the war effort through accepting the scheme. Those who found this unacceptable opted to return to prison. It therefore seems evident that, despite the formally non-criminal status of conscientious objection, its adherents were subject to a range of officially administered sanctions that appeared to be quite consistent with orthodox notions of the legitimate scope of criminal punishment. Imprisonment was not however the only adverse consequence to which objectors found they were subject.

Informal Criminalisation?

Several such consequences were imposed directly by organs of the central and local state. For example, the NCF and other pacifist or anti-war organisations were subjected to surveillance.[78]

---

[74] For descriptions, see Hobhouse S., "An English Prison From Within" (1918) *Quarterly Review*, July, 21–38; and Hobhouse S., *English Prisons To-Day* (1922) (London: Prison System Enquiry Commission).

[75] D. Hayes estimated that in World War One 655 objectors were court-martialled twice, 521 three times, 319 four times, 50 five times, and 3 six times; *Challenge of Conscience: The Story of The Conscientious Objectors of 1939–49* (1949), p. 8. See also Barker R., *Conscience, Government and War* (1982), p. 85.

[76] For a description of the scheme in theory and in practice see Rae, *op. cit.*, Chap. 8.

[77] *ibid.*, p. 167.

[78] See Mitchel D., *Women on the Warpath* (1966), pp. 331–346; and *The Tribunal*, June 8, 1916.

The Home Office kept a file entitled "Anti-Recruiting and Peace Propaganda" which listed 115 organisations and recorded their activities.[79] In addition, the Defence of the Realm Acts[80] were sometimes used to prosecute those who campaigned for objectors" rights. Bertrand Russell, who was too old to be called-up, was sentenced under the Act as the author of an NCF leaflet,[81] and NCF organisers Violet Tillard, Joan Beauchamp and Lydia Smith (editor of *The Tribunal*) were also arrested.[82]

Perhaps the most graphic illustration of the deviant status which objectors had assumed was Parliament's decision to remove their right to vote. The Representation of the People Act 1918 section 9(2) disenfranchised them for five years after the end of the war. This was intended as both a punishment to individuals, and a deterrent to the Absolutist movement.[83] The measure applied to conscientious objectors who had been granted absolute exemption and to those who had been imprisoned by court-martial for an offence committed on conscience grounds. Its enactment implied that those who had not contributed in any way to the war-effort had lost their status as full citizens. Thus, those who had undertaken non-combatant service retained the right to vote, whilst those who had undertaken work of national importance, and could establish this to the satisfaction of the Central Tribunal, could avoid disqualification. A similar denigration was achieved though state employment practices. The Civil Service imposed restrictions upon the promotion and employment of objectors; where objectors were permitted to remain in the service, on the grounds that their jobs constituted work of national importance, their wages were frozen.[84] After the war, reinstatement to Civil Service posts was not guaranteed to objectors even if they had undertaken non-combatant or alternative service. Central government departments were initially unwilling to re-employ objectors unless they had served in the Non-Combatant Corps. Although the rigidity of this position was gradually relaxed, various types of discrimination continued until

[79] Wiltshire, *op. cit.,* pp. 130–131.
[80] Defence of the Realm Consolidation Act 1914 and Defence of the Realm (Amendment) Acts 1915.
[81] *The Tribunal*, June 8, 1916.
[82] See Mitchel, *op. cit.,* pp. 331–346.
[83] See debate on disenfranchisement proposal; *HCD*, November 20, 1917 col. 1135–1274.
[84] CAB 23/4/298(18), December 14, 1917.

1929. The Ministry of Defence, however, maintained a complete bar on objectors.[85]

Objectors who remained in private sector or local government employment also faced discriminatory treatment. This evidently stemmed from a diffuse, but pervasive public concern that such men should not profit from their non-combatant status. Many experienced abuse within the workplace, and a number were dismissed from their jobs, or were forced to resign, because colleagues refused to work with them. This was by no means an exclusively private sector phenomenon; objectors employed by local authorities in teaching posts were in a particularly vulnerable position.[86]

Those who had remained in their jobs throughout the conflict also faced discrimination. Following the cessation of hostilities, such men were often dismissed to make way for those who were discharged from the military. Also, objectors applying for new posts found that their war record was treated like a criminal record.[87] However, this discrimination was, in the majority of cases, relatively short-lived.

The wider insights that this episode of political history might offer to questions concerning the legitimate scope of the criminal law, in both substantive and procedural terms, are addressed in the conclusion. Before broaching this task however, it is helpful to examine the legal status of conscientious objection in the somewhat different cultural milieux of the Second World War and the immediate post-war period.

The Second World War

The introduction of compulsory military service in this conflict, and the inclusion of provisions for conscientious objectors were, not surprisingly, less controversial than in 1916. The experiences of the previous conflict had normalised both concepts.[88] However, the introduction of conscription did not go completely unchallenged; the Labour Party briefly voiced its opposition and

[85] See Report of the Select Committee on the Civil Service (1922) *Employment of Conscientious Objectors* (HMSO); and Treasury Circular E.1206/4 (September 10, 1929) *Civil Service and Conscientious Objectors*.

[86] For examples, see Box: 1918, Cardiff City Council Archives, City Hall, Cardiff and *Birmingham Gazette*, September 27, 1940.

[87] *The Tribunal*, June 12, 1919.

[88] See Prime Minister Neville Chamberlain *HCD*, April 2, 1939 col. 1151–1152, April 26; May 4, 1939 col. 2097–2098.

some pacifist campaigners resisted compulsion.[89] In Scotland, a more novel approach was attempted. Two men challenged compulsion in the courts on constitutional grounds. A Mr Young argued, *inter alia*, that the conscription legislation constituted a material breach in the Treaty of Union 1707, and was therefore of no legal effect in Scotland.[90] The argument that the Treaties of Union are a supra-Parliamentary source of constitutional authority has been sporadically aired by academic commentators,[91] and consistently avoided or rejected by the courts.[92] Young's arguments enjoyed no better success; being rejected both at first instance and on appeal.[93] A similar argument was also dismissed in *Leonard v. Paterson*.[94]

During the Second World War, the British Government's preparations for full compulsion were laid early. The Military Training Act 1939, section 1 of which temporarily introduced limited compulsory military training for males between the ages of 20 and 21, allowed for a new approach to compulsion to be devised before war was declared. The National Service (Armed Forces) Act 1939 (NSA 1939),[95] which replaced it, used an almost identical approach to secure wartime conscription. Section 1 allowed for the introduction of a compulsory scheme of enlistment for all able-bodied men aged 18–41.[96]

The Act also included provision for the exemption of conscientious objectors who objected to being placed in the military service register, to performing military service, or to undertaking combatant duties.[97] Such an objection had to be registered provisionally at the time of call-up. Section 5 provided for a tribunal system to hear applications. Local conscientious objectors' tribunals would then hear the claims and decide whether to

[89] See Moorehead C., *Troublesome People: Enemies of War 1916–1986* (1987) pp. 148–150.
[90] *Young v. Adair,* H.C.J., July 9, 1942 (unreported).
[91] MacCormick N., "Does the United Kingdom Have a Constitution" (1978), *N.I.L.Q.* pp. 1–20.
[92] *MacCormick v. Lord Advocate* [1953] S.C. 396; *Gibson v. Lord Advocate* [1975] S.L.T. 134.
[93] For a discussion of the constitutional issues raised see Smith T. "The Union of 1707 as Fundamental Law (1957), *Public Law* pp. 99–121.
[94] *Leonard v. Paterson,* September 22, 1942 H.C.J., (unreported).
[95] Subsequent wartime National Service Acts (National Service Acts 1939–1947) amended this measure although the basic framework remained the same until 1948.
[96] NSA 1939 s.3. The upper age limit was extended to 51 by The National Service (No. 2) Act 1941 s.2(1).
[97] NSA 1939 s.5.

grant unconditional, partial (non-combatant service) or conditional exemption, or to reject applicants. This decision could be challenged before an appellate conscientious objectors' tribunal.

Efforts had been made to try to avoid some of the criticisms which had been directed towards the First World War tribunals. The experiences of Members of Parliament, who had been involved in the earlier bodies, probably aided this.[98] Thus, both the local and appeal bodies included legally qualified members who dealt only with objectors. In addition, the statute avoided the ambiguities in the substantive law of the Military Service Act, 1916.

There was also statutory provision concerning the treatment of those objectors who found themselves in the military. The Government had accepted the need for explicit legal machinery to discharge from the army any conscripted soldier who committed a military offence for conscientious reasons. The new procedure in the NSA 1939 section 13 allowed a man serving a three months (or longer) court-martial sentence of imprisonment to apply to an appellate tribunal for a hearing which could result in his discharge. This measure aimed to avoid the problem posed by the Absolutists in 1914–1918, but initially it did not apply to men who had become conscientious objectors whilst serving in the military. However, the Secretary of State for War took the unprecedented step of allowing such men the same rights which had been granted to those who had originally registered as objectors.[99]

Conscription in the Second World War was not merely confined to military service. A form of industrial conscription was introduced in May 1940 by an Order in Council, and in 1941 fire-watching became compulsory.[1] In 1941, the National Service Act (NSA) introduced compulsory service in one of the Civil Defence Services. Section 1(1) stated that everyone who was liable to be called-up under the terms of the NSA 1939 could be called-up for civil defence work. The provision also applied to those conditionally registered as conscientious objectors.

The Second World War brought another unprecedented step: the conscription of the female population. In late 1941, the

[98] Prime Minister Neville Chamberlain had been Chairman of Birmingham Local Tribunal, and a number of other M.P.'s had either been tribunal members, or concerned with the treatment of objectors. See Rae, *op. cit.*, pp. 240–243.
[99] Central Board for Conscientious Objectors Papers, 699, October 1, 1942, C.B.C.O. Collection, Friends House, London.
[1] Both were introduced by Orders in Council; See Barker R., *Conscience, Government and War* (1982), pp. 104–107 and pp. 107–111.

National Service (No. 2) Act 1941 made the NSAs 1939–1941 applicable to women, albeit with certain qualifications.[2] The Act included a "conscience clause" similar to the other NSAs. However, in practice if a woman claimed to be an objector she would be offered civilian work; if she agreed to this there would be no tribunal hearing.

The Criminalisation of Belief?

The tighter definition of the substantive law was accompanied by an explicit criminalisation of certain consequences which flowed from objection. Most straightfowardly, objection was not permitted in respect of industrial conscription. Under section 2, men and women who refused to work committed an offence. The NSAs also created several other offences arising from failure to comply with the statutory requirements. The explicit criminalisation of conscientious objection met with little or no comment within Parliament. Instead, the debates centred around compulsion itself, and on the need for adequate provisions for the recognition of genuine conscientious objectors.[3] The criminalisation was clearly intended to act as a deterrent for those who might contemplate non-compliance.

The offences included failure to fulfil the requirements in relation to registration,[4] and, as per section 3(4), refusal to undergo a compulsory medical examination. Such conduct would result in criminal charges under NSA 1939, section 17. This punitive approach was sometimes used in conjunction with the possibility of being handed over to the military: under section 5(8), those who had been granted conditional exemption but failed to observe the tribunal conditions faced the possibility of being removed from the register of objectors and being called-up.

Consistent with this *de jure* criminalisation of objection, empirical evidence suggests that Second World War tribunals conformed in the main to a rather more rigorous notion of procedural due process than their First World War counterparts. The clearer drafting of the new conscience clause reduced the scope for substantive aberrations in the content of decisions,

---

[2] NS (No. 2) A 1941 s.1. Section 3 includes the specific differences in relation to women. The Act applied generally to single women aged 20–30.

[3] For example, see contribution of Arthur Creech Jones M.P. (Labour) *HCD*, May 18, 1939 col. 1689–1690.

[4] These were compulsory for all those to whom the Act applied; NSA 1939, ss.2(3),(7),(9).

while the inclusion of at least one legally qualified member on all tribunal panels enhanced awareness of procedural norms. The Second World War record was not however untarnished. There were still criticisms of tribunal attitudes towards, and treatment of, objectors. For example, F. W. Pethwick-Lawrence M.P. (Labour) complained that some tribunals tended to bully applicants. He was especially critical of Sir Edmund Phipps, a member of the London Local Tribunal, who referred to objectors as "These miserable creatures" during a hearing.[5] Judge Richardson of Newcastle Tribunal was frequently the subject of newspaper articles which questioned his impartiality. On one occasion he told an objector: "I have the greatest contempt for your sort".[6]

The Consequences of Non-Compliance

Conscientious objectors, along with others who refused to cooperate with the requirements of the National Service Acts, frequently faced criminal charges. A wave of prosecutions resulted from the various military service provisions.[7] Individuals were prosecuted for their refusal to register or to undergo a medical examination in relation to civil defence or military service, for failure to undertake compulsory fire-watching and failure to comply with industrial conscription. The lack of provision for those who conscientiously objected to civil defence work added to these numbers. Many objectors who had previously been quite willing to volunteer their services felt unable to continue once compelled to do so; they considered that their co-operation would symbolise a recognition of the State's authority to compel behaviour. Refusal to comply often resulted in the imposition of repeated prison sentences and/or fines.[8]

Despite the fact that objection was now classified as a crime, the official punishments imposed on 'offenders' were, in many senses, less severe than those suffered by the formally non-criminal First World War objectors. The possibility that objectors

---

[5] *HCD*, February 22, 1940 col. 1587–1589.

[6] *The Herald*, April 11, 1940.

[7] Smithies E., *Crime in Wartime, A Social History of Crime in World War II* (1982), p. 18.

[8] For example, George Elphick appeared before Lewes Magistrates' Court repeatedly and was imprisoned five times for refusing to fire-watch. Eventually the authorities decided to cease legal proceedings against him. In total, 555 prosecutions were made against objectors who refused such work. See Chrisp P., *Conscientious Objectors 1916 to the Present Day* (1988), p. 34.

might face execution was non-existent. Nor does it appear that they were as frequently subject to the kind of semi-official physical brutality which characterised their treatment in the First World War. Individual incidents of abuse continued to be recorded, however. Objectors detained in 1940 at the Dingle Vale army training centre in Liverpool were "kicked, beaten with rifle butts . . . dragged from their cells, marched round a square and prodded on with rifles".[9] A more common complaint related to the "forcible" dressing in army uniforms of objectors who refused to remove their civilian clothes.[10] Furthermore, for those persistent objectors who had failed to gain recognition, and consequently found themselves conscripted into the military, the NSA safeguards (of permitting transfer to a civilian jail for objectors whose court-martial sentence was three months or more) did not always prove helpful. Gradually it became clear that some court-martials were by-passing this process by deliberately giving short sentences,[11] which would then be repeated as soon as the objector was released and "offended" once again. Alternatively, objectors would be sentenced to military detention, which did not count as a sentence for these purposes. By 1943, an administrative concession was made to alleviate the situation; individuals could be discharged, on completion of a third sentence, of detention or imprisonment.[12] By the end of 1946, 1,050 objectors had been court-martialled; 1 on 6 occasions, 106 three times, and 210 twice.[13]

For those objectors who found themselves in military or civilian prisons, conditions were generally better than in the previous period of compulsion. However, there were still sporadic instances of cruelty.[14] Harold Jackson who was sentenced to six months imprisonment in Wormwood Scrubs in 1951, recalled being treated with contempt and hatred by both the prison officers and other inmates.[15]

In addition to those offences which related directly to conscription during the war, conscientious objectors and their supporters could have been charged with offences against morale, or restrained under public order laws.[16] In practice, the police

[9] Barker, op. cit., p. 91.
[10] ibid. p. 90.
[11] The New Statesman, July 12, 1941.
[12] See Hayes, op. cit., pp. 106–111.
[13] Moorehead, op. cit., p. 167.
[14] ibid., pp. 163–167 and Hayes, op. cit., p. 73.
[15] The Guardian, March 14, 1987.
[16] Smithies, op. cit., p. 3.

tended to target fascists and communists; anti-war speakers, like Donald (now Lord) Soper, were left to campaign against militarism with few confrontations, although relationships with the authorities were often strained.[17] Nevertheless, the Peace Pledge Union (PPU), an organisation which campaigned for peace and supported conscientious objectors, was threatened with closure on various occasions during the war and lost many of its regional offices because of local pressure on private sector and local authority landlords.[18] In 1940, the display of a PPU poster, which encouraged men to refuse to fight, resulted in six officials being bound over for a year.[19]

The various types of informal sanctions visited upon objectors, from both public and private sources, in First World War were also evident in the Second World War. Winston Churchill had strongly condemned discrimination against objectors in the sphere of employment,[20] and, qua employer, the central State did not adopt a systematically intolerant view towards objectors among its workforce.[21]

Objectors who were employed by local authorities experienced greater problems. A number of councils, concerned by the possibility that they were employing fifth columnists, voted to dismiss objectors or suspend them for the duration of the war regardless of whether an individual had been granted exemption from military service.[22] Other authorities retained objectors but put them on soldiers' pay or withheld bonuses and increments.[23]

Such explicit sanctions were also apparent in the private sector. In this period as in the First World War, many professing to be objectors lost their jobs as a result of the prejudice of other workers and employers.[24] At one firm in Leicestershire, staff went on strike because they refused to work with an objector.[25] Similarly, Lloyd's Bank kept objectors on the work force but ensured that they were not placed at an economic advantage as a

---

[17] Moorehead, *op. cit.,* pp. 171–172.
[18] Smithies, *op. cit.,* pp. 9–11.
[19] Moorehead, *op. cit.,* p. 169.
[20] *HCD*, March 20, 1941 col. 284.
[21] Barker, *op. cit.,* pp. 72–74.
[22] Reading Town Council took this course: *Evening Standard*, April 5, 1940. More generally, see Barker, *op. cit.,* Chap. 5.
[23] Masson, *op. cit.,* pp. 16–17.
[24] For example, A. C. Strange, who had been unconditionally exempted from service, was dismissed from his job in 1940 because fellow employees refused to work with him; *Sunday Graphic*, May 26, 1940.
[25] *The Daily Herald*, March 12, 1940.

result.[26] Those who became unemployed often found it difficult to secure alternative positions. Arthur Smith, who had been placed upon unpaid leave by London County Council for the duration of the war, found it impossible to secure another post.[27]

In addition, Parliament took steps to fashion a positively discriminatory employment regime for citizens who had been conscripted. There were various statutory provisions for the reinstatement to civil employment of those who had served in the military during the war.[28] The Acts placed an obligation upon employers to reinstate ex-servicemen. For those who had not undertaken service in the forces no such guarantees were available. In addition, the NSA 1948 section 39 obliged employers to discharge any individual whose employment did not date back as far as a former employee returning from military service. A number of objectors fell foul of this measure.

Discrimination also took the more diffuse form of social isolation and stigmatisation. As in the First World War, objectors during the 1939–1945 conflict found themselves the subject of vilification in the mass media. Particularly after Dunkirk, objectors were roundly condemned as unpatriotic and cowardly.[29] The *Sunday Pictorial's* declaration of war on all pacifists and 'conchies' was characteristic of this.[30] However, press denunciation was not only, nor even, primarily directed at objectors. If a moral panic can be detected in this period, then it concerned the hidden presence of enemy agents. "Fifth Column Fever" was widespread. The press encouraged citizens to suspect any outsider, or anyone behaving unpatriotically, of being a spy. Conscientious objectors were frequently drawn within this expansive category of evil-doers. In some cities, people formed anti-conscientious objection organisations which campaigned against opponents of conscription: the League of Swansea Loyalists was formed in Wales;[31] the Anti-Conscientious Objector League emerged in Blackpool.[32] In one village in Wales, the homes of objectors and their supporters were covered with graffiti.[33] Once the war ended,

---

[26] Central Board of Conscientious Objectors, Executive Committee Minutes, 11, March 18, 1942, Friend's House, London.
[27] Moorehead, *op. cit.,* p. 170.
[28] NSA 1939 s.14; and subsequently the Re-instatement in Civil Employment Act 1944. NSA 1948 ss.35–49.
[29] For example, see Ursula Masson, "Loyalty and Dissent: War", (1991) *Radical Wales* 29, p. 16.
[30] June 2, 1940.
[31] Masson, *op. cit.,* p. 17.
[32] Moorehead, *op. cit.,* p. 170.
[33] Masson, *op. cit.,* p. 16.

such condemnatory attitudes and practices began to dissipate, but objectors continued to be marginalised.

Conclusion

When viewed through the 'lens'[34] of a late twentieth century liberal democratic political order, the State's reaction to cons-cientious objectors in the First World War appears, in many respects, indefensible. As Ashworth has suggested, a fundamen-tal characteristic of the criminal law is that it is "liberty-depriving, coercive, and stigmatic in its operation".[35] Further-more, Ashworth argues: "the maximimum penalties attached to offences may also be taken to convey the relative seriousness of the types of offence".[36] It is quite clear that objectors were deprived of liberty and coerced by government institutions, and stigmatised by public opinion. Moreover, they found themselves subjected to potentially very severe punishments. They would seem to have been, for practical if not formal purposes,[37] criminals.

Yet objectors were not, in formal terms, so defined. In consequence, they were exposed to punishment without receiving the benefit of the procedural due process protections traditionally associated with the criminal trial. By 1914, the nature and substance of the Government process in Britain had become sufficiently imbued with collectivist concerns to ensure that 'public interest' infringements on some areas of individual auto-nomy were considered legitimate, even in the absence of trial type hearings; town planning and public health protection are the obvious examples.[38] The liberties thereby infringed, however, were of a minor nature, and qualitatively quite distinct from the penalties imposed on objectors. One is, drawn to ask therefore, why Parliament chose to inflict *de facto* severe criminal sanctions through the *de jure* procedurally perfunctory process of an adminstrative law tribunal?

---

[34] See Nicola Lacey's chapter in this volume.
[35] Ashworth A., *Principles of Criminal Law* (1991), p. 28. The question of the threat that objection allegedly posed to the war effort would also seem to fall squarely within the "principle of urgency" that Lacey suggests may be used to justify extension of criminal liability; *State Punishment: Political Principles and Community Values* (1988), p. 100.
[36] *ibid.*, p. 31.
[37] See Lacey in this volume at pp. 20–24.
[38] See Harlow C. and Rawlings R., *Law and Administration* (1984), Chap. 1.

Considerations of cultural specificity are obviously pertinent, whether cast in terms of the then nascent status of the collectivised State, or, more specifically, of the existence of a war of thitherto unimagined intensity. Yet neither context seems fully to explain the evidently paradoxical legal response to conscientious objection. In so far as society was tentatively moving away from a dominant ideology of laissez-faire individualism, one might have expected pursuit of newly defined substantive public interests to be characterised by tenacious adherence to due process constraints, rather than by their enthusiastic abandonment. Similarly, the notion that all normal rules of constitutional propriety are suspended when society's very survival is at stake offers too simplistic an explanation. Sir John Simon's suggestion that, in introducing conscription, Parliament was subscribing to the values against which it was waging war may not have convinced the majority of M.P.'s in 1916, but neither the Asquith nor Lloyd-George governments embraced an ideology of "total war" in the sense of entirely and explicitly disregarding previously dominant notions of the 'correct' content and conduct of citizen-state relations.

There was, perhaps, something special about conscientious objection. It is tempting to draw an analogy with Richardson's study of the War Crimes Act, in which he suggested that if due process norms are indeed being compromised in order to convict Nazi war criminals, then that compromise is justified in order to vindicate fundamental moral values. Asquith's statement to the Commons that objectors would receive no sympathy because they were refusing to honour a fundamental moral obligation suggests that they were seen as deviants in a particularly acute sense. Objection was perhaps one of those acts which Lacey suggests might be already "criminal", irrespective of whether it was formally so defined.[39] In effect, objectors were stripped of various attributes of citizenship. The right to vote, to remain at liberty unless convicted of "a distinct breach of the law before the ordinary courts of the land", and to compete on formally equal terms within the labour market were attributes of citizenship which were withdrawn from objectors.

The juxtaposition of morally "deserving" and "undeserving" litigants is a familiar one in many areas of legal study which examine the actual implementation as well as the formal content of particular laws. Undeserving litigants are frequently found to

---

[39] See Lacey, in this volume at p. 14.

be disadvantaged in terms both of the procedures to which they are subjected, and the outcomes of their particular cases. Such inequity generally operates, however, as a hidden, but effective, source of legitimation for what would formally be regarded as illegitimate behaviour. The unique nature of the conscientous objector in the First World War is perhaps best illustrated by the fact that such departures from due process norms were considered legitimate within the highly visible forum of the legislative process, as well as in the murkier world of implementation.

The marked shift in the formal status and procedural character of the central State's response to conscientious objection in the Second Word War is a subject that remains relatively unresearched.[40] It seems plausible to suggest that Parliament's willingness to offer objectors the greater procedural safeguards contingent upon explicit criminalisation of their refusal to serve, indicated that the substantive legitimacy of conscription was less problematic in 1939 than in 1916. As noted above, this may have been because the First World War normalised the concept of compulsory service *per se*. It may also be attributed to more diffuse political trends. By 1939, the sphere of individual autonomy had become increasingly (and legitimately) circumscribed as government had begun to intervene to an ever greater extent in both the broad sweep and fine detail of social and economic life. The notion that a citizen might be asked to kill or risk death in defence of the public interest then entailed a less severe rupture with orthodox political ideology than had been the case 25 years earlier.

The cultural specificity of both episodes precludes the drawing of any sweeping statements concerning their implications for contemporary debates about the nature and regulation of 'criminality'. Yet one lesson that might be drawn from the history of conscientious objection is that proponents of a functionalist critique of the criminal law[41] might sensibly conclude that the legitimate boundaries of their enquiries may extend not just into the realm of ostensibly civil law dispute resolution, but also into the treacherous and often uncharted waters of the minutae of routine social and economic interaction. In seeking to delimit the the outer limits of societal notions of criminal liability, one should not neglect to examine the equally useful analytical tools that may be offered by that society's innermost workings.

---

[40] Barker, *op. cit.*, p. 1.
[41] See Lacey, (1988) *State Punishment: Political Principles and Community Values*, Chap. 5.

Chapter Four

THE SERIOUS FRAUD OFFICE: NIGHTMARES (AND PIPE DREAMS) ON ELM STREET[1]
by Matthew Weait

"They look upon Fraud as a greater Crime than Theft, and therefore seldom fail to punish it with Death: for they allege that Care and Vigilance, with a very common Understanding, may preserve a Man's Goods from Thieves; but Honesty hath no Fence against superior Cunning: And since it is necessary that there should be a perpetual Intercourse of buying and selling, and dealing upon Credit, where Fraud is permitted or connived at, or hath no Law to punish it, the honest Dealer is always undone, and the Knave gets the advantage".[2]

This chapter discusses the work and objectives of the Serious Fraud Office (SFO). It considers the SFO's role, its organising philosophy, its statutory powers and the problems which it faces in investigating and prosecuting serious fraud. However, before looking at the SFO and its work in detail it is first necessary to look more generally at fraud itself; how it is conceived, what it involves, what its particular qualities are, and what particular problems are presented to those whose task it is to uncover, investigate and prosecute it.

Fraud — the Moral Concept

In *The Prince*,[3] Machiavelli discusses the extent to which rulers should keep their promises and act honestly. He explains that although it is generally accepted as praiseworthy that they live an upright life, he continues:

"Nevertheless, experience shows that in our times the rulers who have done great things are those who have set little store by keeping their word, being skilful rather in cunningly confusing men; they have got the better of those who have relied on being trustworthy."[4]

[1] The Serious Fraud Office is to be found on Elm Street. The fact that Elm Street was also the thoroughfare immortalised in a series of horror films is no doubt merely coincidental.
[2] Swift J., *Gulliver's Travels* (1941) in Davis H., (ed.), *The Prose Works of Jonathan Swift*, Vol. XI, p. 42.
[3] Machiavelli, *The Prince* (1988) (ed., Skinner Q.).
[4] *op. cit.*, p. 61.

Rulers must imitate both the fox and the lion:

> "for the lion is liable to be trapped, whereas the fox cannot ward off
> wolves. One needs, then, to be a fox to recognise traps, and a lion to
> frighten away wolves."[5]

Foxiness, or cunning, is essential for a ruler's survival; but it is
important that this quality should be kept hidden from others.
Man's innate naivety, Machiavelli argues, makes this an easy
task. More importantly, a ruler should *seem* to be merciful,
trustworthy, upright, humane and devout:

> "In these matters, most men judge more by their eyes than by their
> hands. For everyone is capable of seeing you, but few can touch you.
> Everyone can see what you appear to be, whereas few have direct
> experience of what you really are . . ."[6]

Machiavelli was a wise old bird. After nearly 500 years his
observations still resonate, although the walls off which they echo
are no longer those of the stone-flagged council chambers of
Florentine palaces, but rather the plush-carpeted boardrooms of
corporate headquarters. Where once the princes sported velvet
doublets, now they don their sombre suits. Where once their
ambitions were territorial, now their sights are set on increased
market share. Still they seek to dispose of enemies; their militia
now — the corporate financiers, the investment analysts and the
brokers — as skilled, dangerous and hungry for success as those
of their forebears. Even the language of commercial conflict —
takeover battles, price wars, cut-throat competition — recalls the
days when to destroy opponents required their physical
annihilation.[7]

No doubt many of our current princes, the rulers in our
corporate society, possess the positive qualities by which
Machiavelli set so much store. Perhaps they survive and prosper

---

[5] Machiavelli, *op. cit.,* p. 61
[6] *op. cit.,* pp. 62–63.
[7] It was ever thus. As Defoe, railing against the pernicious antics of the earliest
stock-jobbers, put it: "The war they manage is carried on with worse weapons
than swords and musquets; bombs may fire our towns, and troops overrun and
plunder us. But these people can ruin man silently, undermine and impoverish
by a sort of impenetrable artifice, like poison that works at a distance, can
wheedle men to ruin themselves and *fiddle them out of their money* by the
strange and unheard of engines of *interests, discounts, transfers, tallies, deben-*
tures, shares, projects, and the devil and all of figures and hard names." (Defoe
D., (1701) *The Villainy of Stock-Jobbers Detected*).

by playing honestly, according to the rules. Alternatively, as Machiavelli suggests, many who achieve success and appear to be so playing are those who have heeded his advice and are expert in the techniques of deceit. The point is that it is indeed easier to see than to touch, to accept at face value than to inquire. Those who invested with Barlow Clowes, for example, were seduced by the promise of a higher rate of return than that offered elsewhere; and understandably so. Peter Clowes clearly understood, as Machiavelli did, that:

"One must be a great feigner and dissembler. And men are so naive, and so much dominated by immediate needs, that a skilful deceiver always finds plenty of people who will let themselves be deceived".[8]

Indeed, this sentiment was reiterated in similar terms by a former Director of the Serious Fraud Office:

"Fraud arises out of greed by the perpetrators and often by the victims; often it arises out of the naivety of those members of the public who come into sizeable sums of money, such as retirement lump sums, without having the necessary skills or experience to invest it wisely and without the worldliness to recognise that those who offer high rates of interest also offer a risky investment."[9]

Of course, the unfortunate investors whose savings metamorphosed tragically and, in many cases, irreversibly into the various components of Peter Clowes' luxury lifestyle would have found it difficult, if not impossible, to find out the truth had they wanted to.[10] The complexity of the institutions and practices of the City, and of its products and services, conspire to confuse the outsider.[11] As a consequence, outsiders have to rely on others — on insiders. They have to place their trust in those who profess expertise because they have little option to do otherwise. Shareholders, although the owners of companies, are distanced from their management. This they entrust to Boards of Directors, with

---

[8] Machiavelli, *op. cit.*, p.62.

[9] Wood J., "The Serious Fraud Office" (1989) Crim. L.R. 175–184.

[10] In February 1992, Clowes was found guilty on 18 out of 19 counts involving false statements to induce investment and theft of investors' funds. He was sentenced to 10 years imprisonment.

[11] As one nineteenth century commentator put it: "The City is a world within itself. Centred in the heart of the metropolis, with its innumerable capacities for commercial pursuits, it presents at first sight, to a stranger, a most mysterious and unfathomable labyrinth . . . ."; Evans D., *The City: or, the Physiology of London Business* preface (1845).

which they have scarce contact.[12] Many of those who wish to play the markets rely on the advice of brokers as to what should be bought and what should be sold, at what time and at what price; and even those who know what they want must trust that the broker does what he has undertaken to do. Similarly, with companies and other complex organisations, higher management delegates executive responsibilities to others and trusts that they will perform their obligations honestly and loyally. Such delegation is an essential aspect of efficient bureaucracies. Conversely, employees trust that higher management will pursue corporate interests, if necessary at the expense of their own personal ones, in order to create a profitable and secure environment in which to work. In sum, the world of commerce and business is one in which expectation, reliance and trust are both inevitable and essential elements. Yet it is upon these very things that those who perpetrate fraud rely, in order to achieve their own selfish objectives. It is to this which we now turn.

Fraud — the Legal Concept

fraud **1.** deliberate deception, trickery or cheating intended to gain an advantage.   **2.** an act or instance of such deception.   **3.** something false or spurious.[13]

> "Fraud . . . is a difficult thing to define in the ethics of trading, which are essentially the ethics of deceiving the other side."[14]

Fraud is a satisfying, fudgy, word. We use it with abandon and often with no more than a vague sense of what it entails. In fact, such vagueness is not entirely misplaced since it is an inherently problematic concept. There is not space in this chapter to go into the details of the many and various kinds of fraud which can be perpetrated;[15] instead, the emphasis will be on the peculiar characteristics of fraud which mark it out from other kinds of crime and which make its investigation and prosecution particularly difficult.

Perhaps the most important quality of fraud, at least of that kind of fraud with which the Serious Fraud Office is concerned, is

[12] Berle A. and Means G., *The Modern Corporation and Private Property* (1936).
[13] Collins English Dictionary (3rd ed.).
[14] Arnold T., *The Folklore of Capitalism* (1937), p. 232.
[15] Excellent illustrations are found in Leigh L., *The Control of Commercial Fraud* (1982), pp. 15–149. See also, Comer M., *Corporate Fraud* (2nd ed., 1985).

its organisational context. More often than not the corporate form is the vehicle or the means by which fraud is committed.[16] Corporations are bounded environments, both physically and legally, and those who work within them are given access to fraudulent opportunities that are, in many cases, denied to outsiders. Depending on such factors as the level of access which they have to the financial systems within the organisation, the extent of their authority, their knowledge and expertise[17] and, of course, their desire to defraud, corporate insiders have ample opportunity to serve their own interests at the expense of others — whether they be employees, creditors, shareholders or, as with insider-trading, other market players. The functional differentiation of participants upon which organisations rely in order to achieve efficiency[18] also provides those who would commit fraud with the means to achieve their ends. Delegation of authority, and the presumption of trustworthiness in those who exercise it, gives the fraudster a head start. Research on organisations relies upon information passed to them by those lower down.[19] Unable to assimilate and process all the information which an organisation and its transactions generates, reliance is placed on the version of that information which they receive.[20] This may be either a partial representation or an active misrepresentation, but either way it is often impossible, for those who may want to know the truth, to determine it.[21] Indeed, it is arguable that the "truth" of what is happening in a complex corporate structure is fundamentally unknowable to directors and managers, and that information, far from being value-neutral, is always constructed and

[16] Examples include long-firm fraud, a practice which involves buying goods on credit, selling them and then disappearing without repaying suppliers; window-dressing, which involves borrowing money at year-end to give a false picture about a company's financial situation; and insolvent trading, which involves trading with the knowledge that the company is unable to meet its commercial or financial obligations.
[17] This is especially true of computer fraud and that involving advanced information technology.
[18] Weber M., *The Theory of Social and Economic Organization* (1947).
[19] Etzioni A., *A Comparative Analysis of Complex Organizations* (1961); Kriesberg, L., "Note: Decision-Making Models and the Control of Corporate Crime" (1976) *Yale L.J.*, pp. 1091–1129: Vaughan, D., *Controlling Unlawful Organizational Behaviour* (1983).
[20] This is the phenomenon of 'bounded rationality'; see Simon H., *Administrative Behaviour* (1976), pp. 38–41.
[21] Of course, in some cases those in the boardroom may collude with, or actively refrain from taking action against, inaccurate representations — especially when they relate to the financial state of a company which is sliding into insolvency. They may hear what they want to hear.

passed on to achieve a particular result. It is similarly difficult for those lower down in the organisation, or otherwise distanced from its management, to know what is happening in the top corridor — and this goes for auditors, as well as for employees and shareholders.[22] Like a virus, fraud thrives parasitically within the organisation. Undiscovered, it can destroy its host; but discovering it is no easy matter and may depend on the recognition of frequently subtle symptoms.

The complex and serial nature of financial transactions within organisations also affords opportunities for fraud. Many frauds are charged as offences under the Theft Acts of 1968[23] and 1978.[24] Students and practitioners alike are aware of the problems of interpretation with respect to the substantive law in many property offences.[25] These are almost nothing compared to the problems which face those whose task it is to investigate and prosecute such offences as they occur within the corporate and commercial context. First, conduct in the commercial and business sector quite frequently operates on a continuum which ranges from the perfectly legitimate to the wholly unlawful. The point at which it becomes criminal is often a matter of degree. The point at which, for example, the payment of reasonable expenses for services rendered amounts to bribery or corruption of the person concerned is often a matter of fine judgment.[26] Similarly, as Hadden points out, the payment of generous salaries to directors differs only in form from the illegitimate abstraction of similar sums.[27]

Aside from this, determining whether or not particular conduct is criminal when fraud is suspected is made additionally problem-

[22] Auditors, although required to be alert to patterns of irregularity and the consequent possibility of fraud, are under no obligation to act as sleuths.
[23] These include: theft (s.1); obtaining property by deception (s.15); obtaining a pecuniary advantage (s.16); false accounting (s.17); the making of false statements (s.19); the suppression of documents (s.20(1)); and, procuring the execution of a valuable security (s.20(2)).
[24] These include: obtaining services by deception (s.1); securing the remission of a liability (s.2(1)(a)); inducing a creditor to wait for or forgo payment (s.2(1)(b)); and, obtaining an exemption from or abatement of liability (s.2(1)(c). Other offences include those under the *Companies Act 1985*, the *Financial Services Act 1986*, the *Forgery and Counterfeiting Act 1981* and conspiracy to defraud at common law.
[25] The most thorough analysis is to be found in Smith J., (1993, 7th ed.) *The Law of Theft.*
[26] *Prevention of Corruption Act,* 1906, s.1.
[27] Hadden T., 'Fraud in the City: The Role of the Criminal Law' (1983) Crim. L.R., pp. 500–511. The same point may be made about the slippage between tax avoidance and tax evasion.

atic by the fact that frauds are rarely constituted by one-off actions, and are frequently committed by more than one person.[28] To take the first point; whereas the classic deception cases in criminal law textbooks involve discussion of whether the *mens rea* and *actus reus* requirements have been made out in one discrete transaction, fraud often involves actions which, although they do not in themselves constitute a deception, amount to one when taken together. Secondly, and in the same way, more than one person may be involved in the perpetration of a fraud and their individual *mentes reae* may not be sufficient to satisfy the requirements of the particular offence charged against them.[29] As Hadden explains:

"It is difficult enough to apply the established concepts of intention, recklessness and negligence in respect of individual offenders. In cases involving a series of complex transactions which have been carried out by a number of individuals at various levels in a corporate hierachy the difficulty is considerably greater."[30]

The substantive criminal law, whose focus is so firmly grounded in individual intentionality, confronts grave difficulties when the conduct which it seeks to judge has these qualities. Similar difficulties face those agencies whose responsibility it is to investigate and prosecute such conduct, and it is to one of these, and how it manages these that we now turn.

The Serious Fraud Office

Before the SFO was set up there was general agreement that the investigation and prosecution of serious fraud was a haphazard, arduous and inefficient affair. There was little co-ordination

---

[28] A similar point is made in respect of consumer protection offences and corporate manslaughter in the chapters by Scott and Wells in this volume.

[29] Levi observes a particular difficulty in relation to the standard of dishonesty which currently obtains in theft cases. As he explains, the prosecution must prove beyond reasonable doubt that the defendant himself knew that the conduct was dishonest according to the standards of honest and reasonable people (*R. v. Ghosh* [1982] 2 All E.R. 689). In Levi's words, "This imposes serious difficulties and it is far from clear that it is analytically justified, rewarding as it does the ethical psychopath or the person who has so little contact with ordinary honest and reasonable people that s/he has no idea how they think": Levi M., *The Investigation, Prosecution and Trial of Serious Fraud* (1993) (Royal Commission on Criminal Justice Research Study No: 14 at p. 224).

[30] Hadden, *op. cit.*, pp. 502–503.

between the various agencies concerned with it and, although fraud investigators had long term appointments in some of them,[31] and were consequently able to gain a measure of expertise, this was not the case with those members of the police force involved in investigation.[32] There were also legal barriers to the exchange of information between agencies and this made the collation of evidence, sufficient to ground a prosecution, hard if not impossible.[33] Some headway was made in 1985 with the introduction of the Fraud Investigation Group (FIG), which combined the skills of lawyers and police officers, under the direction of the Director of Public Prosecutions (DPP). However, there was understaffing and an increasing caseload for both FIG and the DPP during this period and insufficient funding to enable them to do their work as effectively as they might have liked.[34] As the Roskill Committee's Report stated: "The public no longer believes that the legal system in England and Wales is capable of bringing the perpetrators of serious frauds expeditiously and effectively to book".[35]

As a consequence of the perceived public concern over the inefficiency of the system, Roskill recommended that the Government consider the introduction of an integrated body with authority to both investigate and prosecute serious fraud.[36] This suggestion was taken up rapidly by the government and led to the establishment of the SFO.

The SFO was set up under the Criminal Justice Act 1987[37] with two simply stated objectives: the investigation and prosecution of

---

[31] These included the Inland Revenue, the Customs and Excise and the Department of Trade and Industry.

[32] As Levi points out, the Fraud Squads in local police forces are generally small and so opportunities for internal promotion are remote. Those who gain expertise while working in them tend to move on after a relatively short time, and are replaced by other officers for whom the learning curve is steep (Levi, (1987) op. cit., pp. 150–51).

[33] Such was the case between the Revenue Departments and the police, for example.

[34] Levi, (1987), op. cit. at p. 177.

[35] Fraud Trials Committee (1986) Report p. 1.

[36] ibid., at p. 27. It is interesting to note that the SFO was set up to both investigate and prosecute cases, whereas the Crown Prosecution Service was set up at almost the same time to separate the functions of investigation and prosecution because of concerns about the police wanting a conviction at all costs. This is dicussed further below.

[37] Criminal Justice Act 1987 s.1(1).

cases of serious and complex fraud.[38] It forms part of an increasingly organised network of bodies, some old, some new, which co-operate in the regulation of corporate misconduct.[39] These bodies report to the SFO allegations of serious and complex fraud.[40] The aims of the SFO are two-fold: first, to increase the efficiency of criminal justice within the jurisdiction[41] through the "appropriate and successful" investigation of serious fraud; and secondly, to "deter fraud and maintain confidence in the United Kingdom's financial systems". To achieve these general aims, the objectives of the SFO are, *inter alia,* to pursue the appropriate and prompt investigation and prosecution of fraud; to ensure more effective prosecutions, and where a prosecution results in acquittal, to consider any lessons to be learnt; and to liaise with other organisations concerned with the identification, investigation and prosecution of fraud.[42] As a policy statement these aims and objectives are what one might expect. The question arises, however, as to how the SFO proceeds in realising them. The sections which follow will deal in turn with the aims and objectives outlined above.

Efficiency

It was an understandable assumption that the rather un-coordinated nature of fraud investigation, prior to the introduction of

---

[38] Criminal Justice Act 1987 s.1(2).

[39] Among these are the Department of Trade and Industry, the Bank of England, the International Stock Exchange, the Securities and Investments Board, the Takeover Panel and the various Self Regulatory Organisations; the Securities and Futures Authority, the Life Assurance and Unit Trusts Regulatory Organisation, the Investment Management Regulatory Organisation and the Financial Intermediaries, Managers and Brokers Association.

[40] Other cases of fraud are dealt with by the police and the Crown Prosecution Service through the Fraud Investigation Group, as well as by fraud squads in local police forces.

[41] *i.e.* England, Wales and Northern Ireland.

[42] Its other objectives are: to ensure that the SFO's operations are properly reported, in accordance with the SFO's aims; to put the SFO's resources to maximum effect in investigating and prosecuting serious fraud; to develop financial and information systems able to identify the full costs of investigation and prosecution and to provide appropriate performance measures; to implement an information strategy able to support the SFO's operations and administration; to develop personnel management systems which provide the necessary staff resources and individual career development; SFO (1992) *Annual Report* (1991–92) pp. 8–9.

the SFO, was inefficient. There was duplication of effort, inadequate information exchange and a lack of career professionals in the field. It thus made perfect sense to assume that these problems might be remedied through the introduction of an agency which sought to counter them directly. Nevertheless, measuring the efficiency of the SFO is no easy matter, since it is difficult to know what criteria to employ. It is not possible to measure the efficiency of the Office by comparing like with like, because there is no analogous body with which it can realistically be compared.[43] It is not possible for the same reasons to measure its efficiency through a comparison with the number of successful prosecutions undertaken before the SFO was set up; the work of the DPP and FIG, prior to the setting up of the SFO, was undertaken with fewer resources and in a less co-ordinated way. More fundamentally, the SFO is not directly responsible for the return of any assets which those defrauded may have lost. In measuring the efficiency of tax inspectors, or customs and excise officers, it is possible to calculate the revenue which they have managed to extract and which would otherwise have been lost. The same equation is not possible with respect to the SFO. Its function is to investigate and prosecute; whether that leads ultimately to the return of ill-gotten gains is a matter for the courts to decide.[44]

One way of considering the internal efficiency of the SFO could be in terms of the success rate of its prosecutions, and, it is true that, since its inception, and at the time of writing, 66 per cent. of its prosecutions have resulted in convictions. However, it is important to remember that the SFO only prosecutes those cases where it considers there to be a "realistic prospect of conviction" and so one might argue that it is "inefficient" in one-third of the prosecutions which it brings. Of course, it must be pointed out that the failure of a prosecution may be the result of

[43] Unlike, for example, the relative success of police forces operating in demographically similar areas and with similar staffing and resources, in clearing up crime.
[44] Under s.71 of the Criminal Justice Act 1988 a court may make a confiscation order to deprive convicted offenders of the proceeds of their crimes. The power is permissive, not mandatory, unlike the analogous provision in s.1 of the Drug Trafficking Offences Act 1986. For further discussion see Graham C. and Walker C., 'The Continued Assault on the Vaults — Bank Accounts and Criminal Investigations' (1989) Crim. L.R. pp. 185–206.

factors beyond the SFO's control, such as the refusal of a key witness to testify or, as in one recent case, as a result of a case being dismissed because of the defendant's ill-health.[45]

Another measure of efficiency might be the number of cases which the SFO manages to investigate and prosecute within the budget available to it. In 1990–91, the actual expenditure of the SFO on investigations and prosecutions was £6.57 million and 45 out of 72 defendants were convicted. Measured in this way each defendant "cost" the SFO approximately £91,000, and so the cost of unsuccessful prosecutions was just under £2.5 million (or 37 per cent of total expenditure on investigations and prosecutions). In 1991–92, expenditure of the SFO on investigations and prosecutions was £8.76 million and 38 out of 58 defendants were convicted. Each defendant therefore "cost" just over £150,000 and so the cost of unsuccessful prosecutions was almost exactly £3 million (or just under 34 per cent of total expenditure).[46] On this basis there has been an improvement in efficiency, despite the increased "cost" of each defendant; but it would be necessary to enter two caveats. The first is that the expenditure on investigations and prosecutions, for each of these periods, includes the cost of investigations which were continuing between accounting periods and where no prosecution had yet been brought. This would mean that the cost of prosecutions in any one period would in fact be somewhat lower than these figures suggest (although if the costs for both periods are combined, and assuming that all those whose investigations began in 1990–91 were prosecuted in 1991–92, the cost of unsuccessful prosecutions as a percentage of overall expenditure would still average at about 36 per cent.). The second point to make is that the kinds of fraud, their size and complexity, will inevitably vary from year to year so that any comparison on this basis can only ever be a rough one. It may be, for example, that the apparent improvement in efficiency for 1991–92 is a consequence of the fact that 38 per cent. of defendants in that period pleaded guilty as contrasted

---

[45] This happened, for example, during one of the cases involving Guinness plc's takeover bid for Distillers plc. The judge ruled that the burden of defending himself was affecting the health of Roger Seelig so badly that the trial could not continue. The trial having ended, the Attorney-General entered an order of *nolle prosequi* against Seelig, which placed an irrevocable stay on the existing proceedings.

[46] This provides a graphic example of Lacey's observation that increased expenditure on law enforcement may in fact 'create' more crime; see p. 18 above.

with 31 per cent. in 1990–91, (although it could, of course, be argued that the fact that a greater percentage did plead in 1991–92 is a reflection of the strength of the cases which the SFO brought against them).[47]

Deterrence

One of the principal aims of the SFO is the deterrence of fraud, and, as with efficiency, it is extremely difficult to estimate the extent to which such an aim can be achieved or measured. The ambition is explained by John Wood, the SFO's first Director, in the following way:

> "If the SFO is able to increase the speed and efficiency of investigations and the quality of prosecutions to ensure a greater certainty that they will be convicted it will, without doubt, add to the confidence of investors and ultimately discourage those who are now prepared to take risks in the knowledge that an investigation will be so protracted that the chances of conviction are lessened and, in the event of a conviction, a light sentence will ensue."[48]

The idea is reiterated by the present Director, George Staple, in similar terms:

> "I think it's getting the message across that if you do commit fraud there's a good chance of you being investigated and prosecuted and if it's serious enough, that it will be by the SFO, and if it is by the SFO the SFO is seen by the public at large as an effective and efficient organisation."[49]

---

[47] Although not really an indicator of efficiency, one way of considering the contribution which the SFO makes might be to consider its running costs against the value of the frauds investigated. The cost of fraud is undoubtedly substantial. Levi estimates for example, that the total cost of fraud recorded by the police in England and Wales is about twice that of theft, burglary and robbery combined, and that this does not take into account the cost of frauds dealt with by other agencies, such as Lloyds, the International Stock Exchange or the Securities and Investments Board, or of those which are unrecorded Levi M., *Regulating Fraud* (1987) pp. 23–31. At the end of the 1991–92 period the estimated value of the frauds in cases under investigation by the SFO was £5,300 million. In contrast to the enormous value of alleged frauds, the administration, investigation and prosecution costs of the SFO for the year amounted to just under £18 million, a relatively small proportion.

[48] Wood J., *op. cit.,* at p. 178.

[49] Interview with the author; February 10, 1992.

Several themes emerge from these statements of intent. The first is that the deterrent effect is characterised as being predicated on the SFO's efficiency. In other words, if the SFO is able to present itself generally as an organisation which has "got its act together" this will discourage potential fraudsters from committing their evil deeds. This assumption is perhaps in part the basis for the continued emphasis on efficiency in the Annual Reports.[50] The SFO does, however, face difficulties in that the deterrent impact of its own efficiency must be matched by the efficiency of the courts and trial process as well. If there is delay in hearings taking place, as a result either of the unavailability of judges or of adequate court rooms, then much of the SFO's work will be undermined.[51] The second theme is that the SFO recognises the importance of appearances. Irrespective of the reality of its efficiency, it must be perceived to be efficient by those who may be tempted to engage in fraudulent activity. To this extent the mere fact of the existence of the SFO has, in its view, a deterrent function, since it is an indication of a commitment to the prosecution of serious fraud. The third theme is that the SFO's presentation of itself as an effective deterrent adds to investor confidence and so contributes to the United Kingdom wish to remain a safe and attractive place in which to do business.[52] In so far as the extent to which this is true (the claim is as immeasurable as other claims concerning its contribution to efficiency) the SFO constitutes part of the wider attempt of government in the

[50] It is possible to be at least a little cynical about this, since the SFO's preoccupation with alerting the wider world to its efficiency is also a product of its desire to fend off criticism of both the general and investing public that it is inefficient as an organisation. It is important to remember that the SFO is only a part of the process by which serious frauds are investigated and prosecuted, albeit a high-profile part. The present Director is concerned about the fact that the public often see the prosecution of fraud as being akin to a football match in which both sides are out to win, whereas the prosecution are just as much there to ensure a fair trial as to secure a conviction. It is important that the public understand this, but getting the message across is extremely difficult, especially when the public has made up its mind that a conviction should occur. If it does not then the SFO is often the brunt of subsequent criticism.

[51] These matters are dealt with by the Lord Chancellor's Department and the Circuit and Court administrators. However, the SFO liaises on a continuing basis with these bodies and keeps them informed of the cases which are ready to be heard.

[52] A consideration which adds a further dimension to notions of the extra-territorial impact of the criminal law; see the chapter by Richardson in this volume.

mid 1980s to present the United Kingdom as somewhere committed to the maintenance of high standards in business.[53]

Deterrence is notoriously difficult to measure, and no less easy when considering the deterrent impact of institutions as against, for example, sentencing. In fact, it is almost impossible to imagine a way in which the deterrent effect of the SFO could be assessed. As the present Director put it:

> "You don't know but for the existence of the SFO what the level of fraud would have been in recent years; but I think one can be fairly certain that serious and complex fraud which at the end of the 1970s and in the early 1980s was simply not being investigated and prosecuted is to some extent now being investigated and prosecuted."[54]

It is perhaps only possible to consider deterrence as an understandable aim at a political level. Efficiency and deterrence, combined to generate and sustain the investor confidence necessary for a healthy economy, are aims expressed at the level of political rhetoric and provide the SFO with a way of structuring its activities and justifying its existence.

The SFO in the Courts

The legislation, which introduced the SFO, improved the efficiency of the criminal justice system through the introduction of preparatory hearings. A preparatory hearing may be ordered by a judge of the Crown Court where it appears to him that the evidence on an indictment "reveals a case of fraud of such seriousness and complexity that substantial benefits are likely to accrue from a hearing . . . before the jury are sworn".[55] Its purpose is to identify issues which are likely to be material to the verdict of the jury; to assist their understanding of those issues; to expedite the proceedings before the jury; or to assist the judge's management of the trial.[56] In addition to ordering the preparatory hearing, the judge may order the prosecution to prepare and serve any documents which he considers relevant.[57]

---

[53] The regulatory framework set up under the Financial Services Act 1986 was the other principal attempt.
[54] Interview with the author, February 10, 1993.
[55] Criminal Justice Act 1987 s.7(1).
[56] *ibid.*, s.7(1)(a)–(d). A judge may make an order under s.7(1) on the application of the prosecution, or of the person indicted (s.7(2)).
[57] These include those documents specified in s.9(4) or under Crown Court Rules (s.7(3)).

When such an order has been made and the prosecution have complied with it, the judge may order the person indicted to prepare documentation on the same grounds.[58] For the purposes of the preparatory hearing the judge may order the prosecution to supply the court and the defendant with a case statement including: the principal facts of the prosecution case; the witnesses who will speak to those facts; any exhibits relevant to those facts; any proposition of law on which the prosecution proposes to rely; and the consequences in relation to any of the counts in the indictment which appear to the prosecution to flow from these.[59] The judge may similarly order the defendant to provide the court and the prosecution with a statement setting out, in general terms, the nature of the defence and indicating the principal matters on which he wishes to take issue; to give them notice of any objections to the case statement; and to inform them of any points of law (including the admissibility of evidence) which he wishes to raise.[60]

The preparatory hearing, therefore, allows the trial judge to deal with the preliminary aspect of a case and to familiarise himself with the central issues that it raises. The SFO prepares case statements almost as a matter of routine and, in addition, is committed to the presentation of data in a form which makes it more easily intelligible.[61]

Much of the criticism that has been levelled at fraud trials has focused on their length and consequent cost. The SFO is conscious of its obligations in this respect and has set a target of one year from transfer/committal to the end of the jury trial, as well as a target of one year for investigation from initial acceptance of the case.[62] It is clear that it is not possible to know in advance what an investigation will reveal and it is consequently difficult to estimate the time that a contested trial will take. The SFO has,

---

[58] Criminal Justice Act 1987 s.7(4).

[59] ibid., s.9(4)(a)

[60] ibid., s.9(5).

[61] Such presentation of data may be through flow charts and computer-generated graphics. As part of the case statement the trial judge can order the prosecution to prepare their evidence and other explanatory material "in such a form as appears to him to be likely to aid comprehension by the jury and to supply it in that form to the court and to the defendant . . ."; C.J.A. 1987 s.9(4)(b).

[62] SFO Annual Report 1991–92 at p. 11. The average length of time between the SFO accepting a case and its transfer or committal was just under one year in 1990–91 (Annual Report 1990–91, p. 17). The average length of time in 1991–92 was 15 months (Annual Report 1991–92, p. 23). Each case accepted for investigation has task sheets and a timetable, and progress is now reviewed monthly.

however, attempted to minimise the length of cases, to the extent that it is able. Its first priority is to ensure that the evidence which it has against a defendant is as strong as possible; this strengthens the possibility of a guilty plea. In addition, it has accorded as a matter of priority the use of sophisticated information systems and the clear and accurate presentation of evidence at trial. It has, for example, exercised its powers to seize computers and software in order to secure data for use in evidence. It also makes substantial use of optical scanning techniques as a way of collating and ordering the vast number of documents involved in complex fraud, as well as witness statements and interview transcripts. This enables the otherwise impossible cross-referencing of relevant information. The information thus gathered is then used during the trial and, in some cases, is displayed in computer generated form via screens to the court.[63] This reduces the papers which the jury need to view and ensures that those in court all view the same material at the same time. Such graphical techniques can also be used to show more clearly complicated corporate structures and flows of funds.[64]

Due Process of Law

As Richardson suggested in his critique of the War Crimes legislation, perceptions as to the difficulty of securing convictions led Parliament to compromise certain supposedly normative standards of criminal due process in the investigation and trial of alleged war criminals. Many of those innovations were simply borrowed from the procedural regime introduced in respect of complex fraud cases by the Criminal Justice Act 1987. Richardson suggests that departure from traditional procedural safeguards is legitimate in the war crimes context because of the uniqueness and enormity of the offences[65]; such justification is perhaps more difficult to find in respect of serious fraud.

One of the major problems faced by those seeking to investigate frauds is obtaining the documents necessary for a full investigation. The investigation of fraud is document-based to a

[63] This technique was used in the cases involving County NatWest, Barlow Clowes and Charnley Davies.
[64] In one case during 1991–92 satellite communications were used to enable a witness in Canada to give evidence during a trial in England, an event which provides an unlikely (procedural) parallel between serious fraud and war crimes; see Richardson, above, at pp. 38–43.
[65] Chap. II, above.

large degree, and without access to the information contained in documentation it is almost impossible to evaluate the behaviour of those under suspicion or to bring charges. Fraud is rarely, if ever, transparent. Documentary evidence must be collated and analysed before it can be understood. The process is rather like moving back gradually from a television screen. At first, all that can be discerned are primary coloured dots; it is only when you reach a certain distance that the image becomes clear and you are able to describe with some certainty the image which those dots make up.[66]

The first stage of an investigation, before the critical distance is reached, is to get at the documents — to turn on the television. Extensive powers have been granted to the SFO to enable it to do this. Under the Criminal Justice Act 1987, the Director of the SFO, or a person designated by him, may require in writing that a person under investigation, or any other person whom there is reason to believe has relevant information, answer questions or otherwise furnish information, with respect to any matter relevant to the investigation, and to produce documentation.[67] Where a person fails to comply with a request, a warrant may be issued to enable the documents to be seized.[68] Banks, which owe a duty of confidentiality to their clients, and which are a common source of such documentation, are relieved of their obligations in this respect if the Director, or a member of staff nominated by him, has authorised the requirement.[69] It is an offence not to comply with this requirement or to knowingly or recklessly make statements which are false or misleading, or to falsify, conceal, or otherwise dispose of documentation.[70]

These powers are substantial, and the SFO exercises them with care.[71] Their principal advantage is that they enable relevant information to be obtained quickly and efficiently, thereby speeding up the investigation. Before the powers were introduced it was not possible, for example, to gain access to bank accounts without first having instituted criminal proceedings. An important

[66] An analogy which might be applied with equal facility to Wells' analysis of corporate manslaughter as a multi-component 'crime'; see pp. 123–125 below.

[67] C.J.A. 1987 ss.2(2) and 2(3) as amended by the Criminal Justice Act 1988 schedule 15.

[68] ibid., ss.2(4) and 2(5).

[69] ibid., s.2(10). Legal professional privilege is retained (s.2(9)).

[70] ibid., s.2(13)–(17).

[71] However, as Graham and Walker point out, the only real safeguard for those required to furnish information in this way is the integrity of the Director (Graham and Walker, op. cit., p. 193).

safeguard for potential defendants is that where statements are
made to the SFO under these powers, that information may not
be used in evidence in subsequent proceedings unless the evidence given in them is inconsistent with that which was originally
given to the SFO.[72]

Relationships with the Police

Some concern was expressed during the debate surrounding the
introduction of the SFO as to the proper role in the investigative
process. It was clear that many police officers had substantial, if
in some cases rather under-tapped, skills and resources which
could be put to good use. The problem was that police officers
serve under the Crown,[73] must adhere to specific disciplinary
codes and their conduct is monitored under the supervision of
their Chief Officer. In contrast, civil servants, such as those
directly employed within the SFO, are both servants of the
Crown and employees. It was felt important that the constitutional dependence of the police be maintained, and their existing
accountability structure be continued. This is reflected in the
legislation, which allows the Director, if he so decides, to conduct
any investigation in conjunction with the police,[74] but not to
assign his investigative or prosecutorial powers to them.[75]

The SFO's Approach to Case-Work

It will be remembered that one of the main criticisms of fraud
investigation before the introduction of the SFO was the fact that
there was insufficient co-ordination between those with different
kinds of expertise in the area of fraud investigation. Fraud is
characterised by its organisational context and frequently complex transactions. It is clear that lawyers or police officers
working alone on the investigation of fraud would have inade-

[72] C.J.A. 1987 s.2(8). This is to be contrasted with transcripts of interviews
conducted by DTI inspectors under s.432 of the Companies Act 1985, which are
admissible in criminal proceedings. Since the SFO was set up, over 2,000
notices under s.2 have been issued. There have been six prosecutions brought
against people for failing or refusing to answer questions.
[73] *Fisher v. Oldham Corporation* [1930] 2 K.B. 364.
[74] C.J.A. 1987 s.1(4).
[75] *ibid.*, s.2(11). The police are represented on the SFO's Senior Management
Board by a representative of the Association of Chief Police Officers and the
SFO's two senior police liaison officers.

quate skills to do the job properly. To discover, analyse and prosecute fraud needs a concerted and organised approach, where different but complementary skills can be brought together to construct as full a picture as possible. Forensic accountants are skilled at piecing together transactions and analysing the flow of funds between different parts of an organisation, while lawyers have to determine whether what has taken place amounts to criminal conduct. Both have difficult tasks. For accountants, a principal difficulty is determining whether a pattern of apparent irregularities amounts to something more than just a strange way of pursuing legitimate business. For lawyers, the principal difficulty lies in fitting such irregular conduct into the straitjacket of rigid criminal offences. The SFO has consequently developed a team approach to the investigation of suspected frauds. When a case is accepted for investigation a case team is appointed, under the direction of a lawyer and including accountants and police officers from the relevant force, and this team follows the investigation through to any eventual prosecution. Where necessary, outside experts in specialist fields, such as fund management and stockbroking, are brought in. The team has regular meetings, and is attended from an early stage by prosecuting counsel. At the end of the investigation a meeting is held to go through the case and to establish what lessons can be learned from it, such as how best to handle witnesses, and how to deal with overseas authorities.

The Decision to Prosecute

One of the most crucial decisions which the SFO must make is whether, having investigated a case, it should proceed to prosecution. It is rather paradoxical that the SFO should have this decision, since the Prosecution of Offences Act 1985 removed this power from the police as a consequence of growing concern about the propriety of an investigative agency also having the power to determine whether prosecution was the appropriate outcome. The concern centred on the fear that it was difficult for those responsible for investigation to exercise sufficient objectivity in the decision whether or not to prosecute — that they might be committed to a prosecution at all costs, irrespective of the strength of the evidence against the defendant. The decision to grant the SFO both investigative and prosecutorial discretion was taken because it was felt that, in the case of serious and complex fraud, the benefits to be gained from the co-ordinated approach outlined above outweighed any potential disadvantages.[76] The SFO is, however, conscious of the need to make any prosecution decision as objective as possible and so that decision is always taken by a lawyer not directly involved in the investigation. It might also be added that given the sensitivity of the SFO to criticism about bringing duff cases, there is an understandable tendency to err on the side of caution when making this decision.

The SFO is a Crown Prosector and so bound by the guidelines set out in the Code for Crown Prosecutors,[77] just as the Crown Prosecution Service (CPS) is. These guidelines set out the criteria which should be taken into consideration when deciding whether or not to prosecute. The principal criteria concern the sufficiency of evidence and the public interest in prosecution. As the SFO puts it:

> "Once the case has been investigated, the SFO will consider whether on the evidence against each potential defendant there is a realistic prospect of securing a conviction and whether the public interest requires a prosecution before instituting any criminal proceedings."[78]

The nature of serious fraud cases means that the SFO faces peculiar difficulties in deciding whether or not to proceed to prosecution. As far as evidential sufficiency is concerned it will be recalled that evidence of fraud is usually to be found in complex documentation, and that piecing this together and deciding whether or not the transactions and conduct so identified can be translated into established offences is no easy matter. The problem which the SFO faces is that sometimes there will be a pressure for prosecution, because the public has made up its mind that there should be a prosecution, where there is insufficient evidence. The present Director expressed no doubts when asked whether he would ever proceed to prosecution because there was such pressure, even though there were doubts about the quality of the evidence which could be mustered and admitted:

> "One just has to be as robust as one can about these things. Of course, one is under pressure sometimes either to prosecute or not to prosecute for reasons which aren't really valid reasons in terms of the

---

[76] Roskill had recommended that the SFO have detection powers as well, but these were not thought necessary given the introduction of the Financial Services Act 1986. This legislation created a sophisticated regulatory framework enabling the detection of misconduct by the SIB and SROs.

[77] This is issued by the D.P.P. under s.10 of the Prosecution of Offences Act 1985.

[78] Annual Report 1991–92, p.7.

criteria that we have to take into account; but one just has to be resolute."[79]

The criterion for realistic prospect of conviction is thus paramount, but the Director's comment invites further reflection. The SFO would seem to have an irresoluble dilemma. It recognises that there is substantial public interest in the prosecution of serious fraud, and that it was set up to undertake that function. However, the public interest is not the principal determinant of the decision to prosecute. The present Director argued that it could never be in the public interest to prosecute when there was no reasonable prospect of conviction, because such action would just waste limited resources. If the SFO brings an unsuccessful prosecution it is criticised for being inept, even though this may be for reasons beyond its direct control; if it does not bring prosecutions when the public considers that it should, it is criticised for being too soft. The problem would appear to be two-fold. First, the public are generally unaware of the constraints, both economic and statutory, which affect the SFO's decision-making process. Secondly, the SFO is perhaps the most high-profile component of the prosecution process. Although the courts have just as large a part to play in that process, the SFO has a designated task and a relatively highly-publicised image. Indeed, the SFO fosters that image as part of its desire to act as a deterrent against those who would commit fraud. It also suffers from the fact that in recent trials which have led to acquittals or which have taken a long time to conclude, judges have taken it upon themselves to be public in their criticism of the SFO's handling of cases.[80]

The SFO has not idled in the face of such criticism, however unjustified it considers that criticism to be. It makes it a special priority to only charge the most serious offences where this is appropriate, and only to charge those at the heart of a fraud if, as is usual, there is more than one person under investigation. In doing this, it hopes to contribute to the reduction of time in court hearings; but even so it faces problems. The first relates to the choice of which offences to charge. It is clearly better to charge that offence, or those offences, for which there is the most

[79] Interview with the author, February 10, 1993.
[80] Such was the case in the recent trial of those involved in Blue Arrow plc's bid to purchase Manpower, which lasted from February 1991 to February 1992. It is interesting to note that the SFO, in its summary of this case for the Annual Report emphasised the fact that of the time taken up by legal argument, 25% was by the prosecution as against 75% by the defence.

compelling evidence. This is especially true if it is anticipated that any custodial sentences imposed after conviction will be concurrent rather than consecutive. It is arguable that the retributive function of punishment is equally well served if the total sentence passed is commensurate with the sum of the offences committed. Indeed, there is a principle that sentences should not be consecutive when this leads to punitive over-kill. With this in mind it is clearly more efficient if the limited available resources of the SFO are focused on the most serious charge, or that for which it is most confident of a conviction. The problem is that such focusing and limiting the offences charged may prevent the jury from understanding the context in which those offences took place. This may in turn mean that they are less likely to convict. As the present Director explained:

> "The trouble is that if you only focus on one [charge] you may not be able to tell the whole story to the jury in order to get that one conviction; and if you can't tell the whole story the jury is mystified."[81]

The SFO is therefore caught again, between trying to present as full a picture of the story as possible in order to secure a conviction, and limiting the charges brought in order to answer calls for efficiency.

The second problem relates to choosing who to charge. Serious and complex frauds frequently involve more than one person, and there are always varying degrees of participation and culpability. The public may demand that all those involved be brought to book, but this is not always desirable or possible. Referring to the Code for Crown Prosecutors' criteria, the present Director explained:

> "We are required to charge only those at the heart of the fraud, at the heart of the offence; there are always people on the periphery who carry a degree of blame and could be prosecuted. And as I've said, I think its probably among those people that we would look for involvement by the regulators rather than a full-scale criminal prosecution before a jury."[82]

This demonstrates the extent to which the SFO operates within a wider framework of regulation, and that the way in which a person is found to have been fraudulent may vary. The role of

---

[81] Interview with the author, February 10, 1993.
[82] ibid.

the SFO is specific, concerned with the most serious fraud and the most culpable or central defendants. Provisions under other legislation, such as the Companies Act 1985 or the Financial Services Act 1986, enable others to be disqualified, or have their authorisation to carry on investment business suspended or removed. Such action may not have the same symbolic potency as a prosecution, but to the extent that it prevents fraudsters from having the opportunity to commit further offences, it achieves the same instrumental ends.[83] The fact that the SFO must make this decision, in a sense reinforces its role as the public, deterrent side of fraud control; but, even though it is required to make such a decision, lays it open to public criticism that it is letting people "get away with it".

One of the interesting factors concerning the decision to prosecute concerns its potential political sensitivity. When asked whether he thought that the decision to prosecute was in any sense a political one, the present Director was at his most diplomatic:

> "We're certainly not party political in any sense, but I think it is political in the broader sense in that in weighing the public interest there are often sensitive factors which have to be taken into account which can, if they're given too much weight . . .."[84]

And here he trailed off, perhaps understandably.

Such a cautious response is not entirely unexpected, although it does perhaps give some indication that although there might be sufficient evidence to ensure a reasonable chance of conviction, there are cases in which the public interest might not be served by prosecution. The public interest may not just be reflected in justice being done in relation to the defendant(s), but in the possible social consequences of prosecution. In this respect the SFO faces similar dilemmas to those other public agencies which have the power to prosecute, notably in the field of health and safety, where prosecution is often the last resort. The difference,

---

[83] This means of dealing with fraud has a long history, and because of the inadequacy of investigation and prosecution arrangements prior to the setting up of the SFO was often the principal means. As the present Director put it, "My guess is that in the old days, in many cases, I think it was almost considered enough for a company to go into liquidation and for the directors to be effectively put out of business" (Interview with the author, February 10, 1993).

[84] ibid.

and it is a crucial one, lies in the fact that such agencies typically have a continuing relationship with those whom they regulate, and their main concern is to secure compliance with legislative requirements. They thus adopt a proactive regulatory strategy, based on negotiation, and see prosecution as a failure of that strategy rather than as a success.[85] The SFO clearly does not operate under the same conditions and has no similar interest in avoiding prosecution. As far as being cautious in the prosecution of those at the apex of high-profile companies, there appears to be no such caution on the SFO's part. In the present Director's opinion:

> "Frankly, the prosecution of an individual, say the Chairman of such a company who has been fraudulent in some way, the company will survive normally. It will survive better if the culprit has been identified and taken out of the commercial situation."[86]

He cited the prosecution of Ernest Saunders, Chairman of Guinness, as an example and said that such prosecutions in fact lead to public confidence in the commercial and business sector — one of the SFO's main aims.

Conclusion

The decision to prosecute is clearly a tricky issue for the SFO, with respect both to the evidential sufficiency and public interest criteria. Collating documentation into a form which provides evidence of fraud, and fitting that evidence into established offence categories is a problem which the CPS faces less often. So the principal criterion — that there must be a reasonable prospect of conviction — is often hard to satisfy. There are also, as we have seen, particular issues with which the SFO must deal in relation to the public interest, again ones which the CPS seldom face. The SFO faces criticism if it does not prosecute, and criticism if it does and fails. Even when it succeeds it may face criticism that it is not bringing more prosecutions or that it di''
not proceed against a defendant when it had the opportunity t

---

[85] See for example Hawkins K., *Environment and Enforcement* (1984): Hutter L *The Reasonable Arm of the Law* (1988): Weait M., "The Letter of the Law? An Enquiry into Reasoning and Formal Enforcement in the Industrial Air Pollution Inspectorate, (1989) Brit.J.Criminol., pp. 57–70. See also the chapter by Scott in this volume.
[86] Interview with the author, February 10, 1993.

do so. In a sense, however, it could be argued that as far as the aims of the SFO are concerned it is not the number, or the type, of prosecutions which it brings that matters. The SFO was set up in part to demonstrate a public commitment on the part of government to the investigation and prosecution of serious and complex fraud, to deter would-be fraudsters and inspire confidence. Many of the criticisms which have been levelled against it stem from a lack of understanding about the peculiar problems which it faces in doing the task which it has been set. The fact is that the existence of the SFO is, in a way, as important as the way in which it does its job. As with all institutions which function in the public sector it is subject to resource constraints and demands for improved efficiency. And like other institutions it is just one part of a system which depends upon the other institutions, with which it must interact, to do its job effectively. The high-profile position which it occupies, and the claims which it must make to justify its existence (such as deterring fraud) mean not only that it must suffer the brunt of much criticism, but also that it can, in fact, never live up to the expectations which others may have of it. The SFO's aims are grand, and probably immeasurable. For those who would praise its achievements there will always be others who will say it has failed. Both, and neither, are right.

Chapter Five

CRY IN THE DARK: CORPORATE MANSLAUGHTER AND CULTURAL MEANING
by Celia Wells

"Corporate manslaughter" is a phrase which many people now recognise. When I use it to explain to those polite enough to inquire what sort of law I am interested in, it usually evokes the response "like Zeebrugge you mean". This is personally gratifying since there is nothing worse than having one's interests regarded as effete, obscure or incomprehensible. Yet it is significant in a more general sense, that it evidences a change in public perceptions. Corporate manslaughter is not just a category in a legal textbook (in fact, quite the opposite and that is the other half of the story), it has acquired a cultural meaning. Broadly stated, my thesis is concerned with the idea that there is not yet, and perhaps never will be, a fit between that cultural meaning and the legal construction of the term "corporate manslaughter". While there is nothing very startling or original about demonstrating such a mismatch, this one specifically highlights the complex relationship between blame, risk perception and the criminal process.

Strong resistance within the legal system to the notion that corporations might be criminals has resulted in an under-developed jurisprudence of corporate liability for crime.[1] A number of reasons might be advanced for this. On a politico-economic level it is clear that globally, nationally and regionally, business corporations represent a distinct and powerful force.[2] They wield enormous economic power, they are producers, service providers, media manipulators, political campaigners, advertisers, employers, consumers, polluters, tax avoiders but . . . are they criminals? Related to this, there is the argument that legal structures and mechanisms facilitate rather than hinder

[1] A student textbook dismisses the idea of developing such theories: "No doubt this is one of the many topics which call for systematic research and consideration but it is one of the least urgent"; Card R., Cross R. and Jones P., *Criminal Law* (1991), p. 170.
[2] Calavita K., *et al.*, Dam Disasters and Durkheim: An Analysis of the theme of Repressive and Restitutive Law (1991) *International Journal of Sociology of Law* 407–425.

the operation of corporations. The legal system within which they operate largely serves their interests, corporate personality protects their owners from the full consequences of failure,[3] and the regulation to which they are subject assumes their beneficence. A number of disaster studies show that moves towards corporate blaming are hampered by the tiers of company structure. The local company and its officials may be perceived as under the power of a parent company which is protected by the corporate veil.[4]

When it comes to criminal law, corporations are formally within but symbolically without. Corporations generally encounter criminal law only in its regulatory guise, an experience often characterised by a compliant, client-relationship reinforced by avoidance of condemnatory, denunciatory culpability tests.[5] It is generally accepted that many regulatory agencies use their powers of criminal enforcement as a last resort; they rarely press for trial on indictment and, when they are imposed, fines are often extremely low.[6] No attempt has been made to adapt the range of available penalties to deal with the particular demands of corporate offenders.[7] We should scarcely be surprised that when the Law Commission looked at corporate liability they found that on a number of points there was very little authority.[8] From achieving separate legal personality with its financial security to forging working relationships with complicit regulators, corporations can be seen as participants and creators of law. They are as often proactive in the legal process as passive defendants, sue as much as they are sued.

It is easy enough, in attempting to account for shortcomings and gaps in corporate liability principles, to point to the influence of moral and political individualism in criminal theory generally,

---

[3] A corporation is a group of individuals deemed in law to be a single legal entity, legally distinct from all the individuals who compose it. This has been recognised since the fifteenth century.

[4] This was one reason why the relatives of the Piper Alpha disaster abandoned efforts to proceed against Occidental, see Wells C., *Corporations and Criminal Responsibility* (1993), p. 145. And see Calavita, *op. cit.*, p. 413.

[5] Through the imposition of strict liability.

[6] The average fine for health and safety offences, for example, was £1,134 in 1991/92; Health and Safety Commission (1992) *Annual Report 1991/92*.

[7] An opportunity lost when the Criminal Justice Act 1991 introduced unit fines but confined their application to individual offenders. This attempt to achieve a more equitable distribution of the impact of fines was short-lived; see the Criminal Justice Act 1993 s.65(1).

[8] Law Commission (1989) *A Criminal Code for England and Wales*, Rep. no. 177 Commentary, para. 10.4.

and in particular in ideas about responsibility. Strict liability, prevalent in many regulatory schemes, allows corporate liability to be imposed vicariously. This avoids the doctrinal "problem", and ideological inconvenience, of attributing a mental element to an inert body.[9] The rise of the abstract individual as the appropriate recipient of legal blame can, of course, be traced to political and industrial changes.[10] However, the insinuation and permeation of the abstract individual into legal discourse should not be regarded as the sole explanation of the marginalisation of corporations from criminal law doctrine.[11] Otherwise there would be a danger of stating the obvious — here are corporations (legal groups), here is the criminal justice system ideologically infused with specific ideas about individuals, leading therefore to the irrelation between corporations and criminal liability.

None of these arguments seems to me to get underneath the conundrum that, while corporate manslaughter is a widely recognised cultural phenomenon, criminal doctrine remains very reluctant to acknowledge corporations as criminals for these purposes. To observe that corporations do not measure up to the culpably responsible individual which criminal justice is portrayed as addressing, identifies the symptom rather than the cause. Instead, I seek to identify some of the influences which make up the intricate pattern of criminal law and practice and raise some critical socio-cultural questions about the role which blame plays in the construction of the social institution of criminal justice. This involves considering the part played by perceptions of risk in sustaining the blame process. In other words, rather than hold everything constant while we switch from the individual to the corporation, we should conduct a deeper inquiry into the roles that blame and risk perform in reinforcing social constructions of crime and criminals. Notions of cause, blame and risk are inextricably bound up with the prevailing political and cultural climate, resulting in a symbiotic process rather than a flow in either one direction or the other.

Blaming Corporations

A number of writers assert that we are witnessing an increased tendency towards blaming collective institutions for the misfor-

---

[9] Note that when dealing with regulatory offences before *Tesco v. Nattrass* [1972] A.C. 153, courts were not averse to imposing *mens rea* liability vicariously. See Wells, *op. cit.,* pp. 97–111.

[10] See Williams R., *The Long Revolution* (1965), pp. 90–91 and Yeazell S., *From Medieval Group Litigation to the Modern Class Action* (1987).

[11] Norrie A., *Crime, Reason and History* (1993), Chap. 2.

tunes which befall us.[12] In particular, the argument that there has
been a cultural shift towards blaming corporations has been
eloquently made by Mary Douglas.[13] It is argued that perceptions
of corporate organisations and their responsibilities for mass
death have undergone a change. It is clear that corporate
negligence is more likely to be translated into calls for manslaughter prosecutions. There is less blind faith in the ability or
willingness of corporate organisations to take safety seriously.[14]
Business corporations are increasingly expected to provide compensation for injuries that, in earlier times, would have been
attributed to individual fault or fate.[15] This itself is possibly part
of a move towards greater legalisation resulting from a decline in
confidence in major institutions, business and government.[16]

It is important before attempting to account for this shift, to
examine the evidence to see what support there is for the thesis
that we really are blaming corporations more. Analysis of legal,
institutional and media responses to mass deaths such as those at
Aberfan, Zeebrugge, Kings Cross, and the *Marchioness* riverboat
collision shows an incoherent and incomplete process.[17] There
was little, if any, talk of collective criminal liability following
disasters such as those at Aberfan in 1966 and the Bradford
football stadium fire in 1985. The trend towards responding to
disasters in terms of corporate manslaughter seems to have begun
with the capsize of the *Herald of Free Enterprise* at Zeebrugge in
1987. The reasons for this change are varied and complex but

---

[12] A process anticipated in the debates about tortious principles of causation, see
Bush R., "Between Two Worlds: the Shift from Individual to Group Responsibility in the law of Causation of Injury" (1986) UCLA L.R. 1473–1563. See
also Rabin R., "A Socio-Legal History of the Tobacco Tort Litigation" (1992)
Stanford L.Rev. 853–878.

[13] Douglas M., *Risk and Blame* (1992).

[14] *ibid.* It has been argued that all cultures share the same basic repertoire of
explanations for explaining misfortunes (blaming the victim in a "moralistic"
style, blaming unpopular groups or forces in an "adversarial" style or deflecting
blame in a no fault style); Douglas M. and Wildavsky D., *Risk and Culture*
(1982).

[15] Bush, *op. cit.*

[16] Galanter M., "Law Abounds: Legalisation around the North Atlantic" (1992)
M.L.R. 1–24; Lipset S. and Schneider W., *The Confidence Gap: Business,
Labour and the Government in the Public Mind* (1987); and Giddens A., *The
Consequences of Modernity* (1990). See also Horlick-Jones T., "Modern
Disasters as Outrage and Betrayal" (1993) (paper at *International Institute of
Sociology Congress, Paris*).

[17] For detailed analysis of the inquiry, inquest process, see Wells C., "Disasters:
The Role of Institutional Responses in Shaping Public Perceptions of Death"
(1993) p. 196, in Lee R. and Morgan D., (eds.) *Death Rites*.

they do not seem to flow from any obvious differences, in terms of legal culpability standards, such as negligence, neglect or recklessness. For example, the *Herald* legal story usually opens with the Sheen inquiry's damning criticisms of P&O.[18] Yet there is little difference in the language there than in the Edmund Davies Report after Aberfan, a tip disaster in which 116 children and 28 adults were buried in slag.[19] The Report was persuasive and unequivocal in its condemnation, not only of the National Coal Board (NCB) for failures which led to the disaster itself, but also for the attitude it displayed to the Inquiry.[20] Here is an idea of how the Report saw the Coal Board's culpability:

> . . . [T]he Aberfan disaster could and should have been prevented.[21]
> . . . However belatedly, it was conceded by the N.C.B. that the Aberfan disaster stemmed from their failure to initiate any policy in relation to the siting, control, inspection and management of tips."[22]

> ". . . we cannot escape the conclusion that the Board must at national level also be blamed for its neglect of the stability of tips. Theirs was the overall responsibility for the initiation of policy, which involved that at national level there should have been due consideration of the proper methods to dispose of the waste of the coal-mining industry."[23]

The NCB in its opening statement had claimed that the disaster was due to a coincidence of an unknown set of geological factors:

> . . . [T]his was the starting-point of an attempt, persisted in for many weeks by the NCB, to persuade acceptance of the view that the concatenation of geological features on Merthyr Mountain was such as could not reasonably have been expected to exist. It might conceivably have had some bearing on our task had there ever been an attempt to ascertain what the geological features were; but, since there was no investigation and no thought devoted to the subject, the claim carried one nowhere."[24]

The similarities between the official responses to the Aberfan and *Herald* disasters do not quite end there. After each, both the

---

[18] Sheen Report, (1987) *M.V. Herald of Free Enterprise Report of the Court No. 8074* (London: Dept. of Transport).
[19] (1967) Report of the Tribunal Appointed to Inquire into the Disaster at Aberfan, H.C. 553.
[20] It was clear that the Board was civilly liable, without proof of negligence, under *Rylands v. Fletcher* (1868) L.R. 3 H.L. 330.
[21] Para. 18.
[22] Para. 178.
[23] Para. 178.
[24] Para. 190.

coroners and the relevant law officers[25] displayed the same
resistance to the idea of translating such negligence into criminal
liability. The reasons given were, however, of a different order.
After Aberfan it was accepted that while there might be a basis
for prosecution, to institute proceedings would not be appropriate. The Attorney-General explained to the Commons that those
implicated "have suffered enough by their own neglect."[26] Neither criminal proceedings nor the Chairman's resignation would
be desirable.

A clear distinction between criminal proceedings against individuals rather than the corporate body had yet to emerge. When
the Aberfan Parents and Relatives Association decided that they
did not want to pursue prosecutions because that would be to
bow to vengeance, they appeared to be thinking in terms of
prosecutions of individuals. Also, although the Report clearly
impugned the NCB, I have not come across any suggestion at
that time that a corporate charge should be considered. The
Report itself does not connect its condemnation of the NCB's
negligence with the possibility of this having criminal
consequences.

The Sheen Report into the *Herald* disaster did not mention
criminal liability either but, by the time of the inquest, this was
clearly at the forefront of the Herald Families Association's
agenda. Once started, this was then a clarion call in subsequent
disasters. After the Kings Cross, Clapham, and *Piper Alpha*
disasters, survivor groups spoke of their wish to pursue private
prosecutions. In the end, however, only two prosecutions were
brought, in relation to the *Herald* and the *Marchioness*. The
former ended in directed acquittals and the latter private prosecution did not pass the committal stage.

The next task is to seek to account for this shift in attitudes, to
establish what led to the identification and pursuit of corporate
negligence through the criminal process in the *Herald* and
subsequent disasters.

As with most untoward events, following a disaster a range of
causal levels can be drawn upon. Shall the deaths be blamed on
God or nature (as after Aberfan and other dam type disasters),
or on the rogue stranger (witness the Bradford stadium and Kings
Cross underground fires); shall the finger be pointed at the

[25] The Attorney-General after Aberfan and the D.P.P. after *The Herald*.
[26] We can imagine that many prisoners serving life for murder would have settled
for the option of enduring only self-punishment. For some extraordinary
personal accounts, see Parker T., *Life after Life* (1990).

individual employee (as happened after the *Herald* capsize and the rail crashes at Purley and Clapham), at the safety manager, (Aberfan, *Herald*, Hillsborough); or at company policy (Aberfan, *Herald*, Kings Cross)? Only when the causal level is attributed to company policy will consideration be given to corporate manslaughter. A cultural or social institution perspective can assist in explaining how changing notions of responsibility and blame are translated into legal liability. Cultural selection determines which dangers are recognised, and the institutions of public inquiry and punishment are ways in which this selection is activated.[27] Whether victims are blamed, whether misfortunes are regarded as natural rather than man-made, and the types of official institutional response to them, are functions of the type of social system in which they arise.[28] Blame is only invoked where an event is perceived as unnatural: "If a death is held to be normal, no one is blamed."[29]

The move towards blaming corporations for major disasters bears witness to the theory that blame generally, and criminal blame in particular, is used as a way of people making sense of the world.[30] People select certain risks for attention to defend their preferred lifestyles and as a forensic resource to place blame on other groups.[31] The dingo baby case in Australia illustrates this well.[32] Lindy Chamberlain's baby disappeared from a tent in a camp site at Ayres Rock, a major source of tourism in that part of Australia. Despite the consistency of her claim that the baby had been taken by a dingo, she was found guilty of the baby's murder and remained in prison for three years before new evidence emerged vindicating her claim. Part of the explanation for the refusal to believe her story was that it was deeply threatening to hitherto widespread beliefs about dingos. If indeed they were likely to do as she suggested this would also threaten many people's livelihoods. A further contributory aspect perhaps was the fact that she and her husband were Seventh Day

---

[27] Douglas M., *How Institutions Think* (1985), p. 54.

[28] *ibid.*, p. 64.

[29] Douglas and Wildavsky, *op. cit.*, p. 35.

[30] A number of writers point to the effect of the increasing secularisation of society on perceptions of crime and risk, Taylor I., *Crime, Capitalism and Community* (1983), p. 107: Lee T., "The Public's Perception of Risk and the Question of Irrationality" (1981) in Warner F., (ed.) *The Assessment and Perception of Risk*, p. 5.

[31] Douglas, *op. cit.*

[32] And also explains the enigmatic title to the paper taken from the "cinema verite" film made on the case.

Adventists — as religious freaks they might be seen as double outsiders. It proved much easier to find her wrongly guilty than to bring a successful prosecution against P&O. If the social construction fits, weak evidence can be overcome or selectively ignored. If the social construction does not fit, as with P&O, *Marchioness*, and other potential corporate manslaughters, then it has proved remarkably difficult to initiate or to maintain criminal proceedings.

Culture renders the construction of categories into a seemingly natural, taken for granted, process. It affects the way we look at ourselves and the rest of the universe.[33] Yet, at the same time, in a highly interdependent society, culture is fragmented. Its reflection and refraction through the maze of social institutions will be diverse and enigmatic. One of the things people value most will be the set of social institutions that they personally strongly identify with or participate in. The hazards which most concern them will be those which threaten locally-valued social arrangements.[34]

As the power of collective enterprise to cause harm comes to be recognised, so does the collective interest as a potential victim, of which concern about pollution is an example.[35] "New technology," it has been suggested, "produces new social responsibilities and provokes cultural re-assessment."[36] The salient message is that responsibility and blame allocation are not derivative of individual moral positions. An article in *The Times*, on the 20th anniversary of Aberfan, underlines the array of potential targets:

> "When battles turn to carnage, the field commanders are blamed; in earthquake or famine, God is held responsible. But you cannot blame God for the tragedy of Aberfan; or, if so, only obliquely, for the black monster above Pantglas school was unleashed by man. The Aberfan tribunal made that quite clear."[37]

Two connected trends in recent writing about crime help underline the theme of blame which runs throughout this essay. First, there has been a revival of interest in Durkheim's theory of the

---

[33] Erikson T., *In the Wake of the Flood* (1979), p. 46.

[34] Pidgeon N., *et al.* "Risk Perception", in *Risk: Analysis, Perception and Management* (1992).

[35] Nelken D., "Criminal Law and Criminal Justice: Some Notes on Their Irrelation", (1987) in Dennis I., (ed.) *Criminal Law and Justice.*

[36] Douglas and Wildavsky, *op. cit.*, p. 35.

[37] Michael Watkins, *The Times*, October 17, 1986.

relationship between legal sanctions, social structure and public sentiment.[38] The second trend is the renewed concern with ideas of vengeance and shame and their role in modern society.[39] For Durkheim, punishment is a social institution which reinforces matters of morality. Punishment is neither rational nor instrumental, it is irrational and emotional. However, it is also ultimately functional and, in giving vent to outbursts of common sentiment, it strengthens the social bond.

This connects with Braithwaite's argument for a reintegrative theory of shame, on the grounds that it is crucial to crime control. What is interesting here is the essential functionalism ascribed to shame and to vengeance. Durkheim saw law as either repressive or restitutive. Repressive laws inflict suffering and punishment, and penal laws are therefore characteristic of them. Restitutive laws seek to return things as they were, and their sanctions are characteristic of civil laws. In their study of two dam disasters, Buffalo Creek and the Stava dam in Italy, Calavita *et al* show that, despite calls for condemnation, in both cases the legal response was restitutive rather than repressive. Differences in legal culture meant that criminal proceedings were automatic in Italy, yet their repressive effect was reduced by the imposition of lenient sentences. Despite victims' initial labelling of the Buffalo disaster as "murder", and "criminal negligence", the grand jury eventually decided that no-one should be held criminally liable. The authors argue that restitutive sanctions can emerge, despite an emotional reaction of outrage or shock and, further, that Durkheim underestimated the "nexus between economic and political power."[40]

"While Durkheim . . . correctly predicted an increased use of regulatory law and a decreased public tolerance of violations of it, the Stava and Buffalo Creek cases reveal the inadequacy of his assumption that this public sentiment would produce a new 'apparatus of repression' ".[41]

Braithwaite, on the other hand, uses the notion of shaming as specifically non-repressive. Shame can be used in a reintegrative rather than stigmatising way. Forgiveness, apology and repentance need to be elevated to cultural importance. The connec-

---

[38] Calavita K., *et al.*, *op. cit.*, See also Garland D., *Punishment and Modern Society* (1991), Chap. 2.
[39] Braithwaite J., "Shame and Modernity" (1991) Brit. J. Criminol. 1–18.
[40] Calavita, *et al.*, *op. cit.*, p. 419.
[41] *ibid.*, p. 422.

tion, I think, is that restitutive sanctions can have a place in criminal law. It is a mistake, argues Braithwaite, to see shame as connotative of pre-industrial, folk society with clear networks of relationships. Modern communications and so on may mean more interdependencies rather than less.

Mechanisms of Blame

This cultural shift in blame has bred procedural and substantive tensions in the legal system's responses to mass death. In this section I apply the broad cultural model of blame and responsibility ascription outlined above, first to processes leading to prosecution and then to substantive questions of criminal recklessness.

Procedure

The *Marchioness* story is used to demonstrate the procedural and institutional mysteries which ring-fence the cultural expressions of blame emerging in the last decade. Fifty-one people drowned in the River Thames on a clear moonlit night in August 1989 when the dredger *Bowbelle* (with a gross tonnage of 1,494.94 and a length of 79.91 metres) ran into the pleasure cruiser *Marchioness* (which was 46.19 gross tonnage, 26.06 metres in length). A Department of Transport Marine Accident Inquiry was set in motion but no public inquiry was ordered.[42] The Marine Accidents Investigation Board investigation disclosed previous collisions between similar vessels in 1981 (involving *Hurlingham*, a sister cruiser of *Marchioness*), and two in 1983 (one of which involved *Bowbelle*). The visibility from the wheelhouses of both vessels was restricted (in the case of *Bowbelle* alarmingly so)[43] and this was one of the main factors contributing to the accident.[44] Poor lighting was a further contributory factor and the Report noted that "no particular attention" had been paid by the Department of Transport to consideration of "any steps to improve the conspicuity of passenger launches".[45] However, the

---

[42] See Sheen J.'s criticism of this, prompted by the decision to hold a public inquiry into the Shetland oil spill, in a letter to *The Times*, January 23, 1993.
[43] Department of Transport *Report into the Collision between Marchioness and MV Bowbelle on August 20, 1989* (1991) paras. 7.4, 7.5 and Annex 5, photograph B.
[44] Para. 18.4.
[45] Para. 17.11.

Department was given the benefit of the doubt of hindsight; it was concluded that it would have been unrealistic for it to respond to potential risks from poor visibility.[46] This might be thought to add a whole new meaning to complacency in the face of risk assessment.

Although completed by February 1990, the report was not published until two years after the accident, on August 15, 1991. The explanation for this was that it was necessary to prevent any prejudice to the trial of the captain of the *Bowbelle* for breach of duty under the Merchant Shipping Act 1988.[47] At two successive trials, juries could not agree on the charge that he had failed to ensure a proper lookout. This may well evidence a reluctance to blame the individual for what seemed to be faults of the shipowners and possibly of the Department of Transport.

Meanwhile, in September 1990 the Director of Public Prosecutions had ruled out the possibility of charges against Bowbelle's owners, South Coast Shipping.[48] A private prosecution was launched as soon as the D.P.P. indicated that the case against the captain was being dropped. This prompted the unusual move of the D.P.P. asking for papers from the private prosecutor's solicitor with a view to taking over and dropping the prosecution.[49] Such action before committal is almost unprecedented. The D.P.P. changed his mind and decided not to intervene after all. At this point, the long-awaited publication of the MAIB Report took place. This rendered less credible the claim that it had been necessary to withhold it previously for fear of prejudicing the captain's trial. An interpretation even less favourable to the D.P.P. is that the Report was published at this point precisely so as to prejudice the private prosecution?[50] The defendants attempted to stop the proceedings before committal with an application for judicial review on grounds of abuse of process and lack of *locus standi* on the part of the prosecutor.[51] Neither went

---

[46] *ibid.*

[47] Section 32. No use was made against Bowbelle's owners of the offence under section 31 of failing to ensure the safe operation of their ship, a new provision introduced following recommendations of the Sheen inquiry into the *Herald* disaster.

[48] An application for judicial review of this was rejected, *The Times*, October 31, 1990. Nolan J., however, said it was "entirely understandable that the survivors and . . . relatives . . . and all who are concerned with the safe passage of vessels on the Thames, should seek a full public inquiry . . .". Letter from Louise Christian, *The Guardian*, January 28, 1993.

[49] *The Times*, August 3, 1991.

[50] The Marchioness Action Group certainly believed that publication was an attempt to block the private prosecution; *The Times*, August 15, 1991.

[51] Ivor Glogg, whose wife was a victim of the tragedy: April 13, 1992, Divisional Court, Lloyd L.J. and Waterhouse J.

in favour of the applicants.[52] Committal proceedings finally began
in June 1992 but the case came to an end there.

These tensions between a government department, the legal
officers, the legal system and the relatives and survivors disclosed
a procedural dance for which no-one knew the steps in advance
and in which the lead passed quite unpredictably from one to the
other. This account has excluded the inquest which was opened,
adjourned and almost abandoned as the other institutional forces
took hold.[53]

A number of messages emerge from this unchoreographed
performance. First, it was far from clear who was pulling the
strings. Secondly, the obstacles to the prosecution were largely
procedural and not substantive. Thirdly, the procedures for
public accounting for mass death are both unfamiliar and
incoherent.[54] Fourthly, that when there is a hint of government
incompetence, that incoherence is intensified and fifthly, that
corporate bodies appear to fear criminal proceedings and will
make strenuous efforts to prevent them taking hold.

It is instructive to compare this process with that for a
stereotypical homicide where the structures are more clearly
understood. Most police work involves attaching a person to a
crime, or even a crime to a person, whereas here the issue is
whether to attach the label, crime, to an event. Public inquiries,
inquests and the D.P.P. play enhanced roles,[55] and, as I show in
the next part of this chapter, corporate defendants and the State
play unaccustomed roles. Instead of the defendant being the

---

[52] *R. v. Bow Street Magistrate, ex p. South Coast Shipping Co. Ltd.* [1993] 1 All
E.R. 219. The position may be less favourable in Scotland, where the issue
arose potentially in relation to Piper Alpha. See Ferguson P. and Staunton M.,
"Private Prosecutions" (1991) 135 S.J. 952. Ultimately, the prosecution plan
was dropped for other reasons, see n. 4 above.

[53] The Court of Appeal upheld a complaint of bias against the original coroner's
decision not to reopen the inquest in July 1992, *R. v. Dr Knapman* and another,
ex p. Dallaglio and others, June 11, 1994. Despite his "great reservations" the
West London coroner to whom the decision was then assigned acceded to the
bereaved relatives' request to have the inquest reopened, *The Independent,*
October 19, 1994.

[54] Paul Knapman, who was also the coroner for the Clapham rail crash, has
argued that coroners and juries should be empowered to make safety recommendations; he favours something more like the Scottish Fatal Accident Inquiry
in which a sheriff can determine the cause of any accidental death, reasonable
precautions which might have been taken including examining defects in any
working system which contributed, speech to the Bar Conference, *The
Guardian,* September 30, 1991. See on FAIs, "FAIs After Lockerbie" *Scots
Law Times,* (1991), p. 225.

[55] See Wells, *op. cit.*, n.17.

under-resourced party against an oppressive state, a corporate defendant is a match for the Crown, and, instead of the State being clearly on the prosecution side, it may well itself be implicated in its failure to maintain a more rigorous safety policy.[56]

I have concentrated so far on what or whom to blame. Is an untoward event to be attributed to nature, an act of God, or is the accusation to be directed towards an individual or group? A further dimension to the picture of the interaction between blame and social constructions of crime is the role of risk perception. Risk acceptability can be regarded as the mechanism or instrument of the blaming process.

Risk Perceptions and Recklessness

The assignment of responsibility takes place partly through the emergence of cultural standards of what is to constitute a proper risk.[57] As Douglas puts it; "the cultural coding of responsibility is also the coding for perceiving risks."[58] Risk and danger are not rational objective neutral concepts. Rather than an objective probability being the means by which a decision as to culpability is reached, it is the other way round. Communities use their shared experiences to determine acceptable risk taking.[59]

As Barry Turner argues, the aetiology of many catastrophic events can be traced back to hazards which were foreseen, but inappropriate or inadequate action was taken as a result of that foresight.[60] Further, the perception that such events might have been preventable (and therefore in some way foreseeable) partly contributes to their being viewed as man-made disasters rather than acts of God. Perceiving an event to have resulted from a failure of foresight can be regarded as "the collapse of precautions that had hitherto been regarded culturally as adequate."[61]

The pseudo-scientific assumption of objectivity underlying common (and perhaps legal) usage of the notion of risk is being replaced by awareness that subjective considerations inevitably insinuate expert assessments.[62] Public perception of risk and

---

[56] Report, above, n.39.
[57] Douglas, *op. cit.*, pp. 67–68.
[58] *ibid.*, p. 72.
[59] *ibid.*, p. 69.
[60] Turner B., "The Organizational and Interorganizational Development of Disasters" (1976), 21 *Administrative Science Quarterly* 378 - 397 at pp. 380, 382.
[61] *ibid.*, p. 380.
[62] Lee, *op. cit.*, p. 7.

"objective" risk assessment can be seen as "complementary forms of rationality".[63] Research shows both that experts can be as imprecise as lay people once they go beyond their data[64] and that, once formed, people's beliefs change slowly and persist even in the face of contrary evidence.[65] The opportunities for such biases or subjectivities can be seen from an account of the two main types of risk prediction from statistical data provided by past events. Two types of extrapolation are used. The first, and perhaps more familiar, one is based upon the frequency of past events. However, where there are no, or very few, past records, such as for core meltdown in a nuclear plant, reliance has to be placed on an aggregation of frequency of possible antecedents. This depends both on an ability to identify a potential hazard and to construct a plausible list of causal factors.[66]

Yet "risk" is freely used as a means of determining legal culpability as if there were a common understanding about it. The legal mechanism for this risk perception process is the culpability norm of recklessness. Legal discussion of the concept of recklessness, whether conceived in terms of a known risk or of one which ought to have been known, has ignored the problematic in the concept of risk itself. A simple model of risk has been assumed, with no distinction drawn between risk based on probability and risk involving a utility calculus. This is not primarily an issue about types of recklessness, although it lends support to the view that the subjective/objective debate misses its target.[67] Rather, it questions at a more fundamental level the assumptions made in that debate about the nature of risk. Risk is more complex a phenomenon, while recklessness more simple, than legal doctrine allows.

This can be seen clearly in the abortive trial of P&O for manslaughter following the *Herald* disaster.[68] As the first prosecution for corporate manslaughter in nearly 30 years, its very novelty is significant.[69] The *Herald of Free Enterprise* capsized

[63] *ibid.*, p. 16.
[64] Slovic P., Fischoff B. and Lichtenstein S., "Perceived Risk: Psychological Factors and Social Implications" (1981), p. 21 in Warner, *op. cit.*
[65] *ibid.*, citing Nisbett R. and Ross L., *Human Inference* (1980).
[66] Lee, *op. cit.*, p. 6.
[67] Recent examples of this genre can be seen in the critiques of Duff A., *Intention, Agency and Criminal Liability* (1990); *viz.* Gardner J. and Jung H., "Making Sense of Mens Rea: Antony Duff's Account" (1991) O.J.L.S. 559–573: and Norrie A., "Subjectivism, Objectivism and Criminal Recklessness" (1992), O.J.L.S. 45–58.
[68] *R. v. Alcindor and Others* (Central Criminal Court, Oct 19, 1990).
[69] *R. v. Northern Strip Mining Co.* 1965 (Glamorgan Assizes), *The Times*, February 2, 4, and 5, 1965.

just outside Zeebrugge after leaving port with its bow doors open. The assistant bosun whose job was to ensure that the doors were shut was asleep in his cabin. It was not possible for the captain to confirm from the bridge whether the doors had been shut. The Sheen Inquiry had been strongly critical of the company's attitude to safety.[70] At least one captain had drawn to the attention of management the need for lights to be fitted on the bridge to ensure that ships did not sail while the doors were still open.

With largely undisputed facts, an extremely well-resourced defence team was able to devote its efforts to legal argument. The trial confirmed that a corporation can in theory commit manslaughter.[71] However, given the convolutions and intellectual difficulties which confronted the trial judge once the defence team raised questions about how to prove recklessness, the possibility of a successful prosecution in the immediate future is unlikely. The ending of the trial on the judge's direction that there was insufficient evidence of recklessness, graphically highlights the gulf between popular and legal conceptions of blame ascription. While attribution of culpability is a cultural process, it has to pass through a number of legal sieves, the most important of those tested, before reaching the trial stage, being the inquest and the D.P.P.'s decision to prosecute.[72] At each stage, the institutional hurdles were counter weighted by pressure from the Herald Families group and from public or lay input (for example, in the inquest jury's verdicts of unlawful death).[73] It was at the last stage, before the trial jury could consider its verdict, that the mesh finally tightened and the case was stopped.[74]

Legal usage of the concept of risk operates at two levels. On the one hand, it is left to juries to attribute blame through assessment of risk, but on the other, the legal ground preparation distorts the very process through which a jury is being led. The P&O case illustrates, in an unusually stark way, that inherent in the legal concept of criminal recklessness are hidden assumptions of an underlying objectivity about risk. By allowing judicial guidance on the legal meaning of recklessness, it is assumed that

[70] Above, n. 18.
[71] The legal ruling on this point is reported in *D.P.P. v. P&O European Ferries (Dover) Ltd.* (1991) 93 Cr.App.R. 73.
[72] See Wells, *op. cit.*, n.17 above.
[73] *ibid.*
[74] *cf.* Moran, who sees the case as a reassertion of law as representation rather than simulation; "Corporate Criminal Capacity: Nostalgia for Representation" (1992), *Social and Legal Studies* 371–391.

there is a verifiable minimum; by ultimately giving to the jury the task of assessing "obvious and serious risk" (or, with subjective recklessness, awareness of an unacceptable risk) it is conceded that the question is evaluative.[75]

If the case had gone to the jury, the fluidity of risk as the kernel of cultural coding in "legal" recklessness would have been exposed. Instead, it will now be relatively easy for the D.P.P. to resist any future pressure to bring a corporate prosecution. It is clear that the *Herald* disaster marked the conception of the cultural meaning of corporate manslaughter and the inquest, its date of birth. It was the inquest jury's finding of unlawful killing which exerted pressure on the D.P.P. to prosecute.[76] With the question of corporate manslaughter now at the forefront in the legal aftermath of a disaster, the D.P.P. is likely to adjourn any inquest on the ground that a prosecution is being considered.[77] The difficulties encountered in the P&O trial will lead her to the (not unreasonable) conclusion that a prosecution will be unlikely to succeed and there the matter will rest. An inquest verdict of unlawful killing is procedurally more difficult once the D.P.P. has already announced a decision not to prosecute, and even if the inquest jury were to return unlawful death verdicts, the D.P.P. will be under no pressure to reopen her file.[78]

Conclusion

Failure to recognise the cultural foundations of attributions of responsibility in the general infrastructure of criminal laws is one aspect of the resistance or inability of legal institutions to respond to, or deal with, the cultural shift towards blaming corporations for technological hazard. Risk perception and acceptability are the hidden driving force of recklessness, the standard-bearer of criminal culpability, both figuratively, in the sense of being at the forefront, but also more literally as the setter of a standard. Recklessness, used in the process of attributing blame and assigning responsibility, is not a necessarily sophisticated or critical notion. In terms of blame allocation, risk perception drives both causal attribution and recklessness determinations. Causal attribution reflects whether the focus of attention is God, nature, the individual operative such as the ship's captain, the

[75] See Norrie, *op. cit.*
[76] See Wells, *op. cit.*, n. 17 above.
[77] Coroners Act 1988 s.16.
[78] As occurred following the Clapham Rail crash; see Wells, *op. cit.*, n. 17, 218.

company directors or the company itself. With the increased sophistication of both technology and communications systems, so too are more elaborate, developed chains of causal attribution emerging.

The paradox is that, together with the complex of social and media networks, those interconnections are productive both of the conditions which make disasters a matter of wide public knowledge, as well as of the inevitability of the blaming and shaming process which is invoked in response. This chapter has attempted to open up some of the channels of thinking which can help us to understand where criminal justice fits as a parochial response to large-scale, even global threats.

Chapter Six

THE CRIMINALISATION OF OFFENCES AGAINST INTELLECTUAL PROPERTY
by Alison Firth

Introduction

The protection of property[1] from dishonest or violent appropriation is often regarded as an important function of criminal law in capitalistic societies. This role relates traditionally to tangible forms of property, whether real or personal. However, the development of industrial processes, coupled with increased possibilities of plagiarism, imitation and diversion of profitable information, have led, over the centuries, to the recognition and codification of many forms of intangible property, including those known as industrial or intellectual property. These developments have been international as well as national. The widespread plagiarism which resulted from the Great Exhibition of 1851 led to the creation of the Paris Union for the Protection of Industrial Property, and the Berne (copyright) Union came into being in the same decade.[2] In the modern era, the transnational character of this segment of British law has been given a further impetus by our membership of the European Community.

Even the most cursory of analyses of the creation, enforcement and repeal of criminal offences in this area reveals a fluctuating, evidently incoherent pattern of regulation. Lacey's metaphor of the lens[3] has, as other chapters in this book suggest, a useful role to play in alerting us to the divergent understandings and impact of the criminal law on actors who occupy different vantage points in the socio-economic or political spectrum. This chapter lends

---

[1] On the relationship between the concepts of power and of property, see Lacey in chapter 1 at pp. 13–14.
[2] The Convention for the Protection of Intellectual Property was signed in Paris in 1883; the International Convention for the Protection of Literary and Artistic Property was signed in Berne in 1986 — see Ricketson S., *The Berne Convention 1886–1896* (1987).
[3] At pp. 8–9, above.

127

perhaps a further complication to the metaphor by arguing that the criminal law framework surrounding intellectual property indicates that some actors who might be thought to share the same vantage point (*i.e.* that they have something valuable to protect) are, in fact, treated very differently by the criminal law for no obviously rational reasons.

In addition to the reductionist argument that the criminal law functions to protect "private property", one can discern several plausible "public interest" reasons for the criminal law to play a role in this field. Estimates of losses to "counterfeiting"[4] and "piracy"[5] (and consequential loss of tax revenues), and suggestions that these activities are connected with organised crime,[6] indicate that society at large has an interest in the enforcement of intellectual property rights. Similarly, one can readily identify a societal interest in encouraging creative individuals to invent, and thereafter market, desirable products or ideas — the incentive to do so is likely to diminish if entrepeneurs know their innovations can be "stolen" with impunity.

Yet one can also readily identify a number of factors which might be thought to militate against criminalisation. There is, for example, some difficulty in identifying a "victim" with whose loss we might sympathise. The consumers of illicitly copied products tend often not to be the innocent dupes of fraudulent sellers, but are knowing purchasers, driven by considerations of price, sometimes to the detriment of their own, and others', health and safety.[7] Similarly, societal concerns with encouraging producer innovation may rapidly shift into a suspicion or resentment of the potentially exploitative, monopoly power that owners of intellectual property rights enjoy. This can produce adverse cultural

---

[4] The pejorative terms "counterfeiting" and "piracy" do not have a standard meaning, but are widely used. "Piracy" generally refers to the making of infringing copies of copyright-protected works, whilst counterfeiting usually connotes more or less precise imitation of a product's appearance, especially by use of trade marks. Regulation 3842/86/EEC, which dealt with seizure of goods entering the common market from elsewhere defined counterfeit goods as "any goods bearing without authorisation a trade mark which is identical to a trade mark validly registered in respect of such goods in or for the Member states in which the goods are entered for free circulation."

[5] As above. See also Lord Denning's description of "pirates" in *Island Records* [1978] Ch. 122 at 133; [1978] FSR 505 at 510–511. The label is perhaps inappropriately grave in its connotations, given the rather unique criminal status of piracy in its original form: see Richardson at p. 55 above.

[6] Intellectual Property Newsletter, Vol. 16, Issue No. 11, p. 5 (November 1993).

[7] Fenby J., *Piracy and the Public* (1983), Chap. 9.

understandings of what it is that "owners" are seeking to protect[8]; in particular as to the perceived harmlessness[9] of the conduct proscribed. This diffuse cultural antipathy towards regulation is, to some extent, compounded by the fact that it is comparatively rare for individuals to engage in enforcement in the civil courts, let alone the criminal courts. Rather, actions are pursued by record companies, or by collecting societies which administer rights on behalf of large numbers of individuals, or by corporate owners of patents and trade marks. These organisations are regarded with disaffection by many, or imagined to be well in a position to afford a little diversion of revenues.

To complicate matters still further, one can also discern factors which might lead one to speculate that any criminal law regulation of this field would necessarily be fragmented, sporadic and un-coordinated, both in principle and in practice. The widespread ignorance of the existence and nature of the various types of intellectual property rights amongst lawyers, judges, and legislators also leads to technical difficulties[10] and cultural misunderstanding. This can rapidly lead to the construction of a public sentiment, which provides another example of what Lacey describes as a crime which is not really criminal at all.[11] It appears, for example, that police forces and trading standards authorities accord low priority to these types of offences.[12] Equally important to the *de facto* cultural decriminalisaton of the *de jure* prohibition is the presumption made by many of those carrying on the forbidden activity that any prosecution is unlikely to occur — and in the event that action should be taken, any penalty imposed is regarded as an acceptable "tax" on their activities.[13]

The existence of powerful civil remedies and procedures, such as injunctions and *Anton Piller* orders[14] further tends to divert

---

[8] See Lacey at pp. 14–15, above; Wells at pp. 124–126 above.

[9] See Feinberg, cited in Lacey, above at n.6.

[10] *e.g.* a criminal trial was adjourned to establish whether a copyright notice was essential to the subsistence of copyright in a film [private communication].

[11] See p. 15 above.

[12] For suggestions as to why see Scott's chapter in this volume. However, trading standards officers now have a duty to enforce, (other than in Scotland) Trade Marks Act 1994, s.93.

[13] See Lacey pp. 6–7 above.

[14] Search and seize orders, named after *Anton Piller KG v. Manufacturing Processes Ltd.* [1976] Ch. 55; [1976] RPC 719. Their role in this field is discussed further below.

enforcement from the criminal to the civil courts. The lower standard of proof required to succeed in civil actions may make this form of litigation more attractive than criminal proceedings to powerful owners of intellectual property rights, as would the ready availability of damages to act as both a specific, and general, deterrent.

In the pages that follow, an attempt is made to pick a way through the seeming confusion and incoherence within this sphere of the criminal law. One might note at the outset that this journey is undertaken less in the hope of finding a universally relevant explanation for the current state of the law, but more in the expectation that we will uncover a particularly good example of the "contingency" of criminal regulation. Our first task, however, undertaken for the benefit of those for whom intellectual property remains largely unknown territory, is briefly to sketch its various forms and legal sources.

The Legal Basis of Intellectual Property

Table 1 shows the varieties of right recognised in the United Kingdom as falling within the description of "intellectual property". It should be noted that the statutory provisions referred to are U.K.-wide,[15] whilst the rights recognised at common law or in equity in England and Wales are equally recognised in Scotland and Northern Ireland. However, procedural differences,[16] particularly in the area of interlocutory relief, may lead plaintiffs to choose to start a civil offensive north of the border, where infringement of rights spans the several jurisdictions. As is readily apparent from column 4 of the table, there are ostensibly clear inconsistencies in the reach of the criminal law. Infringment of copyright, rights in performance, and registered trademarks will attract criminal liability, whereas interference with design rights and patents and breach of confidence does not. Quite why this might be the case, is the question to which we now turn.

---

[15] Although differences between English tort law and the Scots law of delict led to difficulty with the application of s.18 of the Copyright Act 1956 ("conversion" damages — now repealed): see McQueen *Copyright, Competition and Industrial Design* (1989), p. 36.

[16] For example the applicant for an interim interdict (interlocutory injunction) in the Scots Court of Session does not have to file affidavits or to give a cross-undertaking as to damages. The right of a wrongly injuncted party to compensation is regarded as a matter of right at common law in Scotland. See Walker D., "Scotland" in Rose N., (ed.) *Pre-emptive Remedies in Europe* (1992).

Table 1: Some Varieties of Intellectual Property in the United Kingdom

An asterisk signifies that registration and/or other formality is required. Many of these rights come into being automatically upon a qualifying event, such as the creation of a literary work having an appropriate connection with the U.K.

Right	Property Protected	Source	Infringement Criminal?
Copyright[1] (relative)	Original works — literature drama, art, films, broadcasts.	CDPA 1988[2]	Yes — ss.107–110 'Piracy'.
Rights in performance (relative)	Economic interests of performers and those having exclusive recording rights with them.	CDPA 1988	Yes — ss.198–202 'Bootlegging'.
Design rights[3] (relative)	Design for configuration or shape of an article.	CDPA 1988	No
registered design* (absolute)	Designshape, configurations pattern or ornament applied industrially to an article.	Registered Designs Acts 1949, amended by CDPA 1988	No
Patent* (absolute)	Invention — a new, not obvious, industrially applicable technical development.	Patents Acts 1977	No — but s.110.
Breach of confidence	Commercial, private or state secrets.	Equity	No — but the process of obtaining may be.
Registered trade mark* (absolute)	Mark registered for specific goods or services.	Trade Marks Act 1994	Yes — s.92.

Notes to Table 1

1. Relative monopolies require actual misuse of the protected subject matter, such as by copying. There must be a causal link. Absolute monopolies may be used to enjoin independent activities, such as independent design. For a more detailed distinction, see Phillips J. and Firth A., *Introduction to Intellectual Property Law* (3rd ed., 1995) paras. 2.3 *et seq.*

2. Copyright, Designs and Patents Act 1988.

3. Note that short-term protection against copying of designs, as well as longer-term protection by registration, is proposed under a new Community Design regime: Proposal for a European Parliament and Council Regulation on the Community Design, O.J. 1994 C37/20, 21 January, 1994; supplemented by harmonisation of national laws: Proposal for a European Parliament and Council directive on the Legal Protection of Designs, O.J. 1993 C345/14, 23 December, 1993.

Judicial Criminalisation: A Conceptual Problem

Any attempt to attach criminal sanction to abuses of intellectual property by simply borrowing the analytical framework applied to more traditional forms of property faces appreciable conceptual difficulties, for intellectual property is a phenomenon whose substance lacks natural exclusivity. A limited number of people may occupy a house or drive a car. Yet information can be shared without being lost to its originator. Works may be copied or performed by thousands without ceasing to exist. Misappropriation of inventions, trademarks or designs may well diminish their value to rights owners, but it does not physically destroy or remove them. It is for this reason that the general law relating to crime against property might be thought to be quite unsuited to the protection of intellectual property. Nor is this a problem necessarily limited to matters of criminal law; it may also preclude the fashioning of effective civil law sanctions through the development of existing common law doctrines.

Confidential Information: A Non-Proprietary Interest Which Cannot Be Stolen

The action for breach of confidence probably does not protect a proprietary interest at all. Although judges in granting relief do refer to plaintiffs as the "owners" of confidential information, Coleman describes this practice as "merely a shorthand description".[17] In opinions handed down in the *Spycatcher* case,[18] the House of Lords approved the view that the action is based on equitable obligations of good faith and not on proprietary rights.[19] This does, however, cause difficulties where there is no relationship between plaintiff and defendant such as to give rise to any obligations whatsoever (in *Spycatcher* there was an employment relationship, albeit a non-contractual one). The courts do seem prepared to grant relief in such cases, at least where the confidential information is acquired by unlawful or surreptitious means, such as telephone tapping.[20] A proprietary basis has recently been used in the High Court of Hong Kong in *Linda Chih Ling Koo v. Lam Tai Hing*.[21] Doubt has been cast, however, on this decision.[22]

The action for breach of confidence has a parallel in civil law jurisdictions under more or less generalised prohibitions against unfair competition.[23] However, the use of unfair competition analogies to circumvent the precise boundaries of intellectual property laws have met limited success in the United Kingdom.[24] In the cases of *C.B.S. v. Amstrad*[25] and *Amstrad v. B.P.I.*,[26] attempts to enlarge the plaintiffs" copyright monopoly (which included the ability to restrain improper authorisation of restricted acts) by alleging incitement to infringe, counselling or procurement of infringement and negligence, were roundly criticised. "Common law copyright", a somewhat nebulous concept had been abolished by section 31 of the Copyright Act 1911. Born out of royal censorship and the restrictive practices of stationers, copyright has been codified and the courts will not, it seems, engage in judicial extension of its boundaries.

---

[17] Allison Coleman, *The Legal Protection of Trade Secrets* (1992) p. 30, citing *Thomas Marshall v. Guinle* [1978] 3 W.L.R. 116.

[18] *A.G. v. Guardian Newspapers Ltd. (No. 2)* [1988] 3 All E.R. 545, citing *Moorgate Tobacco Co. Ltd. v. Philip Morris Ltd.* (1984) 56 A.L.R. 193.

[19] Contrast, for example, *Boardman v. Phipps* [1966] 3 All E.R. 721.

[20] *Francome v. Mirror Group* [1984] 1 W.L.R. 892.

[21] (1992) 23 IPR 607.

[22] Hull J., "Property Rights in Questionnaires — An Academic Question, in the Hong Kong Court of Appeal [1994] 1 E.I.P.R. 404.

[23] For example Spanish law 3/1991; French Civil Code, Art. 1382; Italian Civil Code, Art. 2598. The European Commission is considering a harmonisation programme for unfair competition in the longer term.

[24] "Pre-emption" by specific laws is recognised elsewhere, *e.g.* Art. 14(5) of Benelux Designs Law.

[25] *C.B.S Songs v. Amstrad Consumer Electronics* [1988] 2 W.L.R. 1191; [1988] A.C. 1013.

[26] [1986] F.S.R. 159.

It is not surprising, therefore, that criminal proceedings in respect of the theft of confidential information have failed.[27] In *Oxford v. Moss*,[28] an undergraduate obtained a paper for a forthcoming examination, memorised the contents and returned the paper. He was acquitted of theft — he had not permanently deprived his university of the paper, and the information he had retained was not "property" within the meaning of the Theft Act 1968.[29] *Oxford v. Moss* was followed in *R.v. Absolom*,[30] where the defendant acquired valuable and secret geological information and attempted to sell it; theft could not occur in the absence of property which the accused could appropriate. In *Grant v. Procurator Fiscal*,[31] the Scots Court of Session applied the same analysis, and commented that the criminalisation of breach of confidence was a matter for Parliament rather than the judiciary.

Theft and Criminal Damage of Copyright Works

This judicial disavowal of legal innovation is also evident in respect of copyright. Notwithstanding that the Copyright, Designs and Patents Act 1988 describes copyright as "a property right",[32] "transmissible . . . as personal or moveable property",[33] the courts have reached similarly conservative conclusions in cases of exploitation of works recorded on borrowed media. In *R. v. Lloyd*,[34] films were removed from a cinema by the projec-

---

[27] For a fuller discussion of this topic and proposals for reform, see Coleman A., *The Legal Protection of Trade Secrets* (1992), Chap. 7. Coleman's account has been of great assistance in the preparation of the following paragraphs. Coleman *(op. cit.,* pp. 93–94, 99–100), and Eisenschitz (1984 — 'Trade Secrets and the Criminal Law' E.I.P.R. 226, citing *R. v. Merkin & Hall* (1971) *Lincolnshire Echo*, October 8th, 9th, and 11th) describe a number of historical and recent instances where the process of obtaining confidential information was criminal — in breach of industrial relations or anti-corruption statutes. These laws, however, are not of general application. It should be noted that unlawfulness of process may be highly relevant in a civil action for breach of confidence where a confidential relationship is lacking (*cf. Malone v. Metropolitan Police Commissioner* [1979] Ch. 344; *Franklin v. Giddins* [1978] 1 Qd R 72; Coleman, *op. cit.,* Chap. 6).

[28] (1979) 68 Cr.App.R. 183.

[29] This does not of course preclude the meting out of "informal" quasi-criminal sanction through institutional disciplinary procedures or peer group ostracisation; see Bibbings at pp. 71–74, above.

[30] *The Times,* September 14, 1983.

[31] [1988] R.P.C. 41 (Scot.)

[32] S.1(1).

[33] S.90(1).

[34] [1985] 2 All E.R. 661.

tionist and copied onto video tapes, which were then sold. The films were returned unharmed to the cinema. The Court of Appeal overturned convictions of conspiracy to steal — the films themselves were not removed permanently and the copyright could not be stolen. It is submitted that this analysis is correct. Copyright is a property right distinct from property in the medium on which a work is recorded. One can envisage a case where fraudulent procurement of a copyright assignment might amount to an offence under the Theft Acts, but the borrowing and piracy of films are not such a case.[35] Although it might be argued that infringers siphon off some of the value of the copyright, its ownership remains intact.

It might, however, seem paradoxical to note that while copyright or confidential information cannot constitute property for the purposes of theft, it can achieve that status when the charge in issue is one of criminal damage. In *Cox v. Riley*,[36] obliteration of computer programmes was held to be damage to a control card within the meaning of the Criminal Damage Act 1971. The Cox rationale is perhaps more easily accommodated within traditional criminal law paradigms, in so far as it prohibits physical alteration of a "thing" with a concrete identity. Yet it would not, of course, reach the financial profits made by a "thief's" subsequent disposal of information which was appropriated without physically affecting its source.

One can discern sound reasons of constitutional principle for judicial reluctance to adapt long-established principles to criminalise behaviour, focused on newly emergent technologies. Most variants of the concept of the rule of law which have informed British political morality in the modern era would conclude that it would be highly problematic for a court to subject a citizen to criminal penalties, in respect of behaviour which was not clearly identifiable as illegal prior to the impugned action taking place. This is so even in respect of "crimes" of violence, such as rape

---

[35] "Infringement of copyright is not theft"; *Re: The Drugs Trafficking Offences Act 1986, The Independent,* April 2, 1987. In contrast - "The counterfeiting of films is a serious offence . . . it is stealing property from the copyright owner"; *R. v. Carter* (1992) 13 Cr.App.R.(S) 576; [1993] F.S.R. 303. It is submitted that the latter statement amounts to "judicial shorthand", in recognising the loss to a copyright owner where films are pirated. Carter was convicted of a specific offence under s.109 of the Copyright Designs and Patents Act 1988. Her sentence of 9 months' imprisonment, suspended, and £250 costs was upheld. She had no previous convictions.

[36] (1986) 83 Cr.App.R. 54.

within marriage.[37] As Richardson's critique of the War Crimes Act suggests,[38] accusations of constitutional illegitimacy in respect of retrospective judicial lawmaking are perhaps less forceful than those targeted at legislation with similar effects. Retrospectivity is not an issue which has afflicted Parliamentary efforts to extend the protections of the criminal law to possessors of intellectual property, but this does not in itself mean that the outcome of the lawmaking process has been wholly uncontested.

Statutory Criminalisation: The Rise and Fall of Specific Intellectual Property Crimes

The following pages offer a brief description of the enactment and repeal of criminal provisions relating to specific forms of intellectual property. As already suggested, no clear pattern in respect either of the style or substance of legislative intervention emerges. Sometimes the very elements of an offence are particularly difficult to make out. At other times, the scale of penalties has been overtaken by inflation or the growing profitability of the infringement in question — factors which clearly lead to a *de facto* diminution of the impact of the unchanged *de jure* penalties. In some areas, criminal provisions are repealed, only to be reinstated years later.

Mostly, the advantage to rights owners of criminal provisions — that prosecution of infraction, and hence control of the conduct in question, falls upon the State rather than upon the caprice of private litigants — is outweighed by the potency of civil remedies[39] and undermined by the proper priorities of an overworked criminal system. As civil procedures and remedies are particularly well-developed in the field of intellectual property, many of the disadvantages are shared by all the specific intellectual property crimes and are treated later in this chapter. For the present, attention centres on the contents and enforcement of the criminal laws *per se*.

---

[37] See Chap. 8, in this volume.
[38] Chap. 2 of this volume.
[39] A situation which, quite paradoxically, is in marked contrast to that pertaining to squatting, a generally (in 1993) non-criminal practice which in effect deprives the owner of the use of the most traditional of property rights; see Chap. 10.

Copyright

Criminal penalties for unauthorised copying have a long history. The Statute of Anne of 1709[40] provided for fines and seizure of infringing copies. In recent years, copyright has shown the most marked trend to increasing criminalisation of all areas of intellectual property. From 1956 to 1988 there was a progressive increase in the range of offences and the scale of penalties. Section 21 of the Copyright Act 1956, rendered criminal certain forms of infringement of copyright in literary, dramatic, musical and artistic works. The *actus reus* of each of these crimes mirrored civil forms of infringement. Whereas primary forms of infringement — the unauthorised manufacture of copies, public performance, and so on — are tortious irrespective of context[41] or knowledge,[42] secondary infringements — dealings relating to infringing copies, etc. — were, and are, actionable only on proof of knowledge. Only commercial or public activities constituted offences under the 1956 Act, and all offences required knowledge. The requisite knowledge was actual, rather than constructive, in both civil and criminal provisions. In civil proceedings, however, a letter before action would fix the defendant with knowledge so that an injunction, if not damages for past conduct, would be available. Furthermore, a defendant who shut his eyes to the obvious, and deliberately refrained from enquiry, would not be heard to say that he lacked knowledge.[43]

In practice, the most economically serious forms of copyright infringement, or "piracy," related to works in audio-visual forms and (later) computer programs. The 1956 Act was amended[44] to extend criminal provisions to sound recordings, films and computer programs. A new offence of the commercial possession of infringing copies was created in relation to these latter types of

---

[40] 8 Anne, c.19. See, for example, Cornish W. R., (2nd ed. 1989) *Intellectual Property* paras 9–002 and 9–003.

[41] Some acts are permitted by the legislation, such as fair dealing for the purpose of research or private study.

[42] There were, and are, very limited defences of innocence. For a discussion, see Copinger and Skone James on copyright (13th ed., 1991) at paras. 11–25 to 11–28.

[43] *C.B.S. v. Robinson* [1986] F.S.R. 424.

[44] By the Copyright Act 1956 (Amendment) Acts 1982 and 1983 and the Copyright (Computer Software) Amendment Act 1985.

work, to overcome the difficulties of proving actual dealing. Penalties were increased from a paltry[45] to a more realistic level.[46]

The Copyright Designs and Patents Act 1988 retained all the prior offences and extended the offence of possession to all types of work. The problems of proving knowledge were eased by introducing constructive knowledge — having reason to believe — as an alternative to actual knowledge. Some offences were made summary and some made triable either way. Penalties were aligned with the statutory maxima, save for a maximum of two years' imprisonment on conviction on indictment. In *R. v. Blair*,[47] the Court of Appeal regarded as not excessive a two year conditional discharge, with £400 costs and delivery up[48] of offending material. A fine of £1,750 with £250 costs imposed by Middleton Magistrates has been noted in the press.[49]

Rights in Performances

This area shows the reverse pattern. To protect the economic interest of performers and the value of their live performances from being undermined by the making and exploitation of unauthorised, or "bootleg", recordings,[50] Parliament saw fit to enact criminal statutes, the Dramatic and Musical Performers' Protection Act 1925, later replaced by Acts of 1958–1972. The preamble to the 1925 Act described it as; "an Act to prevent the unauthorised reproduction of dramatic and musical performances". Despite the breadth of this statement, early attempts to found a civil action[51] on the 1925 Act failed.[52] However, a majority of the Court of Appeal in *Island Records*[53] took the view

---

[45] The maximum fine was £50 per transaction, or two months' imprisonment (for a second or subsequent conviction) s.21(7) and (8).

[46] The statutory maximum fine on summary conviction and/or up to two years' imprisonment on indictment for manufacturing or importing; level 5 fine and/or up to two months' imprisonment for dealings with infringing copies.

[47] C.A. (Cr.D) July 27, 1992 (Lexis).

[48] The act contains specific delivery up provisions for both the civil and criminal infringement — ss.99–100 and 107–108 respectively.

[49] *Video Home Entertainment* March 27, 1993, p. 4: four counts of copyright infringement.

[50] For a description of the problem see *Island Records v. Corkindale* [1978] F.S.R. 505 at 510–511; [1978] Ch. 122 at 133.

[51] In which the remedy of an injunction, as well as compensatory damages, would be available.

[52] *e.g. Musical Performers Protection Association v. British International Pictures* (1930) 46 T.L.R. 485 — no civil relief.

[53] [1978] Ch. 122; [1978] F.S.R. 505, citing *Gouriet v. Union of Post Office Workers* [1977] Q.B. 729 (reversed at [1978] A.C. 435). However, there was held not to be an action for breach of statutory duty.

that the civil courts might exercise their equitable jurisdiction to enjoin the commission of offences. In *Lonrho v. Shell Petroleum (No. 2)*,[54] the House of Lords expressed the view that *Island Records* achieved the correct result for performers but doubted that recording companies were entitled to sue. In *R.C.A Corp. v. Pollard*,[55] the latter was confirmed as against the record company plaintiff. The Scots Outer House in *Silly Wizard Ltd. v. Shaughnessy*[56] granted an interdict (injunction) at the suit of performers. A final development was the decision in *Rickless v. United Artists Corp.*,[57] wherein a successful claim was made by Peter Sellers' personal representatives to restrain the exploitation of film footage contrary to his lifetime arrangements.

The Copyright Designs and Patents Act 1988[58] thereafter introduced civil rights of action for performers, and also for those enjoying exclusive recording rights, as against bootleggers. The proof of performers' protection offences was rendered more difficult by repealing a requirement that a performer's consent should be in writing to be effective. The problem for prosecutors of proving knowledge was eased by introducing constructive, as an alternative to actual, knowledge. The 1988 Act retained the offence of false representation of authority to give consent, relaxing a requirement of actual, in favour of actual or constructive, knowledge. This part of the Act, as in the copyright part, fixes individual liability on the officers of a company.[59]

Trade Marks

Having viewed the processes of criminalisation and "civilisation" at work in the areas of copyright and performers' rights, we may now examine an oscillatory process at work in the context of trade marks. Although the offence of bearing (armorial) arms without registration was criminalised by Acts of 1592 and 1672,[60] presumably because of the connection between rights to arms and to property, the general registration of marks used in the course

---

[54] [1982] A.C. 173.
[55] [1983] F.S.R 9. The performer Elvis Presley, had died before commencement of the action.
[56] [1983] S.L.T. 367.
[57] [1987] F.S.R. 362.
[58] ss. 180–212.
[59] ss. 202 and 110 respectively.
[60] See *Sir Arthur Herman Munro of Foulis-Obsdale* [1955] S.L.T. (Lyon Court) 5 — the issue was succession to a Nova Scotian baronetcy.

of trade has a somewhat shorter history.[61] In parallel with the development of a registration system for trade marks, giving actionable exclusivity of use to the proprietor, the interest of consumers was protected by the Merchandise Marks Acts 1887–1958. One offence under those statutes was that of applying a forged trade-mark to goods. The Merchandise Marks Acts were repealed by the Trade Descriptions Act 1968, which contained no specific offence relating to marks. However, the offences of applying a false trade description, and that of selling goods to which a false trade description has been applied, are clearly broad enough to encompass most conceivable misuses of trade marks, because "description" includes marks. Section 34 states that the fact that a trade description is a trade-mark does not take it outside the scope of the Act unless in lawful use at commencement.

The pattern in these statutes is to impose strict liability, coupled with statutory defences which have provided considerable protection to defendants.[62] False trade description was pleaded in the "Spanish Champagne" case, *Bollinger v. Costa Brava*,[63] but the court declined to hold that the acts imposed a statutory duty, breach of which would be actionable. The editors of the *United Kingdom Trade Marks Handbook*[64] describe the successes of trading standards officers in deploying the Trades Descriptions Act against counterfeiters. They recognise, however, that the Acts have their limitations in controlling piracy and counterfeiting. Apart from the general difficulties of criminal, as opposed to civil, proceedings they refer to doubt concerning the effect of a disclaimer[65] and the existence of loopholes. In particular, they point out that the counterfeiting of packaging does not appear to amount to an offence until the goods are packaged. Certainly there seems to be a number of cases in which inappropriate charges have been brought, giving the courts difficulties of interpretation.[66] The Handbook refers to reluctance

---

[61] From 1875.
[62] See Scott, pp. 161–162, 167–168 below.
[63] [1959] R.P.C. 150; [1960] R.P.C. 16.
[64] Gold and Nicholls (eds.) U.K. *Trade Marks Handbook* (1991) Chap. 22.
[65] Citing the example of 'fake Rolex' goods: *Lewin v. Fuell* [1990] Crim.L.R. 658, where on appeal it was held insufficient, to escape liability, to delay disclaimer until customers came to buy. However, in *R. v. Kent County Council, ex p. Price*, May 6, 1993 (unreported) Lexis, the Divisional Court held that written or oral disclaimers *might* negative false trade description.
[66] Such as whether the display of goods with a false mark could amount to "applying a false trade description" *Shulton v. Slough B.C.* [1967] 2 Q.B. 471; or whether a coke delivery driver could be a "person who sells" *Preston v. Albuery* [1964] 2 Q.B. 796.

of police officers to bring charges in the absence of a specific offence. It must also be observed that trading standards officers are responsible for the investigation and prosecution of many matters which imperil the safety of consumers — "clocked" motor cars and dangerous toys — as well as matters such as short weight, which are more urgent or more straightforward than imitation of trade marks.[67] It can hardly be a matter for criticism if, in the pursuit of these other duties, they have given low priority to cases where members of the public are able to satisfy their vanity at low cost by purchasing fake garments or scent.

However, the "fraudulent"[68] application of trade marks was again made a specific offence by section 300 of the Copyright, Designs and Patents Act 1988. This, in turn, was replaced by section 92 of the Trade Marks Act 1994; the marginal note refers blandly to "unauthorised use of trade marks in relation to goods". Infringement in relation to services is not an offence. Offending activities include: the application of marks to goods, labels, packaging or business papers, the commercial possession or use of, and dealing with, improperly marked goods and other materials. If the goods are not those for which the mark is registered, an offence is committed only where the mark has a reputation and the use of it is shown to be unfair or detrimental. The prosecution must show that the activity was carried out with a view to gain, or loss to another. No intention to deceive need be shown but it is a defence to show that the person charged believed on reasonable grounds that his use did not infringe.[68a] This apparently draconian section was intended to overcome the decision in *R. v. Kent CC ex parte Price*,[68b] where a purveyor of counterfeit goods escaped penalty by indicating clearly that the good were "brand copies". The courts may, however, hold such disclaimers ineffective if there is intended to be confusion as to origin further down the chain of commerce.[69]

It should be noted that pretenders to intellectual property rights may fall foul of the criminal law. Section a2 of the Trade Marks Act 1994 creates the offence of falsely representing that a

---

[67] For a case showing difficulty in ascertaining the falsehood of a trade description, see *Kat v. Diment* (1950) 67 R.P.C. 158.

[68] The word was used in the marginal note to the section.

[68a] cf. *R. v. Veys* [1993] FSR 366 — infringement of trade mark relevant to, but not conclusive of, false trade description.

[68b] (1994) 158 JPN 78; noted at [1993] E.I.P.R. D–224.

[69] *R. v. Beaumont* (unreported) Leeds Crown Court, July 12, 1988, cited in United Kingdom Trade Marks Handbook. Eds. Gold & Nicholls, CIPA.ITMA 1991/92 releases para. 22.5.1.

mark is registered.[70] By section 100, the Patent Act 1977 provides criminal sanctions against unauthorised claims to patent rights.[71] Prior to the liberalisation of the profession of patent agent by the 1988 Act, it was an offence to practice as a patent agent without being on the register.[72]

Criminal Versus Civil Procedures and Remedies

"What is worth copying is prima facie worth protecting".[73] This maxim was coined in the context of tests for infringement of copyright, but it also reflects a commercial nexus between the likelihood of piracy or counterfeiting, and the likelihood that an owner of intellectual property rights will seek redress in the civil courts. Economic correlation, combined with the relative ease of proof and the efficacy of civil remedies, may explain why redress is so often sought in the civil rather than criminal courts. A number of comparisons may be made in support of this proposition.

Penalties, Profits and Compensation

The scale of criminal penalties may provide little or no disincentive to profitable infringement. A pirate's or counterfeiter's overheads may be much lower than those of the person, or organisation, who has developed a work or product — there will be no expenditure on research and development, lower material costs, no expensive product control, no costly advertising and brand promotion. Prices will be set lower, perhaps not much lower.[74] Profit margins will therefore be considerable. Until recently, the maximum penalties were such as to provide little disincentive to infringers. Thus in *R. v. Desai*[75] it was argued on appeal against sentence for conspiracy to contravene section 21(1) of the Copyright Act 1956 that the fine should have been limited to the maximum for the substantive offence — £25.

---

[70] This is subject to E.C. free movement provisions where goods originated from a member state where the mark is registered: *Pall v. Dahlhausen*, Case C-238/89, *The Times*, February 4, 1991.
[71] See *Cassidy v. Eisenmann* [1980] F.S.R. 381.
[72] *Institute of Patent Agents v. Lockwood* (1894) 21 R.H.L. 61.
[73] *University of London Press Ltd. v. University Tutorial Press Ltd.* [1916] 2 Ch. 601 at 610, *per* Petersen J.
[74] Fenby, *op. cit.*, p. 98.
[75] Unreported, C.A., June 12, 1981.

The Copyright Designs and Patents Act 1988 now pegs fines to the general scale maxima and has introduced a menu of custodial sentences — up to two years for offences triable either way for criminal infringement of copyright and performers' rights and up to ten years for trade mark offences. It will be interesting to see how the courts avail themselves of these provisions. In *Carter*,[76] a term of nine months, suspended, was held not excessive for a first offence of making and hiring pirate videos. In *Halawa*,[77] fines of £500 per charge and a £3,600 contribution to costs were approved. *Blair's*[78] sentence of 2 years' conditional discharge and order for costs of £400 coupled with delivery up of offending material was not overturned. Yet, even with the extended powers of sentencing conferred by the 1988 Act it seems likely that sentences will rarely, if ever, reflect in full the loss to the rights owner or the gain to the infringer.

In a related vein, the criminal courts have, it seems, little inclination to use powers of compensation[79] where civil remedies are available.[80] Moreover, compensation may only be ordered in respect of losses resulting from offences actually charged or taken into consideration.[81] The practice of specimen charges thus limits the compensation available. By contrast, although civil actions for infringement are fought on specimen allegations, it is customary for discovery and relief to be awarded at an inquiry into damages for all acts of infringement. So financial redress, whether by way of compensatory damages or an account of profits, must be sought in civil proceedings. For copyright owners the possibility of obtaining additional damages for flagrant and profitable infringements was enhanced by the 1988 Act.[82]

Difficulties of Proof

The need in criminal proceedings to establish all elements of the offence[83] beyond reasonable doubt may be contrasted with the

[76] (1992) 13 Cr.App.R.(S) 576; [1993] F.S.R. 303.
[77] *R. v. Wells Street Magistrates, ex p. Halawa*, (1992) November 5 (Lexis).
[78] (1992) C.A. (Cr D) July 27 (Lexis).
[79] See the Powers of Criminal Courts Act 1973, s.35(1) and, generally, Halsbury's Laws of England, 4th issue Vol 11(2) reissue, para. 1238.
[80] In *R. v. Daly* [1974] 1 All E.R. 290 the Court of Appeal urged Criminal Courts considering compensation orders to remember "that the civil remedy for damages still exists".
[81] *R. v. Crutchley, The Times*, January 3, 1994.
[82] s.97(2).
[83] This was reiterated in *Musa v. Le Maitre* [1987] F.S.R. 272, where the court however decided that evidence from the maker of the films in question, or the copyright owner, was unnecessary to establish subsistence of copyright.

standard of proof in a civil action. In *Reid v. Kennett*,[84] the appellant, a part-time employee at a video hire shop, was convicted of possession of illicit material by way of trade. The conviction was quashed on the grounds that it was not enough to show that the films in question had been bought from a pirate. The possession had to be in the course of the defendant's trade. Although the same test as to trade should apply in civil proceedings, one may imagine a civil court being more prepared to make necessary inferences. It can be noted that the relevant civil and criminal sections[85] of the 1988 Act now refer to "*possession in the course of business*" [emphasis added].

Whereas the police may be reluctant to investigate or bring charges if the subject-matter is technical, others may not have adequate knowledge or experience of the complexities of the Police and Criminal Evidence Act (PACE). The 1980s saw the development of two organisations, the Federation Against Copyright Theft (FACT) and the Federation Against Software Theft (FAST). They were instrumental in investigating cases of audio-visual and software piracy and brought private prosecutions.

This *de facto* privatisation of the prosecution process has been given added impetus by several legislative provisions which seem to have removed intellectual property crimes from traditional due process constraints on the conduct of both investigation and subsequent trial. The most potent evidentiary distinction between civil and criminal proceedings for infringement of intellectual property rights stems from section 72 of the Supreme Court Act 1981. This section abrogated the privilege against self-incrimination in intellectual property cases,[86] for reasons which seem to owe more to evidential expediency than to the substantive enormity of the proscribed conduct *per se*.[87] A similar rationale appears to underpin the attempts made in the 1988 Act to improve flows of information between enforcement agencies[88] and

---

[84] [1986] Crim.L.R. 456; 83 Cr.App.R. 63.
[85] ss.23 and 107 respectively.
[86] For the limits of application, see *A.T & T. Istel Ltd. v. Tully* [1992] 3 W.L.R. 344; 3 All E.R. 523 — not shown that information in question protected by "rights pertaining to commercial information"; criticism by Court of Appeal of use of privilege to prevent production of documents in civil cases.
[87] That being the justification advanced by Richardson in Chap. 2 above for the dilution of due process norms contained in the War Crimes Act 1991.
[88] s.300 inserting s.58D(4) in to the Trade Marks Act 1938; see now Trade Marks Act 1944, s.93(4). Similar concerns are evident in relation to the activities of the Serious Fraud Office; see Weait's chapter at pp. 100–102 above.

to make strengthened provision as to search warrants and delivery up prior to conviction in criminal cases.[89]

The judiciary has not wholeheartedly endorsed this trend, however. In *Halawa*,[90] for example, the defendant objected to the admission of evidence gathered in an interview by FACT personnel. The interview had been carried out in breach of PACE codes of practice. The Divisional Court held that challenge to admission of the evidence should have been allowed at an earlier stage in the trial.

The development of *Anton Piller* orders enabled plaintiffs to search for and seize evidence of infringement to preserve it from destruction. However, in *Rank Film Distributors Ltd. v. Video Information Centre*,[91] the defendant successfully claimed that compliance with the order would deprive him of privilege against self-incrimination. The House of Lords held that the plea of privilege was indeed available to defeat an *Anton Piller* order if there was a significant likelihood of facing a serious charge. The decision appeared to give particular protection to the greatest wrongdoers and its effect was reversed for intellectual property cases by the aforementioned section 72.

That section applies even where criminal proceedings are already in train.[92] The offence of which incrimination is feared can be "any offence" — the court refused to give a restricted interpretation of this phrase in *Universal City Studios v. Hubbard*.[93]

Time limits

Limitation of civil actions for infringement is governed by the ordinary period for tort — six years under the Limitation Act 1980. It has not been definitively settled as to whether a continuing course of infringement is better treated as a series of discrete torts or as a continuing cause of action.[94] Whichever view is finally adopted, however, the time limits for bringing proceedings are more generous in civil than in criminal cases. For a case where a complaint of knowing possession of infringing copies was dismissed for delay, see *Carmichael v. Sardar*.[95] In that case, the

---

[89] ss. 108, 109 and 300 [now Trade Marks Act 1994, s.93(2)].
[90] *R. v. Wells Street Magistrates' Court ex p. Halawa* (1992) November 5 (Lexis).
[91] [1982] A.C. 380 (HL).
[92] *Charles of the Ritz v. Jory* [1986] F.S.R. 16.
[93] [1984] 1 Ch. 225; [1984] R.P.C. 13.
[94] See *Banks v. C.B.S Songs* [1992] F.S.R. 17.
[95] [1983] S.C.C.R. 423.

alleged offence took place on December 9th. A warrant to
apprehend the accused was issued on June 7th, just within the six
months time limit for commencement of summary proceedings
under section 331(1) of the Criminal Procedure (Scotland) Act
1975. It was not executed for six days, however. Had the warrant
been executed "without undue delay", proceedings would have
been deemed to commence on June 7th. It was held that in the
absence of explanation, the delay was undue so that the deeming
provision did not apply and the proceedings were time-barred.

The Potency of Civil Remedies

The most powerful reason for instituting civil, rather than criminal, proceedings lies in the availability of injunctions and other
interim and final remedies. The potency of the injunction as
opposed to the effect of criminal sanctions has been described in
a number of cases, notably *Island Records*[96] and *Stafford B.C. v.
Elkenford*.[97]

Apart from final and interlocutory[98] injunctions, intellectual
property litigation has fuelled the development of the *Norwich
Pharmacal* order[99] for discovery against non-parties, the *Anton
Piller*[1] search and seize order, and the "roving" *Anton Piller*
order.[2] Fast on the heels of the Family Division's resurrection of
the writ *ne exeat regno*, a similar *Bayer*[3] order was made in an
intellectual property action.

Industry organisations, like the British Phonogram Industry
Limited and its record industry members, coordinate and collabo-
rate in bringing swift and determined suit against infringers. In
fact, the zeal of the BPI's solicitors was criticised as excessive in
CBS v. Robinson.[4]

---

[96] [1978] Ch. 122 at 136 per Lord Denning: "the criminal law is a broken reed in
some of these cases. At any rate in this particular case".

[97] [1977] 2 All E.R. 519; an injunction would be available even if alternative
remedies (£5 fines) had not been exhausted.

[98] Granted on the criteria laid down in *American Cyanamid v. Ethicon* [1975]
A.C. 396 — arguable case, inadequacy of damages pending trial, balancing the
risks of doing injustice.

[99] After *Norwich Pharmacal Co. v. Commissioners of Customs and Excise* [1973] 3
All E.R. 943; [1974] A.C. 133.

[1] *Anton Piller K.G. v. Manufacturing Processes Ltd.* [1976] Ch. 55; [1976] R.P.C.
719.

[2] *E.M.I. v. Kudhail* [1985] F.S.R. 36.

[3] *Bayer A.G. v. Winter* [1986] F.S.R. 323.

[4] [1986] F.S.R. 424.

European Community Developments

Differing national intellectual property rights, with discontinuities, are seen as disruptive of the single European market. Although their existence and ownership is preserved by Article 222 of the Treaty of Rome, their exercise has been held subject to the rules of competition (Articles 85 and 86) and on free movement (especially Articles 30–36).

Thus, the directorate-general of the E.C. Commission responsible for the internal market is engaged on an extensive programme of harmonisation. One unitary system — the Community Trade Mark — is being established and others — the Community Patent and the Community Design — are proposed, with Community Courts of first instance having E.C. wide jurisdiction. The Community trade mark has been preceded by harmonisation of national laws.[5] Patent law is already effectively harmonised in most Member States, those which have long been signatory to the European Patent Convention. The United Kingdom Patents Act 1977 was designed to bring United Kingdom patent law into conformity with the Convention.[6] Two outstanding member states, Denmark and the Republic of Ireland, are now joining the system. Although patent grant by the European Patent Office at present results in a bundle of national patents, the substantive laws are aligned.

However, even when national laws are harmonised, infringement proceedings are still believed to be a matter for national jurisdiction, notwithstanding the Brussels Convention on Civil Jurisdiction and Judgments.[7] If the proposed unitary systems proceed, another advantage of civil proceedings over idiosyncratic national criminal process will come into play.

Conclusion

The "commonplace, but overly simplistic, assumption" to which Ian Loveland referred in the preface to this volume, that "crime marks an unambiguous boundary of accepted behavioural stand-

---

[5] The 1994 Trade Marks Act has been drafted to conform with Council Directive No. 89/104/EEC of December 21, 1988 to approximate the laws of Member States relating to trade marks.
[6] See s.130 of the 1977 Act.
[7] For an article on jurisdiction in intellectual property cases, see Arnold R., (1990) 'Can One Sue in England for Infringement of Foreign Intellectual Property Rights?" [1990] E.I.P.R. 254.

ards, constructed and policed by a monolithic state which legitimises its action by presenting itself as the transmitter of pervasive societal values,"[8] is manifestly misplaced in respect of the regulatory framework protecting intellectual property. While some of the chapters in this book suggest that this assumption breaks down when one seeks to trace the path between formal legal proscription and practical implementation, such fragmentation between the *de jure* and *de facto* impact of the government process has also been adverted to in this chapter. Yet analysis of this area also indicates that one may encounter quite profound fragmentation even at the formal level. The erratic, ad hoc nature of both legislative (whether domestic or European) and judicial responses to the rapidly changing nature of "property" in the final decades of the twentieth century, dramatically emphasises the contingent nature of criminal regulation.

In concluding her chapter Nicola Lacey questions whether we should begin to view the demarcation and policing of the frontiers of criminal liability as a sub-branch of an increasingly expansive definition of "public law".[9] In respect of the criminal regulation of intellectual property, that advice may prove particularly compelling. This is due in part to the simple institutional issue of the E.C.'s increasing importance in this field. However, it also has a conceptual dimension. Much of the evident inconsistency of the criminal law in this area might be thought to stem from the essentially cultural question of deciding what kinds of property are being constituted by contemporary technological developments, and thence what kinds of legal processes are best suited for their regulation. For public lawyers, the issue of "new property" has long been a familiar one in structuring the nature of the legal response, in both substantive and procedural terms, to newly emergent social and economic relationships.[10] That public lawyers have found answers to their question elusive does not mean that the search is without merit. For intellectual property lawyers, it will perhaps not be until we begin to address this question more systematically in our own sphere that we will be able to understand both why present criminal laws are so variegated in scope, and, more importantly, how we might plausibly go about lending them a more coherent character.

---

[8] At p. iv–v above.
[9] At pp. 132–134.
[10] The starting point being Charles Reich's seminal (1964) article "The New Property" Yale L.J. 733–787.

Chapter Seven

CRIMINALISING THE TRADER TO PROTECT THE CONSUMER: THE FRAGMENTATION AND CONSOLIDATION OF TRADING STANDARDS REGULATION[1]

by Colin Scott

It might be argued that the study of law in context, or law in action, in the 1960s and 1970s, progressively eroded the textbook view of criminal law as being exclusively concerned with "traditional crimes" against the person and against property. Early research on administration of criminal statutes relating to workplace safety, trading standards, and food control demonstrated the economic and social significance of a wide range of regulatory regimes, and sought to develop new methods for understanding them.[2] Equally interesting work on the structure of regulatory legislation, and in particular of the role of strict liability offences and of defences, sought to challenge the doctrinal emphasis on "traditional crimes".[3] Parallel with this shift in the pattern of intellectual inquiry there has been a substantial growth in the

[1] I am grateful to participants at staff seminars at the School of Law, University of Warwick, and at the Faculty of Law, University of Glasgow, at the *Frontiers of Criminality* seminar at Queen Mary and Westfield College, London and to Neil Duxbury, Robert Baldwin, Ross Cranston and Imelda Maher for comments on earlier drafts of this chapter.
[2] Carson W., "Some Sociological Aspects of Strict Liability and the Enforcement of Factory Legislation" (1970) M.L.R. 396–412: Cranston R., *Regulating Business — Law and Consumer Agencies* (1979): Smith M. and Pearson A., "The Value of Strict Liability" (1969) Crim.L.R. 5–16: Paulus L. *The Search for Pure Food* (1974). A more recent study of enforcement in a number of areas is Rowan-Robinson J., Watchman P. and Barker C., *Crime and Regulation — A Study of the Enforcement of Regulatory Codes*. For an evaluation of the empirical research generally, see Richardson G., "Strict Liability for Regulatory Crime: the Empirical Research" Crim.L.R. 295–306. See also the survey by Lidstone K., Hogg R. and Sutcliffe F., for the Royal Commission on Criminal Procedure, *Prosecutions by Private Individuals and Non-Police Agencies* (1980).
[3] Hadden T., "Strict Liability and the Enforcement of Regulatory Legislation" (1970) Crim.L.R. 496–504: Leigh L., *Strict and Vicarious Liability — A Study in Administrative Criminal Law* (1982). But see also Howells G., "An Evaluation of the Role of Defences in Consumer Protection Statutes" (1988) *Trading Law* 244–259.

number of criminal law statutes which fall within a newer regulatory law paradigm.[4]

What I will call here the "regulatory crime paradigm" has a number of characteristics.[5] First most of the offences involved are offences of strict liability, requiring no proof of intention to convict. Secondly, it is generally assumed within the paradigm that the central state retains a monopoly over the criminalisation of conduct. Thirdly, enforcement authorities, whether elected local authorities, central government departments, or private sector organisations, are given considerable discretion as to how they investigate and deal with infractions of the statute. Fourthly, it is possible, within the paradigm, to imagine a non-uniform pattern of enforcement policy and practice. Fifthly, the ambivalence of the courts to the use of criminal law is recognised, and some scholars have been keen to emphasise additionally the role that defences play in limiting the absolute liability for offences.[6]

This chapter explores the characteristics of this regulatory paradigm in the context of the setting and enforcement of trading standards. It focuses primarily on trade descriptions and pricing, and food and product safety. The analysis seeks to marry understandings of administrative activity in relation to trading standards inspection and enforcement, with analysis of the structure of legislation and judicial interpretation. With regard to actual standard setting in trading standards regulation, it is argued that there has been a significant fragmentation of legislative authority. Furthermore, non-legislative mechanisms have increasingly been used to define offences. Whereas the traditional focus has been on central government's exclusive power to legislate criminal law standards, any analysis of standard setting today must recognise the central role of the institutions of the E.C. in legislating for consumer protection measures, and the fact that any domestic consumer protection measures are required to be consistent with the objectives of the Community. Fragmentation has also been effected through the way in which legislative instruments are framed and standards within those

---

[4] Although as Nicola Lacey points out in her chapter in this book, many law students may complete their legal education with only the sketchiest of exposures to this substantial area of criminal liability.

[5] See, for example, Carson, *op. cit.*, Cranston, *op. cit.*, Rowan-Robinson, *et al.*, *op. cit.*; Richardson, *op. cit.*, Hawkins K. and Thomas L., "The Enforcement Process in Regulatory Bureaucracies", (1984) in Hawkins K. and Thomas L., (eds.) *Enforcing Regulation* pp. 4–22.

[6] Leigh, *op. cit.*, Chap. 4.

instruments defined. The trend towards specifying only broad legislative standards seems to be of particular importance as it leaves the detail of standards to be followed, to secure compliance, to be filled in either by codes of practice issued by government, by agency practice, by judicial interpretation or by industry self-regulation. It should be noted that this trend does not represent a move toward generalisation *per se*, but rather a particularisation in which the function of setting of detailed standards is reallocated to agencies and institutions other than the executive and the legislature.[7]

In the case of agency practice, a pivotal role in developing the interpretation of legislation has been taken on by a private body, the Institute of Trading Standards Administration (ITSA), which also administers the professional accreditation of trading standards officers, and by the Local Authorities Coordinating Body on Trading Standards (LACOTS). Judicial interpretation has always been a source of fragmentation in relation to trading standards legislation as judicial attitudes have generally been shaped by the classical values of individualism and moral responsibility associated with a "traditional crime" paradigm. This dominant ideology is only slowly giving way to the more functional regulatory paradigm in the trading standards area. The structure of modern defences in relation to strict liability crime was developed to protect offenders not actually at fault themselves. Judicial interpretation of defences has, with legislative encouragement, greatly increased the role of industry self-regulation. We are likely to see increasing deference to self-regulatory systems of various sorts which will satisfy legislative requirements, effectively filling in the detail of the broad legislative standards. Finally, the paper argues that fragmentation has the potential for being exploited by large businesses which may be favoured by regulatory systems, which have the effect of restricting competition.

This process of fragmentation, however, is accompanied by a process of consolidation of enforcement practices. This consolidatory trend may be explained in two ways. First, the autonomy of enforcement authorities and diversity of enforcement practices in England and Wales, identified by research in the mid-1970s,[8] is gradually being eroded by pressures from the Community to be

---

[7] Cotterrell R., *The Sociology of Law* (1992) pp. 165–166: Teubner G., "Juridification — Concepts, Aspects, Limits, Solutions", (1987) in Teubner G., (ed.) *Juridification of Social Spheres* pp. 3–48.

[8] Cranston, *op. cit.*

able to show uniformity of enforcement of Community Law.[9] Secondly, the pressure of work and increasing complexity and range of consumer legislation has required fragmented enforcement agencies to seek economies of scale in interpretation and coordination. The fragmented pattern of enforcement responsibilities in England and Wales provides a very significant challenge to the E.C., which has belatedly become concerned that a pattern of harmonised consumer protection standards is dependent upon there being a harmonised pattern of enforcement practices and expectations if the internal market objectives are to be furthered. Consequently, there have been a number of moves which, though they fall short of centralised enforcement, nevertheless tend towards greater concentration and coordination. These measures include the establishment of LACOTS in 1979, the developing role of the Office of Fair Trading in monitoring and publishing information about local enforcement, and, for the first time the issue of Codes of Practice on the administration and enforcement of trading legislation under the Food Safety Act 1990 to comply with the E.C.Food Control Directive.

Fragmentation

Fragmentation in Standard Setting

Received wisdom leads us to believe that labelling of any conduct as criminal is such an important thing, that the power resides exclusively with central government acting through the legislature. However, the shaping of social and economic regulation is increasingly coordinated through the E.C., and in practice, and unusually within the Community, local authority enforcement departments in the United Kingdom have had considerable autonomy in designing and implementing enforcement policies. Furthermore, both Community and domestic legislation are increasingly using broad legislative standards to define that which is criminal, relying on administrative codes of practice, public and private standard setting institutions, and industry self-regulation, to determine what conduct complies with the broad standard, or the terms of any defence offered in the legislation. The deregulation initiative announced by the Government in the autumn of

---

[9] Dehousse R., Joerges C., Majone G. and Snyder F., *Europe After 1992* (1992) pp. 22–23 (Florence: European University Institute Working Paper Law No. 92/31).

1992 has involved a questioning of the necessity of detailed regulation which is likely to accelerate the trend towards the use of broad general standards and self-regulation.[10]

The Community's role in relation to consumer protection has primarily been one of addressing the adverse effects on trade of different levels of consumer protection in the Member States.[11] Thus, its objective may be said to be not consumer protection *per se*, but rather uniform levels of consumer protection throughout the Member States. The scope of the Community's jurisdiction in this area has been extended beyond promotion of the internal market by Article 129a of the Treaty on European Union.[12] Thus, the central role of the Community in relation to food standards is being replicated in relation to product safety generally and, in due course, in relation to trade descriptions and other areas of consumer protection hitherto solely within the jurisdiction of the Member States.

The primary focus of Community activity, historically, has been concerned with standard setting. The Community's largest contribution has been concerned with food standards, particularly on composition and labelling. Historically, the Community's approach has been based on a concept of vertical regulation in which particular food stuffs have been regulated by specific compositional regulations or labelling requirements. However, increasingly, the requirements of the completion of the internal market programme have led the Community to resort to the new approach, based on mutual recognition rather than full harmonisation, which involves the setting of broad horizontal standards relying on standard-setting institutions, at the Community level or in the Member States, to fill in detail.[13]

---

[10] Director General of Fair Trading (1993) Annual Report, 1992, pp. 8–9.

[11] See Lasa H., "Free Movement of Foodstuffs, Consumer Protection and Food Standards in the European Community: Has the Court of Justice Got it Wrong?" (1991) E.L.Rev. 391–415.

[12] Article 129a confirms the Community's role in consumer protection legislation under article 100a of the EEC Treaty (completion of the internal market), but will, for the first time, explicitly authorise "specific action which supports and supplements the policy pursued by the Member States to protect the health, safety and economic interests of consumers and to provide adequate information to consumers."

[13] E.C. Commission, *Removal of Technical Barriers to Trade, Com (80) 30 Final; Completing the Internal Market*, Com. (85) 310 Final, point 58. See Dehousse L. "1992 and Beyond: the Institutional Dimension of the Internal Market Programme" (1989) *Legal Issues of European Integration* pp. 109, 112–114. See also McGee A. and Weatherill S., "The Evolution of the Single Market — Harmonisation or Liberalisation" (1990) M.L.R. 578–595.

This trend is also noticeable in relation to product safety, where historically the Community has used vertical regulation of particular product sectors, such as toys and electrical equipment. The Product Safety Directive, adopted in 1992, uses the notion of a general safety requirement, to prohibit the sale and supply of unsafe products.[14] The Directive effectively creates a hierarchy of standards, at the top of which are specific sectoral standards set by the Community (reflecting the old vertical approach to product safety regulation). Where there are no specific Community provisions governing the safety of a product, the "product shall be deemed safe when it conforms to the specific rules of national law of the Member State in whose territory the product is in circulation . . .".[15] In the absence of such specific national rules relating to the safety of the product:

> "the conformity of a product to the general safety requirement shall be assessed having regard to voluntary national standards giving effect to a European Standard or, where they exist, to Community technical specifications or, failing these, to standards drawn up in the Member State in which the product is in circulation, or to the codes of good practice in respect of health and safety in the sector concerned or to the state of the art and technology and the safety which consumers may reasonably expect."[16]

Thus, in the absence of specific sectoral rules, responsibility for setting standards is progressively delegated to Community institutions such as Comité Européen de Normalisation (CEN) and Comité Européen de Normalisation Electrotechnique (CENELEC),[17] national institutions such as the private British Standards Institution, relevant industries (through codes of practice, best practice and assessment of the state of the art), and finally consumers, through a consumer expectation test, to be administered by the courts. This approach to standard setting by the Community creates an extensive delegation of standard setting powers, which though it may be efficient, has implications

---

[14] Council Directive 92/59/EEC of June 29, 1992 on General Product Safety, O.J. L228, August 11, 1992.

[15] Council Directive on General Product Safety, Art. 4(1).

[16] *ibid.*, Art. 4(2).

[17] Burrows N., "Harmonisation of Technical Standards: Reculer Pour Mieux Sauter" (1990) M.L.R. pp. 597–615 at pp. 601–603.

for the democratic control and accountability of Community activities.[18]

The shifting pattern from specific standards to broad standards in relation to food and product safety is also observable in the United Kingdom. While powers remain in the Food Safety Act 1990, and the Consumer Protection Act 1987 Part II to make detailed sectoral regulations,[19] the Acts introduce for the first time a Food Safety Requirement and a General Safety Requirement in relation to products.[20] It should be noted that in relation to trading standards there has always been a general standard, based on the concept of giving a false or misleading trade description.[21] However, attempts to precisely define pricing offences in the Price Marking (Bargain Offers) Order 1979 were abandoned in the new pricing offences created in section 20 of the Consumer Protection Act 1987. Accompanying the shift from detailed to general requirements, has been a delegation of powers to fill in the detail left out in the legislative standards.

Thus, in relation to product safety we find three different ways in which the General Safety Requirement in section 10 of the Act may be satisfied. First, any potential hazards inherent to the product may be adequately warned against, and here the Department of Trade and Industry has issued guidance in the labelling of products in relation to hazards.[22] Secondly, the producer can show that it complied with any safety standard authorised by the Secretary of State. In practice it is the safety standards of the (private) British Standards Institution that will satisfy the requirements. Thirdly, the defendant can show that having regard to the costs of making the product safe, and likely benefits of such improvements, the goods were as safe as it was reasonable to expect. Thus, in this case the power to make a cost-benefit analysis is delegated to our ill-equipped courts. So in each case the effective power to determine standards is delegated, either to civil servants, to standard setting institutions or to courts.

In relation to pricing offences under section 20 of the Consumer Protection Act 1987, the detail of the offences is, in effect, to be filled in by a Code of Practice issued by the Secretary of

---

[18] Dehousse, *op. cit.*, Lenaerts K., "Regulating the Regulatory Process: "Delegation of Powers" in the European Community" (1993) E.L.Rev. 23–49.

[19] Food Safety Act 1990 s.16: Consumer Protection Act 1987 s.11.

[20] *ibid.*, s.8; Consumer Protection Act 1987 s.10. See postscript.

[21] Trade Descriptions Act 1968 s.1. S.1 relates to the sale and supply of goods. The provisions relating to supply of services in s.14 are differently framed.

[22] Department of Trade and Industry, *Instructions for Consumer Products* (1988).

State.[23] This development is rather similar to that witnessed in the employment legislation of the 1980s, and as labour lawyers know, the Picketing Code has, in effect, become determinative of the rights of employees to picket as far as the courts are concerned. The Pricing Code provides guidance and the Act makes clear that failure to follow the code does not of itself prove that an offence has been committed. However, looking at the converse position, it seems unlikely that anyone would be convicted who had complied with the terms of the Code.[24]

Further fragmentation in standard setting may be anticipated as an effect of the Goverment's deregulation programme, which is the subject matter of a Bill before Parliament at the time of writing.[25] Clause 1 of the Bill permits a Minister to repeal or amend burdensome regulatory legislation by means of statutory instruments which are the subject of positive resolution procedure in both Houses of Parliament. The powers include the creation of new criminal offences and the abolition or amendment of existing criminal offences within prescribed limits.[26]

Fragmentation in Enforcement

As has been noted, local authorities charged with enforcement of the various legislative provisions are afforded appreciable discretion. For most consumer protection purposes the enforcement authority in England and Wales is the trading standards department of the County Council or Metropolitan Borough Council. Some aspects of the food legislation, notably relating to hygiene, are enforced by local authority environmental health departments, and in certain spheres such as misleading advertising and unfair trade practices powers are retained by a central agency, the Office of Fair Trading. The discretion exercised by trading

---

[23] The Code of Practice is issued under the Consumer Protection Act 1987 s.25 (1):

"for the purpose of—

a) giving practical guidance with respect to any of the requirements of section 20 . . .; and

b) promoting what appears to the Secretary of State to be desirable practices as to the circumstances and manner in which any person gives an indication as to the price at which any goods, services, accommodation or facilities are available or indicates any other matter in respect of which any such indication may be misleading."

[24] Consumer Protection Act 1987 s.25(2).

[25] Deregulation and Contracting Out Bill, H.C. 1993–94 session, Bill no. 33.

[26] Cl. 2(1) and (2). See postscript.

FRAGMENTATION

standards departments is of at least two types. First, there is an interpretative discretion to decide whether particular conduct constitutes an offence under the relevant legislation. Secondly, there is discretion to decide whether or not to prosecute a case which officers believe constitutes an infraction under relevant legislation. Little attention has been paid to the first form of discretion, but evidence in relation to the second is more readily available. Cranston's study of trading standards enforcement in the mid-1970s found that in many local authorities, where infractions were discovered, prosecutions were rarely resorted to. Rather, there was a hierarchy of measures ranging from education and advice, to informal warnings and cautions, which would be used; prosecution was saved only for those who repeatedly offended, or where dishonesty was suspected.[27] Thus, many authorities adopted what has subsequently been called a "'compliance approach" based on education and advice. Only a small number of authorities were found to prosecute a higher proportion of cases using what has been described as a "deterrence" strategy.[28]

Reiss has argued that in regulatory environments generally, a number of different factors lead to compliance strategies being adopted. Many enforcement officers feel that the most effective method of achieving the objectives of the legislation, given limited resources, is to retain good working relations with businesses, and to seek to advise and educate where infractions are found.[29] Regulatory offences are often continuing, rather than discrete, acts. Compliance approaches may therefore seem more appropriate to enforcement officers.[30] Many regulatory agencies

[27] Cranston, *op. cit.*, p. 101 refers to the importance of cautioning as a technique of manipulating uncertainty.
[28] Reiss, *op. cit.*, pp. 23–24.
[29] Cranston, *op. cit.*, p. 50.
[30] Hawkins and Thomas, *op. cit.*, p. 13. The appropriateness, or otherwise, of regulatory agencies pursuing compliance strategies in preference to strict enforcement of legislation has been the subject of an acrimonious debate. See Pearce F. and Tombs S., "Ideology, Hegemony, and Empiricism" (1990) Brit.J.Criminol. 423–443: Hawkins K., "Compliance Strategy, Prosecution Policy and Aunt Sally — A Comment on Pearce and Tombs" (1990) Brit.J.Criminol. 444–466. Wells has argued forcefully that "the failure to rigorously enforce regulatory schemes taken together with the paucity of available penalties can be used to support the argument that crimes of the powerful are condoned and effectively or even deliberately decriminalized"; Wells C., *Corporations and Criminal Responsiblity* (1993) p. 29. She urges that the views of enforcement officers that compliance strategies are best should not be permitted to stifle debate.

actually use a mix of both compliance and deterrence strategies.[31] There has been considerable judicial encouragement for the discretionary prosecution policy.[32] In relation to trading standards, deterrence strategies tend to be reserved for cases of clear dishonesty, and when dealing with the small class of businesses which agencies tend to characterise as unscrupulous. Second-hand car dealers have headed this list. It is unclear, however, whether an empirical basis really exists for the characterisation of the majority of businesses as intending always to comply with the trading standards law. A very imprecise indication of the extent to which trading standards departments prosecute can be secured by comparing reported consumer complaints relating to areas covered by the Trade Descriptions Act 1968 with numbers of convictions under that Act. In the year to September 30, 1990, for example, there were 127,317 complaints received (by both trading standards departments and advice agencies such as Citizens' Advice Bureaux) in relation to: "selling techniques; misleading claims; representations of advertisements (price, quality, etc); presentation of goods or services (availability, labelling, packaging); lack of information", but there were only 1,129 convictions under the Act.[33]

Further fragmentation in enforcement may result from the Government's aforementioned deregulation programme. Clause 58 of the Deregulation and Contracting Out Bill proposes to permit a very wide range of local authority functions to be contracted out to private companies. Specific amendments to the Food Safety Act 1990 are proposed which will permit private companies to hold the same enforcement powers as are presently vested in local authorities.[34]

Fragmentation Through Judicial Interpretation

As with all legislation creating criminal offences, in the comparatively few instances where there is a prosecution under trading standards legislation, courts have various forms of discretion in relation to interpretation of legislation and imposition of

---

[31] Reiss, *op. cit.,* pp. 25–28.
[32] *Wings v. Ellis* [1985] A.C. 272: *Smedleys v. Breed* [1974] A.C. 839.
[33] Director-General of Fair Trading (1991) *Annual Report* 1990 pp. 66–68. The most recent report available, for 1992, does not present the figures in such a way that complaints relating to matters probably within the scope of the Trade Descriptions Act 1968 may be isolated.
[34] Schedule 13 of the Bill. See postscript.

sentence.[35] We have very little evidence as to how magistrates' courts decide whether infractions have occurred and what is the appropriate sentence because the processes of magistrates' courts are hidden and trivialised. Furthermore: "[e]ven within the triviality of lower court justice . . . trading offences were seen as even more trivial, and these perceptions further hid such offences, particularly from the press."[36] Where the defendant pleads guilty, of course, judicial discretion only relates to sentence. With the exception of an interesting study by Croall,[37] the only evidence of the courts' approach to trading standards offences is from the decisions of the appellate courts, the Divisional Court (where reports are available) and, more commonly, the Court of Appeal and House of Lords. Even with this very limited and unsatisfactory evidence of judicial activity and ideology, it is apparent that there are conflicting views within the judiciary as to the appropriateness of using criminal sanctions in trading cases, and perhaps, more fundamentally, between the judiciary and the legislature on the same issues. These tensions are manifested in ways which could be said to detract from the functional orientation of the relevant legislation.

The main source of tension lies in the way in which the offences are framed.[38] The majority of the offences in modern trading standards legislation are strict liability offences, requiring no evidence of dishonesty or intention to secure a conviction. In many instances the offences laid down in legislation overlap with civil liability for negligence, misrepresentation, or breach of contract. In these areas the imposition of criminal penalties represents a recognition by the legislature of the inadequacy of private law remedies as techniques for regulating market conduct. In most cases the strict liability is not absolute as legislation provides defences in various forms, most commonly where the defendant can prove some form of due diligence in seeking to

---

[35] McBarnet D., *Conviction* (1981) Chap. 7.
[36] Croall M., "Mistakes, Accidents and Someone Else's Fault: The Trading Offender in Court" (1988) *Journal of Law and Society* pp. 293–315 at p. 296.
[37] Croall, *op. cit.*
[38] Though much of the research into white collar crime generally suggests that the cultural homogeneity between court officials and defendants is also a source of tension between functional objectives and judicial attitudes. Croall's study of trading offences in the magistrates' courts challenges this assumption. Her study found that defendants, rather than being articulate middle class business persons, were more typically "corner shop proprietors, restaurateurs, dealers in second hand cars, and market traders . . ."; *op. cit.*, p. 294. She suggests that the assumption of sympathetic treatment may therefore be questionable.

avoid committing the offence. Criminal lawyers of a more traditional frame of mind have long been critical of what they perceive to be an abuse of criminal law.[39] The abuse is said to be a breach of the voluntary act principle, that criminal offences should only be those acts which are intentionally done.[40] The ambivalence of the courts is further, partly, explained by the widely held view, shared in Cranston's research by agencies and businesses alike, that the majority of businesses are honest and attempt to be law abiding.[41] The pattern of sentencing, under the Trade Descriptions Act 1968 at least, has tended to reflect the judicial view that only the dishonest should receive prison sentences.[42] In the year ending September 30, 1992 only 41 of the 1,612 traders convicted under the Trade Descriptions Act 1968 were imprisoned. The average (mean) fine was £549, and the average (mean) compensation award was £61. A very large proportion of the convictions, fines and compensation awards were in relation to second-hand cars.[43]

There is some further evidence, mainly coming from the perceptions of enforcement officers, that lower courts are influenced by a sense that criminal sanctions are inappropriately used to deal with trading offences. Courts may apply rules of criminal procedure too strictly. In some cases, courts have been reluctant to convict where they perceive no fault.[44] Additionally, Cranston suggested that the courts are too willing to accept that a due diligence defence has been made out.[45] This argument should be contrasted with the findings of Croall's study of magistrates' courts, indicating that many defendants, particularly small businesses and employees, were unrepresented, and were unable to plead the statutory defences, which are complex to establish and need to be notified to the prosecution before the hearing. Typically, arguments which might have grounded defences were used in mitigation by unrepresented defendants.[46] Even where the

---

[39] Hogan B., "Strict Liability" [1978] Crim.L.R. pp. 593–598.

[40] See *R. v. Gammon* [1985] 1 A.C. 1.

[41] Cranston, *op. cit.,* p. 150.

[42] *R. v. Haesler* [1973] R.T.R. 486: *R. v. Hammerton Cars* [1976] 3 All E.R. 758: *R. v. Kuldip Gupta* [1985] Crim.L.R. 601: *R. v. Southwood* [1987] 3 All E.R. 556; Roberts D., "Sentencing Under the Trade Descriptions Act" (1991) *Trading Law* pp. 36–42.

[43] Director General of Fair Trading (1993) *Annual Report 1992* pp. 54–55.

[44] *R. v. Hammerton Cars* [1976] 1 W.L.R. 1243: *Cottee v. Douglas Seaton* [1972] 3 All E.R. 750.

[45] Cranston, *op. cit.,* p. 114.

[46] Croall, *op. cit.,* pp. 297–298.

due diligence defence has been pleaded it has been argued that the prosecution ought generally to be able to show further steps that could have been taken to avoid committing the offence.[47] The complexity of criminal procedure and this perception of the attitude of the courts has meant that trading standards departments in Cranston's survey generally only prosecuted straightforward cases where they were confident of conviction.[48]

Thus, it may be argued that the use of criminal law significantly affects the pattern of functionalist legislation in a dysfunctional way.[49] At least with regard to the attitude of the appellate courts there is evidence to support the view that there is growing acceptance of the use of criminal law in trading standards regulation, and an increasing willingness to promote its functional aims. At a theoretical level one can attempt to reconcile the voluntary act principle with strict liability, by arguing that the business that sets an enterprise in motion is at every stage making choices about the organisation of the business, the methods of working and the training of staff, etc. It is true that if one looks at the moment immediately before the offence is committed then there may be no voluntary act by the offender, but by expanding the timeframe to take in the wider questions of business organisation, then it can be argued that a series of voluntary acts led to the commission of the offence.[50] Such an argument has even been accepted, at least implicitly, by the House of Lords in order to bring together the *mens rea* and *actus reus* requirements of section 14 of the Trade Descriptions Act in relation to misleading information about services, which, unusually, has a *mens rea* requirement. In *Wings v. Ellis,*[51] a travel operator had put out a brochure offering holidays to be purchased through travel agents, which at the time of publication was apparently correct in its

---

[47] See Anon "The Evolution of Statutory Defences" (1982) *Trading Law* 181–183; and *Garrett v. Boots the Chemist* (1980, unreported).
[48] Cranston, *op. cit.*, p. 117.
[49] Lord Scarman in *Wings v. Ellis* [1985] A.C. 272.
[50] The exploration of the wider context of criminal offences is developed by Kelman M., "Interpretive Construction in the Substantive Criminal Law" (1981) Stanford L.R. 591–673; (1987) *A Guide to Critical Legal Studies* p. 360. The Deconstructive implications for strict liability have been explored by Alexander L., "Reconsidering the Relationship Among Voluntary Acts, Strict Liability, and Negligence in Criminal Law" (1990) *Social Philosophy and Politics* 84–104 and picked up in the British context by Wells C., "Restatement or Reform" (1986) Crim.L.R. 314 and Richardson, *op. cit.* See also the chapter by Wells in this volume, particularly her discussion of risk assessment at pp. 121–124.
[51] [1985] A.C. 272.

details that a particular hotel had air-conditioning. The defendant tour operator subsequently discovered that, in fact, the hotel in question did not have air-conditioning and attempted to pass this information on to all travel agents handling the relevant holidays. However, at least one prospective holiday-maker did not learn of the correction to the details until he actually reached the hotel and the local trading standards department decided to prosecute for contravention of section 14 of the Trade Descriptions Act 1968 which makes it an offence for someone acting in the course of business to make a statement which he/she knows to be false as to the provision of any services, etc. On an ordinary understanding it would appear that, at the time the statement was made, the defendants did not know the statement was false, and therefore the mental element and the *actus reus* were apparently not both present at the same time. However, Lord Scarman, in particular, made it clear that the purposes of the Act, in promoting the ability of consumers to rely on statements as to services, would be best served by holding that a statement was made whenever a consumer read it, and so when the particular consumer in this case read the statement at a time by which the defendants knew it to be false, the offence was committed. Lord Scarman supported the view that the House was not dealing here with "'real crime'" but rather a regulatory offence. Lord Hailsham had doubts on the appropriateness of bringing the prosecution in this case, but nevertheless held that the interpretation was correct.

With regard to pricing offences it is now explicitly provided that, where a price indication becomes misleading after it has been published and consumers might reasonably be expected to rely on it after it has become misleading, then an offence is committed unless the defendant can show that he has taken all reasonable steps to prevent such consumers relying on it.[52] In *Warwickshire County Council v. Johnson,*[53] a case decided under the 1987 Act, the House of Lords held that a notice claiming that a retail store would beat any price in town for identical products by £20 was a continuing offer, the truth of which was only tested when someone took it up. Therefore, the act of the shop manager in refusing to honour the offer turned the previously

---

[52] Consumer Protection Act 1987 s.20(2). Bragg R., *Trade Descriptions — A Study of the Trade Descriptions Act 1968 and Part II of the Consumer Protection Act 1987* (1991) p. 124.

[53] [1993] 1 All E.R. 299. See also the note by Oughton in [1993] J.B.L. 43 on this point in the Divisional Court.

innocent notice into a misleading price indication under section 20 of the Consumer Protection Act 1987, which does not have a *mens rea* requirement. Lord Roskill said:

> "[t]o hold otherwise would be seriously to restrict the efficacy of this part of the consumer protection legislation. Seemingly innocent notices could be put up and then when such notices were followed by a refusal to honour them by a person acting in the course of his business no offence would be committed."[54]

Such flexible and functional interpretation in the higher courts, however, does not necessarily indicate that lower courts act likewise. In this particular case, the Stratford-upon-Avon justices had refused to accept that a misleading price indication had been given, and the Divisional Court misunderstood the meaning of clear statutory words to the effect that employees were not to be prosecuted. It is arguable that the source of the mistake was being over-fond of notions of individual responsibility which section 20 of the Consumer Protection Act 1987 offends by stating that only the employer, and not the responsible employee, can be prosecuted.[55] Very few cases under the main trading standards legislation reach the appellate courts, so it is certainly true in respect of both the Consumer Protection Act 1987 and the Food Safety Act 1990, that there is very little guidance for lower courts on how to interpret the provisions. There is a more established body of case law on the interpretation of the Trade Descriptions Act 1968.

Fragmentation Through Self-Regulation

Today, the structure of the modern due diligence defence provides considerable encouragement for businesses to regulate their own compliance with legislative standards, either collectively through trade associations or by means of functional differentiation within large business organisations.[56] This encouragement of

---

[54] [1993] 1 All E.R. 299, 302j.
[55] See the letter by Francis Bennion, (1993) New L.J. 356: Scott C., "Pricing Offences and Statutory Interpretation after *Pepper v. Hart*" [1993] J.B.L. pp. 490–505.
[56] It should be noted that there is no due diligence defence at common law in England; Leigh, *op. cit.*, p. 54. This may be contrasted with the position in Canada; See Tuck-Jackson A., "The Defence of Due Diligence and the Presumption of Innocence" (1990) *Criminal Law Quarterly* 11–42 and *R. v. Saulte Ste Marie (City)* [1978] 2 SCR 1299.

self-regulation reflects a delegation to industry itself to determine what conduct may be taken to meet the standards of the legislation. The usual explanation for the presence of the defences is that they mitigate the harshness of strict liability imposed on innocent traders.[57] However, turning the argument round it can be said that only those who commit the offence with intention or gross negligence are intended to be prosecuted.[58] The gradual refinement of defences in criminal statutes has been slowly shuffling towards the aim of promoting self regulation. It is, of course, arguable that this will result in a more cohesive, coherent and responsive body of standards than the legislature can achieve. Once again, however, it raises questions as to how such standard setting is to be monitored and made accountable.[59]

The form of defence least capable of promoting self regulation is, perhaps, the general warranty defence formerly provided in section 102 of the Food Act 1984, but repealed with the passing of the Food Safety Act 1990. This defence permitted a retailer to escape liability if he/she could show that he/she had received a warranty from the supplier that the product complied with all regulations and he/she had no reason to believe that it did not. The retailer's defence, a form of which can be found in the Consumer Protection Act 1987 in relation to unsafe products,[60] is a positive encouragement to retailers to make no investigation at all into the quality of a product, and not to introduce their own systems for checking product quality even where they are able to do so. The first limb of the two limbed defence contained in the Trade Descriptions Act 1968, that the commission of the offence was due to a mistake or to the fault or omission of another person, has also been criticised on the basis that it is too easy to satisfy, for example by showing that the fault of an employee had

---

[57] Leigh, *op. cit.*, p. 79.
[58] Cranston, *op. cit.*, p. 106.
[59] See Braithwaite J., "Enforced Self-Regulation" (1982) *Michigan L.R.* 1466–1507 for the most developed argument as to how industry could regulate itself through enforced self-regulation, under which compliance teams within firms would have duties to draw up regulations, to be approved by a regulatory agency, which the compliance team then has to enforce, with a duty to report all violations to the regulatory agency.
[60] Consumer Protection Act 1987 s.10(4). Here the defence is based on a retailer proving that he/she "neither knew nor had reasonable grounds for believing that goods failed to comply with the general safety requirement . . .". This defence is clearly an invitation to retailers to fail to inquire into the safety of goods supplied to them. Whether it would be possible to interpret this section in such a way as to hold that a large retailer, with resources for in-house testing of products, should have a proper testing regime is unclear.

caused the commission of the offence. A particular difficulty, which seems to have arisen unnecessarily in the prosecution of many trading offences, is the identification of the appropriate person or company to prosecute. Where an offence is committed often both the employee concerned and the company employing him/her may be guilty of the offence. Generally speaking trading standards agencies are reluctant to prosecute employees.[61] Indeed, it now appears to be legislative policy, at least with regard to pricing offences, to ensure that an employee cannot be successfully prosecuted.[62] Yet the first limb of the defence in section 24 of the Trade Descriptions Act 1968 has permitted employers to escape liability, arguing successfully that an employee, unless he/she is the controlling mind of the company, is another person for the purposes of the defence. More recent legislation has abandoned this limb in favour of a simple due diligence defence.[63]

The due diligence defence, which is to be found in the vast majority of trading standards statutes, provides positive encouragement to businesses to put systems in place and to ensure that they are working.[64] The leading case remains *Tesco v. Nattrass*,[65] in which the defendant supermarket chain succeeded in showing both that they had a system of training their managers to get pricing correct, and that the particular manager responsible for committing the offence had undergone this training, and thus the company had satisfied the due diligence defence. It has been recently emphasised on several occasions that magistrates courts will generally need to hear expert evidence on what steps other businesses in the relevant industry take in order to avoid committing the offences.[66] The extent of the systems required is likely to depend on the size of the business concerned.[67] Due diligence requirements can usually be satisfied by small retailers who use reputable suppliers and who check that they receive what they

---

[61] Cranston, *op. cit.*, p. 115.
[62] See *R. v. Warwickshire County Council, ex p. Johnson* [1993] 1 All E.R. 299: Scott, *op. cit.* (1993).
[63] Anon "The Evolution of Statutory Defences" (1982) *Trading Law* 181–183 at p. 182: Howells, *op. cit.*
[64] See for example *Tesco v. Nattrass* [1972] A.C. 153: Leigh, *op. cit.*, p. 76: Lawson R., "On Being Diligent" (1985) *Trading Law* pp. 333–337.
[65] [1972] A.C. 153.
[66] *P&M Supplies (Essex) Ltd. v. Devon County Council* (unreported, 1991 CO/249/90): *Dudley Metropolitan Council v. Roy Firman Ltd.* (unreported, 1992 CO/1541/91).
[67] *Garrett v. Boots the Chemist* (1980, unreported).

ordered.[68] However, for large manufacturing companies satisfaction of the defence may require the introduction of management systems which reduce risk of contraventions at every stage at which such risks occur.[69] Thus, through industry associations, companies and groups of companies are encouraged to introduce systems to regulate themselves and, where they do, they will be able to satisfy the requirements of the defence. Furthermore, most modern statutes, for example section 23 of the Trade Descriptions Act 1968, contain "by-pass" provisions to the effect that where some other person's fault has caused the commission of the offence then that other person may be convicted of the offence instead.[70]

Fragmentation and Function — Law as a Resource for Businesses

One effect of using criminal law in the trading area is to add legitimacy to those who broadly comply with the law, and reduce the legitimacy of those who do not. Typically this effect can serve to cast the large chain of retail outlets as the "'good trader" following best practice, while small local traders, lacking the resources to implement the systems of checks to ensure compliance, may increasingly be seen as "fly-by-night" businesses. It is possible to hypothesise that large retail groups favour additional regulation in areas where they find it easier to secure compliance than smaller businesses, such as pricing, product safety, etc. Larger businesses find it easier also to secure legal advice and representation to prevent infractions, or to deal with infractions when they do occur.[71] It is possible to conclude that apparently impartial criminal law can be used by large businesses as an extremely effective economic resource. While there is considerable American literature outlining the potential of regu-

---

[68] Howells, *op. cit.*, p. 245.
[69] Scott C., "Continuity and Change in British Food Law" (1990) M.L.R. 785–801 at p. 792: Howells, *op. cit.*
[70] The origins and evolution the "by-pass" provisions are explored in Wasik M., "Shifting the Burden of Strict Liability" (1982) Crim.L.R. pp. 567–574.
[71] Croall, *op. cit.*, pp. 297–8 indicates that small businesses are rarely represented in magistrates courts when charged with a trading offence and are often bewildered by the procedure and legal argument. Small businesses are much less able to internalise compliance and infraction costs.

latory law as a resource for big business,[72] such work is less well developed in the United Kingdom.

Consolidation

Two major changes have occurred which have affected the extent of local authority autonomy in trading standards and thus the fragmented pattern of enforcement. First, the complexity and range of legislation which local authorities were required to enforce forced them to seek economies of scale in adaptation to, and interpretation of, new law.[73] Secondly, membership of the E.C. put upon the United Kingdom, obligations to secure effective implementation and enforcement of E.C. measures.[74] Vigorous enforcement approaches in some Member States may create trade barriers not present in Member States where resources do not permit such enforcement, or where compliance approaches are favoured. As the recent Sutherland Report makes clear, problems of uneven enforcement of trading laws which are, in theory, approximated within the E.C., will increasingly need to be addressed.[75]

The need for economies of scale was, to some extent, addressed by local government reorganisation in 1972 which

---

[72] See, e.g. Kolko G., *Railroads and Regulation* (1965): Peltzman S., "Towards a More General Theory of Regulation" (1976) *Journal of Law and Economics* pp. 211–240: Posner R., "Theories of Economic Regulation" (1974) *Bell Journal of Economics and Management Science* pp. 335–358: Wilson J., "The Politics of Regulation", in Wilson J., (ed.) *The Politics of Regulation* (1980). See for the U.K. Ogus A., *Regulation* (1994).

[73] Hunter N., "Trading Standards"; Co-ordination, Co-operation and a Look at the Future" (1985) *Trading Law* pp. 171–176.

[74] To the extent that in the event that the central government of a Member State fails to properly implement an E.C. Directive, the direct effects doctrine may require a local authority to ensure that the Directive is given proper effect in matters within their jurisdiction. See *R. v. London Boroughs Transport Committee, ex p. Freight Transport Association Ltd.* [1990] 1 C.M.L.R. 229.

[75] *The Internal Market After 1992 — Meeting the Challenge* (The Sutherland Report) Report to the E.C. Commission by the High Level Group on the Operation of Internal Market, (Brussels 1992) recommendation 38: E.C. Commission (1992) *The Operation of the Community's Internal Market After 1992 — Follow Up to the Sutherland Report* SEC (92) 2277 Final (Brussels 1992), points 21–28: Joerges C., "The Instruments of Product Safety Policy and the Process of European Integration", (1989) in Joerges C. (ed.) *Product Liability and Product Safety in the E.C.* p. 37 (EUI Working Paper No. 89/404, Florence: EUI): Scott C., "Regulating for Consumer Safety in the United Kingdom within the European Communities" (1993) in Weick G. (ed.) *National and European Law on the Threshold to the Single Market*: Rhodes G., "From Weights and Measures to Trading Standards", (1981) in Rhodes G. (ed.) *Inspectorates in British Government*.

reduced the number of Weights and Measures Authorities from 280 to 88.[76] The logical next step in the United Kingdom context might be to replace local with central enforcement. However, any centralised enforcement system would still need to be operated through local offices, and therefore carries with it the same risks of lack of uniformity that arise with full decentralised enforcement, and, would in any case, prove wholly unacceptable to those presently charged with enforcement.[77] Rather, a number of alternative options have been pursued which pull enforcement towards a more centralised and concentrated pattern. Firstly, on Britain's entry into the EEC the Government encouraged the local authority associations to establish a mechanism for coordination of local enforcement throughout the country.[78]

The professional body of trading standards officers, the Institute of Trading Standards Administration (ITSA), had for a long time provided a focus for coordination of responses to new legislation, policy making and development of professional standards. However, in 1977 this was supplemented by a local authority association scheme, called the Local Authorities Coordinating Body on Trading Standards LACOTS. LACOTS' main functions are providing coordination on technical issues, to coordinate operational practices to provide a centralised point for collection and exchange of information.[79] LACOTS' jurisdiction was extended in April 1992 to cover for the first time the coordination of food hygiene enforcement.[80]

A core development in this context, which exploits the coordinating potential of LACOTS to deal with nationwide businesses, is the Home Authority Principle. Under the terms of the principle, businesses receive advice on trading standards matters from the local authority in the area in which their head office is located.[81] There is a directory of home authorities for major traders, and normally the home authority will be involved if any authority seeks to take action against a major company. It seems likely that in due course the home authority principle will be applied to the E.C. as a whole. ITSA additionally established a National Information Service in 1983,[82] which boasts a 100 per

---

[76] Beckett B., "The Problems of Uniform Enforcement" (1981) *Trading Law* pp. 18–19.
[77] Circus P., "The Headaches of Consumer Law Enforcement" (1983) *Trading Law* pp. 25–27.
[78] Beckett, *op. cit.*, p.18.
[79] *ibid.*
[80] Roberts D., "Five More Codes" (1992) *Trading Law* pp. 66–73.
[81] Beckett, *op. cit.*, p. 19.
[82] Hunter, *op. cit.*

cent. takeup among trading standards authorities, is now available on-line as TS Link, and includes a database of information on interpretation of law and information on businesses, and an e-mail system.

A second instrument designed to secure more uniform enforcement is the issue of Codes of Practice for food authorities under the terms of section 40(1) of the Food Safety Act 1990. Central Government had never before provided such guidance on enforcement for trading standards authorities.[83] The main objective of the Codes is to ensure compliance with the Food Control Directive of 1989.[84] To this end, the Secretary of State has power to enforce the codes by seeking an order of mandamus (section 40(2)). However, concerns about resourcing levels dogged the introduction of the new Act and remain a significant concern.[85] Code 1 provides for greater coordination of trading standards and environmental health departments in enforcing food law. Increasingly they will have to work in teams, rather than as separate departments.[86] The code of main interest to lawyers will perhaps be Code 2 on Legal Matters which sets out in detail the factors to consider in deciding whether to prosecute. These include: the seriousness of the offence; the previous history of the party; the likelihood of the due diligence being established; ability and willingness of the party to cooperate; the willingness of the party to prevent the contravention recurring; the probable public benefit of prosecution (for example establishing a precedent); whether formal caution or an improvement notice would be more appropriate or effective; and any explanation offered by the party. Though these factors are not binding on an authority, it has been suggested that where one or more is not given proper weight this may act in mitigation for a defendant.[87] It is interesting to notice that the Codes make no reference to the requirements of the Police and Criminal Evidence Act 1984, even though these apply as much to trading standards and environ-

---

[83] *cf.* the Code for Crown Prosecutors issued under s. 10 of the Prosecution of Offences Act 1985 in Director of Public Prosecutions (1991) *Annual Report* HC 487 1990–91 pp. 37–41, which deals principally with guidance on whether there is sufficient evidence to proceed with a prosecution, and whether it is in the public interest so to proceed.

[84] Council Directive on Official Inspection of Food Stuffs 89/397/EEC O.J. 27.5.89, 89/C131/07. See also Dehousse *et. al., op. cit.,* pp. 23–24.

[85] Roberts D., "Codes of Practice Under the Food Safety Act 1990" (1991) *Trading Law* pp. 212–225.

[86] Roberts, *op. cit.,* p. 215.

[87] *ibid.,* pp. 216–217.

mental health officers as they do to the police.[88] The other main innovation in the Codes is the requirement in Codes 8 and 9 on food standards and food hygiene inspections respectively, that the food authorities use a risk assessment to put each business into one of a number of risk categories which will determine the minimum frequency of visits, between six months and five years. These provisions are designed to address the very poor record on frequency of inspection discovered by an Audit Commission report in 1990.[89]

It is clear that the Community has a continuing concern with promoting uniformity of enforcement of Community consumer protection laws, and legislation will increasingly be framed in such a way as to meet this concern. Framework Directives typically now contain provisions requiring Member States to report on the implementation process.[90] The recently adopted General Product Safety Directive[91] makes extensive provision for techniques of monitoring, inspection, prohibition and withdrawal of consumer products which Member States will be required to show in order to comply with its provisions.[92] Building on earlier information exchange initiatives, the Directive also makes provision for rapid exchange of information and action by the Commission in the event of dangers being presented by products across national borders.[93]

Conclusion

This chapter started with a picture of trading standards regulation in which standard setting processes were assumed to be relatively homogeneous, and enforcement processes relatively fragmented. However, close scrutiny of the substance and implementation of consumer protection legislation suggests that the standard setting

---

[88] *ibid.*, p. 225.
[89] Audit Commission (1990) *Environmental Health Survey of Food Premises.*
[90] See, for example, the Council Directive on the Official Inspection of Foodstuffs, 89/397/EEC, O.J. 27.5.89. Scott, *op. cit.* (1990) Council Directive on General Product Safety, Article 5.
[91] Council Directive 92/59/EEC of June 29, on General Product Safety O.J. L228, 11/08/92 p. 24.
[92] Art 6.
[93] Council Directive on General Product Safety, Article 8–11. See Sutherland Report, *op. cit.,* Recommendation 32: OECD Committee on Consumer Policy (1991) *Consumers, Product Safety Standards and International Trade* p. 42: Joerges C., "Instruments of Product Safety Policy and the Process of European Integration" (1989) in Joerges, (ed.), *op. cit.*

process is becoming increasingly fragmented, while there is evidence that enforcement processes are being consolidated. The explanations for such changes are complex. Fragmentation in standard setting can be identified with a more general fragmentation of power associated both with the linkage of technical expertise to economic power within major national and multinational corporations, and with the growing jurisdiction of the European Community.

It might be argued that expertise in matters such as food safety and administration developed initially within government, as part of the nineteenth century scientific revolution. During the twentieth century, expertise in such areas has increasingly been developed by growing corporations, so that the State is no longer in a position to identify and set standards relating to safety, organisation and marketing techniques.

It would, however, be overly simplistic to assume that the drift away from detailed legislative control is solely a consequence of technological determinism. The process also has a clearly constitutional dimension. This is most evident in the substantive lawmaking role played by the E.C., but it is also discernible in the choice made by the British Parliament to exercise the discretion it enjoys under E.C. law in a manner which devolves substantial authority both to local government and to "private sector" organisations, albeit under the ostensible supervision of the supra-national E.C. Commission and European Court of Justice.

One may also assume that the shift reflects wider perceptions concerning the correct role to be played by central government bodies in all matters of economic regulation. It may be that recent developments in this particular area of criminal law represent a partial response to the relative decline in the capacity of the central governments of a nation state to regulate trading behaviour in an increasingly international economic environment. The substantial and continuing Europeanisation, decentralisation, and privatisation of consumer protection laws may be seen as a cross-national attempt to secure economies of scale both in the organisation of state institutions, and the monitoring and regulation of economic activity.

If this argument is correct, the consolidation of enforcement practices may be entirely consistent with the fragmentation of standard setting authority, each being a response to the impossibility of regulation: first, to devolve regulatory power to the most appropriate level, and secondly to provide for greater uniformity of instruments for monitoring the exercise of that devolved power. At present, this is a speculative conclusion. The testing of such a hypothesis would require further empirical investigation, presumably on a pan-European as well as intra-national level, into the link between self regulation and state enforcement, and the role of the courts in promoting or hindering such a new form of instrumentalism. This chapter began by observing that empirical studies in the 1970s played an important part in highlighting the poor fit of consumer protection measures with traditional criminal law paradigms. It may be sensible to conclude that the radical changes in the formal substance of consumer protection laws, and the equally profound shifts in the institutional structures of enforcement and compliance, reinforce the need for contemporary insight into the realities of this somewhat murky backwater of the criminal law.

Postscript

Since the completion of the text of this Chapter the Deregulation and Contracting Out Act 1994 has been enacted. Chapter 1 of the Act makes extensive provision for the removal and reduction of burdensome regulation by ministers (sections 1–4), and for improvement of enforcement procedures by ministers (sections 5–6), in each case acting through the issue of statutory instruments. Also, the E.C. General Product Safety Directive of 1992 has been implemented in the United Kingdom by the General Product Regulations 1994 (S.I. 1994 No. 2328). The Regulations, issued under section 2(2) of the European Communities Act 1972, substantially modify section 10 of the Consumer Protection Act 1987, and withdraw the approved standards regime established under that Act. Section 7 of the Regulations creates a new general safety requirement applying to all products placed on the market. A new defence of due diligence is introduced in section 14 of the Regulations.

Chapter Eight

REGULATING SEXUAL OFFENCES WITHIN THE HOME[1]
by Lucia Zedner

This chapter will explore the significance of the distinction made between "public" and "private" spheres for the criminalisation of sexual offences within the family home.[2] In traditional, liberal discourse, notions of the "private" were conflated with the "family". Accordingly, sexual offences committed within the family home were deemed to be outwith the legitimate ambit of the law. This was never entirely matched by the realities of regulations and more recently, feminist legal theorists, among others, have advanced a different view; that the division between public and private is not a well-delineated boundary but little more than a line drawn in sand, constantly shifting in response to political and other pressures.[3] The normative account which claims that the law should not enter the private sphere conceals a strategic truth. As O'Donovan has argued:

> "it is for the state to decide how, where, and in what manner it will regulate individuals' lives. Zones can be mapped out as being inside or outside the state's purview. The placement of an aspect of life inside or outside the law is a form of regulation."[4]

The private sphere, far from occupying some tangible space on the social map, becomes little more than a justificatory device for legal non-intervention.

However, we would be mistaken in concluding that an absence of formal law represents an absence of regulation. Instead, the

---

[1] I would like to thank Joe Jacob, Nicola Lacey, and Les Moran for reading and commenting on earlier drafts of this chapter.

[2] This chapter will focus on heterosexual offences within the heterosexual family. It would be interesting to see how its argument would be modified by consideration of the historic regulation of homosexual offences within the private sphere.

[3] O'Donovan K., *Sexual Divisions in Law* (1985): Smart C., *Feminism and the Power of Law* (1989): Kaganas F. and Murray C., 'Law Reform and the Family' (1991) *Journal of Law and Society* 287–302: Lacey N., 'Theory into Practice? Pornography and the Public/Private Dichotomy' (1993) *Journal of Law and Society* 93–113.

[4] O'Donovan, *op. cit.*, p. 7.

lack of law may reflect the greater strength of other quasi or non-legal regulatory mechanisms of social control which operate outside the legal context and state bureaucracy. In the field of sexuality we would do well to heed the maxim that "analysis of law is the wrong place to start if one wishes to understand regulatory strategies".[5] It would be precipitous, therefore, to assume that the historical reluctance to criminalise sexual relations within the family home implies lack of concern or interest by the state. Rather, the means of regulation are differentiated. The coercive powers of the criminal law in the public sphere are supplanted in the private sphere by the more subtle but no less powerful dominion of the family. Seen this way, the family is not beyond the purview of the state, but is itself an important means of regulating sexual morality.[6]

The legal framework which surrounds and shapes the family recognises it as the site of procreation and of motherhood. Before the advent of effective contraception, and even since then, sexuality was inseparable from its reproductive consequences. In order to protect both patriarchy and property, the family was constituted as the sole site in which sexual relations might legitimately be pursued. Reflecting on this, Smart argues that "the law on sexual behaviour, although defined as part of the criminal law and subject to a very different mode of enforcement to civil law, is analytically much closer to family law".[7] Yet one might go further and question whether any branch of doctrinal law represents the most important means of regulating sexual behaviour. In exploring the regulatory powers of the family, we will argue that where the range of law is most limited, other ideological and social institutions may play a more determinative part in policing the sanctioning of aberrant sexuality.

In this chapter we will explore the contention that the family has been constituted historically as the primary means of regulating that which lies outside the liberal definition of legitimate state interference.[8] A brief incursion into the historical development of the family reveals high expectations of its capacity for self-regulation. However, and this is where the liberal account really

---

[5] Rose N., 'Beyond the Public/Private Division: Law, Power and the Family' (1987) *Journal of Law and Society* 61–76.

[6] Robertson Elliot F., 'The Family: Private Arena or Adjunct of the State?' (1989) *Journal of Law and Society* 443–463.

[7] Smart C., 'Law and the control of women's sexuality: the case of the 1950s', in Hutter B. and Williams G. (eds.) *Controlling Women: The Normal and the Deviant* (1981) p. 45.

[8] Donzelot J., *The Policing of Families* (1979).

fails, when these expectations were not met, intervention at a myriad of levels quickly followed. The mythology of the Victorian family home as a site enjoying privileged status, free from the state's disciplinary gaze, seems to rely on a deliberate misreading of the past.[9]

The Family and Victorian Values

In analysing the relationship between the state, family, and the regulation of sexual relations, one is immediately struck by the centrality of nostalgic visions of the family in the calls for a return to "Victorian values" which have dominated political discourse over the past 15 years. It is perhaps instructive, therefore, to begin by reflecting briefly upon the place and role of the family in Victorian society. In this way, we can employ history as a means of analysing the present, to determine how that which may now appear as a given is, in fact, socially constructed. Against the claim that the Victorian family represented the apotheosis of privacy, we will question whether it has ever been wholly free from scrutiny or regulation.

The traditional account goes something like this. Against a backdrop of industrialisation and urbanisation, the family came to be lauded as a haven from the corrupting influences of the harsh world outside.[10] In contemporary discourse, the family became the very definitional shell of the private sphere and according to conservative ideologists like Ferdinand Mount,[11] occupied a privileged space, protected from intervention by the state. This account relies on a profound misreading of the historical development of the family and is to misunderstand its form and role. Certainly Mount is right to recognise that the evolution of the family entailed the mapping out of a separate domestic terrain. During the nineteenth century, the family was transformed from a loose grouping spanning generations, embed-

[9] On this point see Foucault M., *The History of Sexuality: Volume One* (1978). It relies also on a narrow conception of the state as a unitary, monolithic edifice. In our view the development of modern government is better read as a network of institutions, agencies, and associations promoting differing purposes according to varying, often competing, philosophies.

[10] The idea of the family was gendered — for women, paradoxically, the family home provided the sphere in which their status as citizens was located; Hall C., 'The Early Formation of Domestic Ideology, in Burman S. and Harrell-Bond B. (eds.) *Fit Work for Women* (1979).

[11] Mount F., *The Subversive Family: An Alternative History of Love and Marriage* (1982).

ded in, and barely distinct from, the surrounding community, to its recognisably modern form — a nuclear unit physically and functionally separate.[12] This transformation derived, in part, from increasing social and geographical mobility but, and this is where we part company with Mount, it arose also from the ideological constitution of the family as one among an array of apparatuses of the modern state. The modern family was not *outwith* regulation but rather constructed as a *means* of regulation.

In the agonised sphere of sexuality, the family was to play an especially important role. Crudely put, the family was constituted as a means of curtailing "rampant" male sexuality and the widely condemned dangers of "moral debasement" and "physical degeneration" to which, unchecked, it would lead.[13] Carefully maintained fictions as to women's chastity before marriage, and lack of sexual appetite thereafter, were used to demand male restraint. In its most exalted form, this ideology sought to limit sexual activity to procreation within marriage, to minimise the dangers of overcrowding by keeping unmarried adults segregated from one another, and to raise children in as near an approximation to innocence as was possible. As I have argued elsewhere; "the importance of the family lay in its ability to lessen the demoralising effects of overcrowding and, above all, to police its own members".[14] Although the family was endowed with regulatory powers, their exercise became the subject of a battery of ideological directives and constraints. Much of this took a literary form, from etiquette manuals and advice books to religious pamphlets. Highly prescriptive in tone this literature peddled an image of the ideal middle-class family which permeated down into all but the poorest slums. Over the course of the nineteenth century the working class family in particular became a focus of increasing attention by middle-class philanthropists, evangelicals, and charitable reformers.[15]

Far from residing beyond the purview of the state, then, the family was the subject of intense intervention throughout the nineteenth century. As Donzelot has argued in *The Policing of Families*, the family may best be seen as a point of intersection

---

[12] Of course the form and organisation of the family varied significantly by class and between rural and urban communities — the overarching trend, however, holds true.

[13] Cominos P., 'Late Victorian Sexual Respectability and the Social System', (1963) *International Review of Social History* 18–48, 216–250.

[14] Zedner L., *Women, Crime, and Custody in Victorian England* (1991) p. 13.

[15] Harrison B., "State Intervention and Moral Reform", in Hollis P. (ed.) *Pressure from Without* (1974).

between the public and private. It was both the subject of social intervention and was itself a moralising agent. Or rather women as wives and mothers were assigned responsibility for creating of the family a haven for religious and moral values. In effect, women were expected to act as the moral police of their menfolk and their offspring. This role required that women themselves were seen to be morally superior. Yet, maintaining this artificially elevated position itself relied upon informal regulation of another, more pernicious, kind. Women were subject to the "normalizing gaze" of their community.[16] Working class women in particular were subject to the scrutiny and sanction of "hierarchical female networks" which articulated and enforced social and sexual norms.[17] A range of subtle measures from moral pressure, through prescriptive teachings, to religious and social sanctions, were employed to regulate female sexuality. Most important of all these measures was that of stigma.[18] Historically, as today, there was less need to invoke the coercive powers of police or prison to secure women's conformity. Fearful of critical scrutiny, of being labelled promiscuous or "loose" for behaviour that would pass without comment in men, women could be called upon to ascribe to the ideal of "the angel in the house".[19]

These notions of "good" and "bad" women, and of sexual respectability, added innumerable proscriptions and taboos to the legal code which impacted with varying force at differing levels of society and which were in any case mediated through local culture and value systems.[20] It would be wrong, therefore, to interpret this informal policing solely or unproblematically as a tool of repressive middle-class morality. For many women, especially amongst the most vulnerable — young girls, domestic servants, or overburdened wives and mothers — these standards of sexual propriety were a positive force, a protective shield which helped to guard against sexual exploitation by male employers, against incest in overcrowded homes and against debilitating sexual demands by their husbands.[21]

---

[16] Foucault M., *Discipline and Punish* (1977) p. 170 ff.

[17] Walkowitz J., 'Male Vice and Feminist Virtue' (1982) *History Workshop* 79–93.

[18] Note the testimony of a working class Lancashire woman regarding the power of local matriarchs over a woman who became pregnant outside marriage: "[they] would talk about it and she would probably know and be ashamed. It was the shame that was the worst part"; Roberts E., *A Woman's Place: An Oral History of Working Class Women 1890–1940* (1984) p. 79.

[19] Christ C., "Victorian Masculinity and the Angel in the House", in Vicinus M., (ed.) *A Widening Sphere* (1977).

[20] Interesting oral testimony on these points is provided in Roberts, *op. cit.*

[21] Rover, Love C., *Morals and the Feminists* (1970).

Yet the regulatory force of Victorian morality was limited; even as the family was portrayed as a site of purity, evidence abounded of a darker side of family life — as a harbour of sexual immorality and a cover for abuse.[22] Investigative journalists like W.T. Stead appalled and attracted the public imagination with exposés of mothers selling their daughters into prostitution.[23] Early social investigators and social scientists published more sober, but no less terrifying, qualitative and statistical evidence of the extent of incest in working class homes.[24] Respondents to government enquiries, like the Royal Commission on the Housing of the Working Classes (1884), furnished evidence suggesting that precocious sexuality and incest were the common consequence of poverty and overcrowding in working class families.[25]

Loath to concede that notions of the family as a haven of chastity, and protector of innocence, were misguided and influenced by an emerging psychiatric literature of deviance, many contemporaries tended to pathologise those aspects of family life which did not accord with the invented ideal. They engaged in a twofold strategy. First, by defining sexual abuses within the family as "unnatural vices" they could be dismissed as aberrations which did little damage to the true image of family life. And secondly, where, at the very bottom of the social scale, the family's resemblance to the middle class ideal became hopelessly attenuated, it was condemned to a "pariah class which exists in our state as something fearfully rotten and polluted".[26]

The residuum, as it became known, was stigmatised as wholly distinct from the rest of humanity, not merely culturally distinct but almost a separate species.[27] Whilst it caused concern, its identification left the ideal of the Victorian family relatively unscathed.[28] Middle and upper class families remained the guardians of the domestic ideal and it is significant, but perhaps not surprising, that they were immune from such enquiries. Intervention, even if it had been feasible, remained unthinkable.

[22] One might argue that the maintenance of purity requires a 'darker side' as its legitimating device.
[23] 'The Maiden Tribute of Modern Babylon' by W.T. Stead was published in *The Pall Mall Gazette,* July 7, 8, 10, 1885.
[24] Mearns A., *The Bitter Cry of Outcast London* (1883): Booth W., *In Darkest England and the Way Out* (1890).
[25] Mort F., *Dangerous Sexualities* (1987) p. 105: *Royal Commission on the Housing of the Working Classes* (1884–1885) Cmnd. 4402, Vol. 30.
[26] Carpenter M., *Our Convicts* vol. ii, (1864) p. 208.
[27] Zedner, *op. cit.,* p. 78.
[28] Indeed, one might argue that maintaining the 'ideal' of the family relied upon the 'other' or 'deviant' family — fictive or real.

It would be convenient for the liberal account if our history stopped here. However, towards the end of the century evidence of sexual abuses extending far into the "respectable" working classes began seriously to undermine the faith in the self-regulatory capacity of the family. These abuses became the subject of intense scrutiny, debate, and finally, legal intervention. A thumbnail sketch will suffice here to describe this change. In the 1880s and 1890s, the impact of severe cyclical depression generated a deepening social crisis. The residuum were increasingly seen, not as a pitiable "outcast" group but, as posing a decisive threat to decent society.[29] The corrupting potential of the residuum crystallised around the contagious evil of sexuality. The Criminal Law Amendment Act 1885 sought to protect those whose sexuality and innocence was seen to be most at risk. It raised the age of consent to 16 and made sexual intercourse with a girl under 13 years of age an offence punishable with penal servitude for life. Though it was not explicitly framed as an intrusion into the private sphere, its criminalising of sexual intercourse with adolescent girls was clearly prompted by concern about risks to their purity and virginity from male family members. In introducing the bill, the Home Secretary, Richard Cross, declared "this is a question that has stirred England from one end to the other [because] there is nothing more sacred to the English people, as the purity of their own households".[30] A still more explicit intrusion was forged in the Punishment of Incest Act 1908, which, for the first time, extended the jurisdiction of the criminal law over that which had formally been only an ecclesiastical offence.[31] It made sexual intercourse between people within specified blood relationships a crime punishable with penal servitude of between three and seven years.

Significantly, pressure for the criminalisation of incest came not from central government but from pressure groups, like the National Vigilance Association (NVA) and the National Association for the Prevention of Cruelty to Children (NSPCC), set up in the 1880s in the wake of the Criminal Law Amendment Act 1885.[32] The NVA, a high profile campaigning body, drew together a curious alliance of Salvation Army activists, "purity"

---

[29] Stedman Jones G., *Outcast London: A Study in the Relationship between Classes in Victorian Society* (1971).
[30] Quoted in Walkowitz J., *City of Dreadful Delight: Narratives of Sexual Danger in Late-Victorian London* (1992) p. 103.
[31] Bailey V. and Blackburn S., 'The Punishment of Incest Act 1908: A Case Study of Law Creation' (1979) Crim.L.R. 708–718.
[32] Mort, *op. cit.*, p. 104.

workers and early feminists all of whom were committed to the introduction of a more explicit policy of sexual regulation. Their motivations differed markedly. Feminist campaigners were primarily concerned to protect vulnerable family members from abuse. Religious activists and "social purity" workers were determined to raise standards of morality. Eugenicists sought to prevent the creation of degenerate progeny which might result from such liaisons. The NSPCC's interests were also split, concerned both for the moral welfare of children and alert to the more tangible harms caused by physical and sexual abuses within the family.

This fragmentation of interests was smoothed over by the social cohesion of the leadership and membership of these campaigning bodies.[33] They were drawn from a narrow band of closely interconnected middle and upper class social reformers. Both the NVA and NSPCC were committed to ensuring the effective criminalisation of incest by actively prosecuting fathers under the Criminal Law Amendment Act. When the strictures of that Act proved to be a hindrance,[34] both were instrumental in campaigning for the 1908 Incest Act. According to Bailey and Blackburn, those in governmental and parliamentary circles remained loath to recognise, still less to legislate against incest for fear of tarnishing the reputation of the family. They were pressed to do so only by the sustained efforts of campaigning bodies such as the NVA and the NSPCC in persuading those within the Home Office of the need for legislation.

This brief history of the 1885 and 1908 Acts furnishes us with several interesting insights which might profitably be noted as we go on to explore more recent history. First, that to make an activity the subject of the criminal law does not automatically lead to its effective criminalisation unless the law, its powers and procedures are adequate and are acted upon (the difficulty of securing convictions under the 1885 Act was a major impetus to further legislation). Secondly, criminal law creation is not necessarily the consequence of the actions of a monolithic, centralised state determined to extend its regulatory powers; the 1908 Act was pushed through against the background of governmental indifference and parliamentary opposition. Thirdly, the campaigning efforts of pressure groups may be influential in achieving

---

[33] Bristow E., *Vice and Vigilance: Purity Movements in England since 1700* (1977).
[34] Prosecution had to be brought within three months of the commission of the offence and medical examination of the alleged victim needed parental consent; Bailey and Blackburn, *op. cit.*, p. 711.

the single end of criminalisation but we would be wrong to assume that they necessarily share a single aim. Feminist groups, "child savers", eugenicists, and social purity campaigners shared a desire to see incest criminalised but, as we have seen, their construction of the problem, their motives and even the purposes of their shared solution were diverse. Important too was the impact of social research by an emerging band of social scientists and the persuasive powers of statistical evidence which, arguably, did more than any single political argument to bring opponents of legislative change around.[35] Significantly, research was not carried out by the state nor even as a function of the state government, but rather shaped and directed the development of government policy itself.

Most importantly, this brief historical overview gives the lie to current rhetoric about the inviolability of the Victorian family from state interference. The family was a social and political construct whose very form derived from a highly contrived ideal of domestic life. Moreover, the working class family, at least, retained its freedom from interference only for so long as it accorded with the normative ideal. To the extent that its departures from this model came to public notice, it rendered itself potentially subject to disciplinary intervention and the loss of autonomy.[36] Middle and upper class families were far more resilient to the scrutiny of the state, and perpetrators of incest within them were less liable, therefore, to face prosecution. Some families, it would seem, are more private than others. As a coda we might suggest that legislation, overtly passed to recognise and sanction criminal harms, was as much concerned with the "policing of families" (or rather a certain class of families), as with protecting victims from abuse.

The Regulation of Sexuality
Through the Twentieth Century

If, in the nineteenth century, regulation of sexuality within the family was expressed primarily through moral and religious values, over the course of the twentieth century it has become increasingly secularised. The emerging professionals of the welfare state — doctors, psychologists, social workers — have, in the name of welfarism, increasingly taken on this policing function.

---

[35] Abrams P., *The Origins of British Sociology 1834–1914* (1968).
[36] Harrison, *op. cit.*

With secularisation, the moral content of regulation has been progressively submerged under an apparently anodyne vocabulary of protection and treatment. Yet, this vocabulary should not obscure either the true subject nor the regulatory intent of much that is done in the name of welfarism. The delinquent girl who is taken into local authority care on the grounds that she is in moral danger, the divorcing mother, denied custody of her children, who is deemed unfit because of her sexual history are examples of the way in which female sexuality in particular has been made the covert subject of regulation.

The emergence of welfare and psy-professions have also had a profound impact on attitudes to sexuality within the family. During the first half of the twentieth century, the family was reinvented less as a site of sexual restraint and more a locus of legitimate "healthy" heterosexuality. Sexual education of the 1920s and 1930s taught that sexual relations were a normal and necessary building block of married life. This "eroticisation" of the family[37] continued into the post-war period as sexual relations became the legitimate expression of marital love. The fact that this sexual liberation eroded ideological constraints on male sexuality, which had done much to protect female family members from unwanted sexual attentions, passed almost without notice. One reason may be that sex within marriage was applauded less as a source of pleasure than as a means to securing monogamy and so maintaining the stability of the family.[38]

The need to bolster the family came to be seen as particularly pressing in the face of powerful countervailing forces. The destructive impact of the Second World War, and the rise in divorce and illegitimacy in its aftermath, fostered fears of its erosion. It is in the light of this desire to restabilise the family in the immediate post-war era that the report of the Wolfenden Committee on Homosexual Offences and Prostitution (1957) should be read. Largely because of its progressive move to decriminalise homosexuality between consenting adults in private, the Wolfenden Report has been hailed as a enlightened liberal document.[39] Yet in respect of heterosexuality, its tone and purpose was more ambivalent. In Victorian England, maintaining the purity of the family home relied on the provision of sexual

---

[37] Shorter E., *The Making of the Modern Family* (1977).
[38] Smart, *op. cit.,* (1981) p. 48.
[39] Though one should recognise that the Sexual Offences Act 1967 went on to promote heterosexuality as the norm.

services outside but, by the 1950s, the prostitute's offer of sexual services free from obligations was seen as a threat to the proper expression of sexual love within marriage. Wolfenden's endorsement of the public/private divide sought, therefore, to reserve sexuality to the private sphere by criminalising the public activities of the prostitute.

The philosophy underlying Wolfenden was that the criminal law might properly be invoked in the public sphere where it was necessary "to preserve public order and decency, to protect the citizen against what is offensive and injurious, and to provide safeguards against corruption and exploitation".[40] By this logic, private immorality was not the proper subject of the criminal law. This conclusion relied upon a distinction made between law and morality. Enforcing moral standards was, according to Wolfenden, neither a defensible nor a practicable role for the law:

> "Unless a deliberate attempt is to be made by society, acting through the agency of law, to equate the sphere of crime with that of sin, there must remain a realm of private morality which is, in brief and crude terms, not the law's business."[41]

Accordingly, while it was deemed defensible to regulate prostitution and homosexuality to the extent that they offended against "public order and decency", sexual activities between consenting adults in private should not be subject to legal sanction.

Others argued against legal intervention on more pragmatic grounds, that "laws against private immorality are difficult to enforce and that their enforcement, therefore, tends to be haphazard and to result in inequality".[42] Yet, given the difficulties of access and proof which pervade many areas of criminal law, these practical objections cannot satisfactorily explain the resistance to legal intervention here.[43] Rather, they reflected a more generalised view that, although sexual immorality or abuse within the family was wrong and itself constituted an attack on the sanctity of the home, to invoke the criminal law to punish such action would constitute an invasion of privacy which ultimately might be more damaging. Moreover, law enforcement was deemed liable to inflict further costs; the trauma of involvement in the legal process, the imposition of stigma, the disruption of family life and, at worst, its possible break-up.

---

[40] Fitzgerald P., *Criminal Law and Punishment* (1962) p. 81.
[41] Wolfenden Report 1957, quoted in Lee S., *Law and Morals: Warnock, Gillick and Beyond* (1986) p. 26.
[42] Fitzgerald, *op. cit.*, p. 82.
[43] Atkins S. and Hoggett B., *Women and the Law* (1984) pp. 74–77.

Minimum legal intervention was thus justified on the grounds that a therapeutic approach was more appropriate, and arguably more effective, than a punitive one in responding to sexual abuses within the family. In the hey-day of 1960s welfarism, when such abuses were identified they tended to be diverted out of the criminal justice system into the welfare-orientated civil sphere. Evidence of the sexual abuse of a child was more likely to lead to care proceedings than prosecution. A woman alleging sexual assault by her husband was more likely to become the preserve of social workers than the police. The effect was to divert attention from the criminal character of such actions and to prevent their formal recognition as crimes. Coincidentally, it removed subjects like child sexual abuse or rape within marriage from the sphere of criminological knowledge. During this period research on these topics came to be located within the disciplines of social administration and sociology and not within criminal law or criminology. The therapeutic model condoned widespread intrusion into family life by welfare, psychiatric and medical agencies, with minimum regard to due process, and few limits to discretionary treatment, by promising a cure for crime.[44] Ironically, "rehabilitative optimism" justified intervention to a degree unthinkable on grounds of legal regulation alone.[45]

Challenging the Safety of the Family Home

In the 1970s, declining faith in the rehabilitative ideal, and scepticism about the efficacy of treatment, prompted increasingly strident calls for a return to justice. In the 1979 general election campaign, the Conservative manifesto promised a new emphasis on "law and order" and the promotion of criminal sanctions over "protection" and "treatment". The status of the family, and all that went on within it, underwent a similar series of transformations. Under the new Conservative Government and particularly under the leadership of Margaret Thatcher, the institution of the family became again a central tenet of political discourse. The Thatcherite rhetoric of "Victorian values" exalted the family as a "place of refuge" which should enjoy a privileged space free from

---

[44] Morris A., et al., Justice for Children (1980): Taylor L., In Whose Best Interest? (1980).
[45] Cavadino M. and Dignan J., The Penal System (1992) p. 49.

the interference of the "nanny state".[46] Paradoxically, just as a hundred years earlier, the high value placed upon the family as a "building block" of society exposed it to renewed scrutiny and rendered it once more a subject of intense political debate.

The demand for knowledge generated by this debate was of unprecedented urgency, penetrating the family home in a way that even Victorian social purity workers had not achieved. A curiously eclectic array of factors combined to furnish this knowledge. Right-wing concern about the health and stability of the family coincided with the determination of feminists to expose the damaging effects of sexual abuse on women and children. In 1983, *The Guardian* published a series of secret state papers of the Family Policy Group within the Cabinet which revealed the centrality of the family to all government policy.[47] At the same time, feminist organisations like the Rape Crisis centres set up in the 1970s and 1980s were committed to educating and informing the public about the effects of sexual assault. Their work contributed to a more general project of exploding myths about male and female sexuality, about the character of women who allege rape, and about the impact of rape on its victims.[48] By providing 24-hour helplines, counselling and support, Rape Crisis centres enabled many women, who would not otherwise have done so, to report their experience to the police and face the trauma of the courts.

Evidence as to the impact of sexual assaults was also generated by the growth of interest and concern for victims of crime more generally. Victim surveys carried out by Central Government, local authorities, and academic institutions revealed a "dark figure" of sexual offences which had never been reported to the police.[49] One landmark study, carried out in London in 1985,

[46] Margaret Thatcher speaking to the General Assembly of the Church of Scotland, May 21, 1988, quoted in Frost N., 'Official Intervention and Child Protection: the Relationship Between State and Family in Contemporary Britain', in Parton N., (ed.) *Taking Child Abuse Seriously* (1985). Though it should be recognised that this 'freedom' from interference was also a means of justifying doing very little for the family in social or welfare policy.

[47] Frost, *op. cit.*, p. 32.

[48] Temkin J., *Rape and the Legal Process* (1987): Anna T., 'Feminist Responses to Sexual Abuse', in Maguire M. and Pointing J., (eds.) *Victims of Crime: a New Deal?* (1988).

[49] Hough M. and Mayhew P., *The British Crime Survey: First Report* (1983); *Taking Account of Crime: Key Findings from the Second British Crime Survey* (1985): Jones T., *et al.*, *The Islington Crime Survey* (1986) amongst many others. Though it is likely that many sexual offences remained undisclosed even to these victim surveys.

reported that one in seven respondents who had been married claimed to have been raped by their husbands; even if one confined the definition to those instances involving the use of physical force, ten per cent. had been raped.[50] These figures were affirmed by a later survey of 1,007 married women which revealed that 14 per cent. claimed to have been raped by their husband at some time during their marriage.[51] Studies such as these played a significant part in reconstituting the public picture of sexual crimes, recognising their frequency within the marital home and revealing the extent of the physical and psychological trauma inflicted. This new knowledge, or rather these different, coinciding bodies of knowledge, did much to transform largely hidden activities into publicly recognised wrongs.

The effective criminalisation of sexual offences within the family was also furthered indirectly by changes brought about in the police response to victims of sexual assault. In 1982, a highly controversial television documentary about the Thames Valley police carried the eye of the camera into a police station where officers were investigating an alleged rape in a brutal and unbelieving manner. Television became the medium of reform in much the same way that journal articles of the nineteenth century popular press had prompted public outrage and demands for state action. As a direct consequence of the programme, all police forces were called upon to review their treatment of sexual assault victims.[52] Many forces introduced special interview suites in police stations and trained teams of women officers to respond more sensitively to claims of sexual assault. These changes led to somewhat higher levels of confidence in the police amongst sexual assault victims, and increased the willingness of women to report such offences to the police.[53] Without legal reform, the effective remit of the law was expanded into areas of what Stanko has termed 'hidden violence'.[54]

As a century before, the initiators of criminalisation were heterogeneous, ranging from right wing moralists, to feminist

---

[50] Hall R., *Ask Any Woman* (1985) pp. 88–89.
[51] In 44 per cent. of these cases violence was used, and of these rapes half the wives had been raped 6 or more times; Barton C. and Painter K., 'Rights and Wrongs of Marital Sex' (1991) New L.J. 394–395.
[52] Home Office Circular 25/1983.
[53] Shapland J., *et al.*, *Victims and the Criminal Justice System* (1985) p. 87: Temkin, *op. cit.*, Chap. 1.
[54] Stanko E., 'Hidden Violence Against Women', in Maguire and Pointing (1988), *op. cit.* Its efficacy remained inhibited, however, by the failure to extend this more sympathetic treatment of victim-witnesses into the courtroom.

activists, to voluntary bodies, to the media. Their respective projects were, at the same time, diverse in motive and aim, yet overlapping in substance and outcome. Demands that we should recognise the importance of political and legal pluralism would seem to be well founded here. As Rose has argued:

> " 'pluralism' entails genuine conflicts of interest, struggles for political ascendency and labile alliances. Familialised concerns have arisen in relation to different issues across these networks: inheritance of property or of pathology; vice and delinquency; health and efficiency; motherhood and femininity".[55]

We would look in vain, therefore, for a single unifying theme or purpose behind developments in the regulation of sexual offences within the home.

Two Areas of Sexual Abuse

The re-politicisation of the family in the 1980s and the bright light thrown on sexual offences, their incidence and impact, collided on two distinct areas of criminal activity; the sexual abuse of children and the immunity of husbands from rape within marriage. The "moral panic" over child sexual abuse which absorbed so much media and political attention in the latter years of the 1980s is instructive in our bid to understand how the "frontiers of criminality" are delimited. We are accustomed to recognising that the boundaries of criminality relating to fraud, to environmental offences, or public safety are determined as much by the politics of regulation as by changes in the criminal law. We are less ready to recognise the importance of enforcement policies in respect of "real crimes" (activities which entail culpable individuals perpetrating moral wrongs which inflict grave harms on identifiable victims). Yet, the response to child sexual abuse during the so-called "Cleveland Crisis" in 1987 is one, above all, of the vagaries of regulation. Sexual abuse or assault on children, whether carried out by a member of the household, other relatives, family friends or outsiders, is covered by a number of statutory offences.[56] Until the past decade, however, it only rarely came to light, mainly because, except in the most violent cases, it generally leaves little tangible evidence of its occurrence. Its

---

[55] Rose, *op. cit.*, p. 68.
[56] Rape, unlawful sexual intercourse, indecent assault or gross indecency and, of course, incest itself.

victims rarely have the means to instigate prosecution and too often become entangled in a familial conspiracy of silence. Bringing these crimes to light relies, therefore, on active intervention by an array of agencies, from family G.P.s, social workers, voluntary agencies or the police. Intervention is thus scattered across a range of professional bodies each with its own operational philosophy, its own definition of the problem it seeks to tackle and of the child's best interests. The tensions created by this dispersal of responsibility, of judgement and of aim combined in an explosive cocktail in Cleveland in the spring of 1987. Impelled by growing evidence that far greater numbers of children were being sexually abused than had been previously known, key professionals in Cleveland identified more than 100 cases of sexual abuse in 5 months (March to July) compared with only 2 in the whole of the previous year.[57] The children were taken immediately into local authority care following a series of dramatic dawn raids.

If the story stopped at this point we might conclude that here was an example of heavy-handed intrusion on the part of an all-powerful state intent on undermining the sanctity of the home. Instead, what emerged was evidence of an extraordinary fragmentation of authority. There was an absence of agreed diagnostic guidelines, disagreement over the implementation of place of safety orders and of criminal proceedings, and conflict among medical, welfare, and criminal justice agencies each seeking to stake out their territory against the intrusions of the others. Even within areas of expertise, disagreement raged; for example, medical opinion differed about the reliability of techniques for determining whether abuse had taken place (in particular in respect of the highly controversial reflex anal dilatation test). Paradoxically, the very politicians whose endorsement of family values had done so much to expose abuse to the public gaze now supported parents trying to secure the return of their children through a series of distressing court battles. The courtroom became an arena, in the full glare of national media attention, in which rival medical, welfare and legal expertise competed for ascendency.[58]

---

[57] DHSS (1988) *The Report of the Inquiry into Child Abuse in Cleveland 1987.*

[58] A few headlines from the period give some flavour of the kaleidoscopic lenses through which the Cleveland story was viewed: 'Does the law help the sexually abused child?', 'Flawed Protection', 'Put Children first", says Mackay', 'Confronting Disbelief', 'Crisis in care for our abused children'. It is perhaps significant that 'sexual abuse' is not a term of criminal law.

The Cleveland affair prompted a major inquiry by Lord Justice Butler-Sloss which, in turn, made sweeping recommendations for managerial and regulatory, but significantly not legal, change. It prompted, too, the proliferation of preventative initiatives, help-lines, and innovations in the workings of welfare and criminal justice agencies. Yet, pressures for a more proactive role by police and prosecutors clashed irreconcilably with equally insistent demands for the protection of the family from state interference.[59] Even those of us who demanded that "the criminal law should not stop at the door of the family home", were obliged to concede that criminal proceedings and penal sanctions are far from being an unproblematic solution to the sexual abuse of children.[60]

The recent history of rape within marriage offers yet another opportunity of illuminating the complex of issues involved in criminalising sexual offences within the home. In the 1970s, a series of cases had sought to test the limits of the marital rape immunity by exploring those circumstances in which the marriage could be said to be effectively at an end and the wife's consent revoked.[61] Curiously perhaps, these cases constituted a judicial attempt progressively to undermine that which had never had formal legal authority.[62] These attempts at judicial subversion were sharply checked by Parliament in the Sexual Offences (Amendment) Act 1976, which, by the insertion of the word "unlawful", was seen to reaffirm the statutory definition of rape as denoting non-consensual intercourse outside marriage only. This stretching and contracting of the definition of rape, in respect of the hallowed institution of marriage, reflects the ambivalence of the state about legal intervention in the family. It is suggestive also of a fracturing of authority and outlook between the judiciary and Parliament.

In 1984, marital rape was subject to particular scrutiny by the Criminal Law Revision Committee (CLRC) in its *Review of*

[59] Frost, *op. cit.*
[60] Morgan J. and Zedner L., *Child Victims: Crime, Impact and Criminal Justice* (1992) p. 115. See also Adler Z., 'Prosecuting Child Sexual Abuse: a Challenge to the Status Quo' (1988) in Maguire and Pointing, *op. cit.*
[61] R. v. O'Brien [1974] 3 All E.R. 663; R v. Steele (1976) 65 Cr.App.R. 22.
[62] The marital rape exemption derives from the writings of an seventeenth century jurist Sir Matthew Hale C.J. in *History of the Pleas of the Crown* (1736 reprint) which declared that the 'husband cannot be guilty of rape committed by himself upon his lawful wife, for by their mutual matrimonial consent and contract the wife hath given up herself in this kind unto her husband, which she cannot retract'. Over time, it acquired the patina and quality of a quasi judicial maxim.

Sexual Offences. Adopting the approach established by Wolfenden, the CLRC concluded that the intervention of the criminal law should be as limited as possible in family cases, on the grounds that to recognise sexual abuses would be to undermine the institution of marriage.[63] Accordingly, and to the disappointment of feminist observers, the majority of the CLRC recommended that the law relating to the marital rape exemption should remain unchanged.[64]

Struggle for its removal continued unabated, founded this time on a curious alliance between feminist organisations like Rape Crisis and WAR (Women against Rape) campaigning on ideological grounds and the Crown Prosecution Service seeking clarification of a particularly muddied area of law. In response to these increasing pressures, the Law Commission was requested in 1990 to undertake a major review of the legal approach to rape within marriage. By 1991, opposing camps were setting out the lines of battle in a series of cases whose judgments were wholly contradictory. The Crown Prosecution Service had sought to test the limits of the law by charging a series of cases of non-consensual sex within marriage as rape. In *R. v. J.*, Rougier J. at Middlesborough Crown Court held that the Sexual Offences (Amendment) Act 1976 was clearly intended to reaffirm and retain the marital rape exemption.[65] In *R. v. C.*, Brown J. at Sheffield Crown Court came to exactly the opposite view.[66] The final showdown came in the case of *R. v. R.*.[67] On appeal to the House of Lords, the interpretations variously ascribed to the word "unlawful" were examined and the conclusion reached that "no satisfactory meaning at all could be ascribed to the word". In taking this view of the wording of the 1976 Act, it was possible simply to declare the exemption an anachronistic and offensive fiction and to sweep it away entirely.

The propriety of such free judicial interpretation of a statute need not concern us here. What is of note is the diversity of stances taken even within the legal profession. Any attempt to see legal change as the product of a systematic state-driven programme quickly collapses in the face of this diversity. Moreover, whereas in the Cleveland story we observed power diffused

---

[63] Criminal Law Revision Committee (1984) *Fifteenth Report: Sexual Offences.*
[64] Wells C., 'Law Reform, Rape and Ideology', (1985) *Journal of Law and Society* 63–75.
[65] *R. v. J.* (Rape: Marital Exemption) [1991] 1 All E.R. 759.
[66] In *R. v. C.* (Rape: Marital Exemption) [1991] 1 All E.R. 755.
[67] *R. v. R.* [1991] 3 W.L.R. 767.

amongst a number of different, competing professional bodies here we find competing ideologies, conflict, and inconsistency within the law itself.[68]

Remnants of the Public/Private Divide

We should not assume that to make an activity criminal in law will automatically be to criminalise it effectively. Even where there is legal reform, or a change in policy, seeking to sanction sexual abuses within the family home, they remain highly impervious to effective legal regulation. Objections on political or ideological grounds are perhaps the most potent source of resistance. Commenting on the Law Commission's Working Paper on the marital rape exemption,[69] Glanville Williams condemned the recommendation that the exemption be abolished, arguing that to stretch the legal category of rape in this way would be to deny it meaning. His argument rested primarily on his perception of the differential quality of the act claiming that: "in my estimation it cannot be nearly so traumatic for the wife as a stranger-rape".[70] Denying that non-consensual sex within marriage could ever be comparable with the paradigmatic "stranger-rape", Williams concluded that: "the fearsome stigma of rape is too great a punishment for husbands".[71] He suggested also that to apply the label of rape to this "lesser" offence would tend to downgrade its seriousness in the public mind and so diminish its stigmatising capacity. Williams' views can be criticised on a number of grounds. First, that the perpetrators of rape are more often known to their victims than not and, in this respect, rape by a husband is not of a significantly different quality from other rapes. Secondly, the fact of a prior relationship does not mitigate, and may in fact exacerbate, the severity of the trauma caused, not least because rape in such circumstances constitutes a betrayal of trust. Finally, far from rape within marriage constituting a trivial misdemeanour "most probably resulting from the fact that the pair have had a tiff"[72] it is commonly a manifestation of a long-term abusive, often violent relationship.[73] Yet, the fact that

---

[68] Parallels may usefully be drawn with the excellent account of the failure of law reform in South Africa by Kaganas and Murray, op. cit.

[69] Law Commission (1990) Working Paper No. 116.

[70] Williams G., 'The Problem of Domestic Rape', (1991) New L.J. p. 206.

[71] ibid.

[72] ibid.

[73] Barton C. and Painter K., 'Rights and Wrongs of Marital Sex' (1991) New L.J. p. 394.

we can reject Glanville Williams assertion that rape within marriage is not comparable to "real" rape may do little to undermine the powerful resistance of those like him, to its effective criminalisation.

We have argued throughout that sexual offences are as much political and social constructions as legal categories. The fact that an activity falls within the frontiers of criminal law may not be sufficient to endow it with the status of crime in the public mind. As Allison Morris has argued: "most of us believe we know what rape is, but our knowledge is derived from social not legal definitions".[74] Unwanted sexual intercourse within established relationships, however painful and distressing, remains highly resistant to being conceived as, or acted upon, as a crime. Even where sexual offences are formally recognised by the law, effective criminalisation may be rendered impossible by the victim's lack of access, unwillingness, or inability to make use of legal processes. If we accept Smart's description of the law as "a bastion of male privilege and power",[75] it is perhaps hardly surprising that it has proved less accessible to groups such as women and children. Its institutions have not been designed for, and its processes are poorly adapted to, the needs of those whose usage was probably not contemplated. This exclusion from law has a circularity — the impoverished or vulnerable victim cannot, or will not, make themselves known to the legal process and so the very hindrances to their access remain unknown and unchallenged.[76] Only when others intervene on their behalf or enable them to speak out can this circularity be broken and the criminal law be rendered effective.

Finally, fear of crime remains one of the most obstinate barriers to reconstituting popular acceptance of the legal recognition of sexual offences. In the public mind, sexual offences, and in particular rape, still occur only outside the family home. Tabloid press and, paradoxically, government personal safety literature continually reinforce the message that for as long as women remain within the domestic sphere they have little to fear.

Fear of rape or sexual assault has always restricted women's movement at night and proscribed other forms of potentially hazardous behaviour.[77] Stanko has demonstrated how fear of

[74] Morris A., *Women, Crime and Criminal Justice* (1988) p. 165.
[75] Smart C. and Brophy J., 'Locating Law: a Discussion of the Place of Law in Feminist Politics', in Brophy J. and Smart C., (eds.) *Women-in-Law: Explorations in Law* (1985) p. 16.
[76] Genn H., 'Multiple Victimisation' (1988), in Maguire and Pointing, *op. cit.*
[77] Crawford A., *et al.*, *Second Islington Crime Survey* (1990): Young J., 'Risk of Crime and Fear of Crime' (1988) in Maguire and Pointing, *op. cit.*

sexual crime amongst women is constructed around notions of vulnerability in public, typically associated with being alone outside the home.[78] Historically, the discourse of personal safety has been mediated primarily through parental advice to young girls, education, gossip and peer group discussion. More recently, it has been promoted increasingly through more formal means. Home Office personal safety advice to women focuses solely on the dangers of the public sphere and enjoins them to limit their movements outside the home, to travel by private rather than public transport, to avoid situations of potential vulnerability and so on.[79] Seen one way, such advice is simply "good sense". Seen another, it serves to deny the risks of sexual abuse within the home.

The message sent out via this literature has been voiced even more explicitly in a number of highly publicised rape cases in which judges have castigated women complainants for wearing "seductive clothing", for frequenting bars alone, or for hitch-hiking at night.[80] All have been characterised as instances of contributory negligence in which the victim, by moving freely in public, in the words of one high court judge "is in the true sense asking for it".[81] Such views have been endorsed and perpetuated by the media whose reporting of rapes commonly throws doubt upon the claims of women whose experiences do not fit the prescribed pattern.[82] The paradigm of real rape remains located far from the safety of the family home. Real rape is that carried out by a stranger in a dark alley using threats or violence upon a sexually inexperienced victim who, in the struggle, suffered bruising or other signs of physical injury. The effect of such injunctions is to narrow dramatically the effective ambit of the law.

The fear which inhibits women's movement within the public sphere, and the social and judicial siting of rape in the dark alley, relies on positing the family home as a haven of security. At a time when those in government circles speak of the breakdown of family life as the cause of juvenile delinquency, drug abuse and a myriad of other social ills, preserving the unity of the family is applauded even at the cost of sacrificing the autonomy of women

[78] Stanko, *op. cit.*
[79] Home Office *Practical Ways to Crack Crime: the Handbook* (1989) p. 2.
[80] Temkin, *op. cit.*, p. 7.
[81] Sir Melford Stevenson, a retired High Court judge, quoted in Temkin, *op. cit.*, p. 7.
[82] Soothill K. and Walby S., *Sex Crime in the News* (1991).

and children within it. This said, the political impetus to shore up the family as a "building block" for modern society is in increasing conflict with the counterweighting pressure to ensure its true health by recognising and acting upon abuses within it.

Conclusion

We began with the premise that, historically, the state has constructed the private sphere as a space beyond the legitimate purview of the criminal law. In this chapter we have sought to show that this traditional liberal account is flawed in the following respects. First, that the state is not a monolithic, centralised entity, but rather takes many guises and operates through a multiplicity of projects often in conflict with one another. Secondly, that the very framing of the private sphere, far from inhibiting regulation, might be better understood as itself a form of regulation. At the heart of the private sphere, the family has been promoted as an agent of social and moral management endowed with substantial disciplinary powers. Where the family failed to accord with this ideal, it was quickly assailed by incursions, whether state or voluntary, religious or secular, social or legal. Evidence of sexual abuses within the home has repeatedly undermined faith in the family's self-regulatory capacity and opened it up to demands for more traditional policing through formal legal channels. Important, too, are changes in public discourse, in the priorities and working practices of voluntary and state agencies, in judicial interpretation, as well as legislative reform, which have at different times shifted the boundaries between the public and the private. Formal criminalisation is then but one amongst an array of means by which sexual offending within the family home has been categorised, policed, and sanctioned.

Chapter Nine

MODERNITY, KNOWLEDGE, AND THE CRIMINALISATION OF DRUG USAGE
by Wayne Morrison

"We live in and by the law. It makes us what we are: citizens and
employees and doctors and spouses and people who own things. It is
sword, shield, and menace: we insist on our wage, or refuse to pay
our rent, or are forced to forfeit penalties, or are closed up in jail, all
in the name of what our abstract and ethereal sovereign, the law, has
decreed .... We are subjects of law's empire, liegemen to its
methods and ideals, bound in spirit while we debate what we must
therefore do."

(Ronald Dworkin, *Law's Empire* p. vii).

For some time now the empire has been at war. We have been
called upon to wage a long campaign and enter into great battles.
As loyal vassals we have fought one enemy above all. From the
time it has been criminalised we have been spurred on against
one foe in particular — whatever the cost we cannot weaken, for
the continuation of civilization is at stake. This enemy has
penetrated into our deepest sanctums — drugs. But how was this
war engaged? And to what methods and ideals are we bound?
What goals are to be achieved? Who, or what, is the enemy?

Philosophy as the Spirit of the Empire

"Lawyers are always philosophers, because jurisprudence is part of
any lawyer's account of what the law is, even when the jurisprudence
is undistinguished and mechanical."

(Ronald Dworkin, *Law's Empire* p. 380).

Can we ask; "is the war a rational war? A creation of reason?"
Does obedience to our abstract and ethereal sovereign know any
limits? Can we demand that our sovereign limit herself by self-
discipline? Can we turn to philosophy to guide us, in case the
sovereign has been rash, mistaken, or ill advised? What does it
mean to ask for a philosophical account of this war? What are the
consequences if philosophy said this war should not be? What
would happen if the empress' decision was illegitimate? Could
this be so? Can this sovereign's commands ever be illegitimate?
And who would ask such a question? For while there is general

agreement that the war is a vital concern there is little agreement on philosophical understanding of the issue. Are not those writers who have dissented from the official position — "drugs are the enemy, and we must wage a full scale war to eradicate their usage" — not anarchistic, hippy-like, or downright dangerous?

What of those who urge dissent based on the pragmatic argument that the war on drugs simply cannot be won and that the harm caused by the anti-drug policies outweighs the likely harms of decriminalisation? Surely they argue a consequentalist position in a purely materialist frame of cost-benefit analysis rather than expressing any progressive (constructive) philosophical or sociological thesis? The empress cannot listen to mere consequentalist arguments. Is not the empire an empire of spirit? And of pride?

Spirit? Or Rhetoric?

What are drugs? The empress has identified good and evil drugs. The illegal are poisons that can produce deadly habits; not only is their use a crime *per se*, it also occasions other crimes and accidents. These drugs threaten the life and health of the individual user, and of those who come into contact with him/her, and of the general social fabric. Only recently the empress' lieutenant, Ronald Reagan, contingent overseer of the USA, the strongest territory of the empire, successfully depicted the drug problem in his 1980 campaign as a murderous epidemic, a threat of such a scale that it required even more resources for the war waged against it. At a time when our poor multiply, when we have to cut back on education services, more resources must be found to combat the menace. However, in these demands upon our services, are we summoned in the spirit of philosophy or rhetoric?

Before we begin our analysis, however, one major caveat; the war on drugs is a misnomer. It is a fallacy, a rigged mode of description which obscures the reality. The war on drugs is not a war on drugs — which are after all but chemical and herbal substances — but on those who use drugs and those who make money producing, transporting, buying and selling them. Articles that begin with the need to fight drugs end with demands to lock up the drug traders, and show no leniency to the drug taker. Hawkins, for example, begins her analysis of the problem with images of disaster:

> "In the absence of quick remedial action, epidemic levels of drug
> abuse and drug-related violent crime threaten to cripple our youth

and our nation. . . . The threat drugs present to the youth of America is particularly distressing."[1]

She then moves through some essentialist claims; "one of the most worrisome aspects of the drug culture is its inevitable association with the criminal world",[2] which lead, through examples of lenient sentencing of drug traffickers, to policy recommendations with both international and internal perspectives. Internationally:

"1. U.S. economic and military assistance to drug-producing countries must be linked to eradication of drug supplies.

2. Additional Drug Enforcement Administration (DEA) agents must be supplied to source countries. After drugs are harvested abroad and enter the trafficking network, interdiction and enforcement are more difficult. DEA help to source countries is an effective use of limited resources.

3. The Central Intelligence Agency (CIA) should be directed to upgrade the priority for gathering and analyzing intelligence data concerning illicit drugs.

4. The U.S should make high-level efforts to enlist our major European allies and Japan, and other nations, in the war on drugs.

5. The U.S. Agricultural Research Service should be directed to undertake special research projects aimed at controlling illicit narcotics crops."

On a national level, the criminal law should be amended to accomplish the following four goals:

"1. To increase substantially the fine levels for drug trafficking.
2. To increase significantly the penalties for trafficking in large amounts of the most dangerous drugs.
3. To increase the penalties for offences involving the most dangerous non-narcotic drugs, such as LSD, PCP, and the

[1] Hawkins P., 'Drugs and Crime: possibilities for reform' in McGuigan P. and Rader R., (eds.) *Criminal Justice Reform: A Blueprint* (1983) p. 57.
[2] *ibid.*, p. 60.

amphetamines, to bring such penalties into line with the penalties for offences involving narcotics, such as heroin and the opiates.

4. To eliminate inconsistencies between the Controlled Substances Act and the Controlled Substances Import and Export Act and permit state and foreign drug convictions to be considered under the enhanced federal sentencing provisions for repeat drug offenders."

Under American hegemony, this approach has been adopted throughout the empire; a mixture of supply side international moves and legal measures to hit at the trafficker. The results have been less than successful. By 1991, it was suggested that:

"The 74 years of federal prohibition since the passage of the Harrison Act of 1914 were not only a costly and abject failure, but a totally doomed effort as well . . . drug laws and drug enforcement have served mainly to create enormous profits for drug dealers and traffickers, overcrowded jails, police and other government corruption, a distorted foreign policy, predatory street crime carried out by users in search for funds necessary to purchase black market drugs, and urban areas harassed by street-level drug dealers and terrorised by violent drug gangs."[3]

The war has entailed massive government expenditure, mostly on supply reduction, and captured large amounts of illegal drugs. In the United States, 5.3 million kilograms of marijuana were seized between 1981 and 1987, while cocaine seizures increased from 2,000 kilograms in 1981 to 36,000 in 1987. Yet the United States Drug Enforcement Administration officials estimate these seizures amount to only 10 per cent. of the drugs entering the United States In the face of this massive programme aimed at elimination of the substance, the price of the major drugs has decreased and their purity increased. Worldwide production has increased dramatically and certain countries seem either unwilling or unable (or both) to take successful stands against drug traffickers. And while drug usage in the United States appears to have stabilised, the growth markets now are in Europe and Asia. Moreover, as others argue, the effects ranged beyond material considerations:

"the true extent of the war on drugs cannot be measured in quantities of dollars spent or numbers of defendants punished. The enforcement

[3] James I., *The Drug Legalization Debate* (1991) p.12.

of drug laws has diminished precious civil liberties, eroding gains for which Americans have made major sacrifices for over two centuries. Increasingly common are evictions, raids, random searches, confiscations of driver's licenses, withdrawals of federal benefits such as education subsidies, and summary forfeitures of property."[4]

Yet, does this not mean that the empire weakens itself in the course of this war? That the operation of one aspect of legality counteracts the forms and operations of others? What is the response of the empress' advisors?

The Debate?

Two separate kinds of responses have developed — a deontological one and a consequentalist one. The deontological builds upon certain philosophical positions while the consequentalist presents images of the empirical results of continued criminalisation or decriminalisation. Both sets of responses are divided on the issue of policy. The purported philosophical foundation for the deontological can either be (i) a moralist position which either defines the taking of (illegal) drugs as a moral evil which requires a prohibitive legal policy and the strict enforcement of the criminal law to prevent the lowering in intensity of its effect; or (ii) argues for a radical freedom for the individual to engage in whatever activity that individual desires. For this second approach, the goal of modern government is to allow individuals to follow their preferences so long as no great social harm results. Thus, most discussions of drug policy, cast in a philosophical frame, counterpoise doctrines of paternalism or political liberalism to policies of prohibition and control by means of the criminal law. To back up the moralist stance a range of absolute proscriptions are made; while those scholars who prefer the second course turn to arguments built on Mill's harm principle. Thus, Bakalar and Grinspoon begin their *Drug Control in a Free Society* with reference to the famous principles of John Stuart Mill's essay *On Liberty* (1859):

> "for all its flaws 'the clearest, most candid, most persuasive and most moving exposition of the point of view of those who desire an open and tolerant society' "
>
> [quoting Berlin, 1959].[5]

---

[4] Husah D., *Drugs and Rights* (1992) p.12.
[5] Bakalar J. and Grinspoon L., *Drug Control in a Free Society* (1984) p. 1.

Mill's basic principle (the harm or liberty principle) is that adults should be free to live their lives in whichever way they choose; coercive instruments, such as criminal laws, should only interfere to protect others, not for the individual's self-protection.

The weakness of this line of argument is that Mill viewed drug use as the free, rational act of an autonomous person. Conversely, we accept that drug use is often associated with ignorance, impulsiveness, addiction — empirical conditions which severely limit the user's freedom. To accept the second, libertarian, argument appears to ask us to accept a vision of human individuality which contradicts empirical reality.

The consequentalist responses build upon the understanding that a policy choice or even discursive categories do not exist in some neutral space but are intimately bound up with institutions, and are the product of socio-cultural history. Arguments for decriminalisation usually begin with the statement that the war against drugs is being lost and that the criminal prohibitive approach to the drug problem is ineffective and counterproductive.

Both the deontological and consequentalist approaches appeal to different sentiments and fall victim to different fears. The strength of the deontological approach is its appeal to particular views we hold as to what humans ought to be like, and how governments ought to relate to the population. The moralist appeals to our feelings (irrespective of how they are empirically aroused) that humans ought to do the good and avoid the bad; the libertarian appeals to our distrust of government and our desire for freedom. Both fall foul of our understanding that the world is a vastly more complicated place then their clean lines suggest; that there is a range of conditions impelling individuals into trading in and using drugs. While some profit, others suffer in conditions which mean that they deserve sympathy, not blame, and imply that the supposed freedom of individuals is often a fiction in which it is difficult to claim that individuals own their preferences. The strength of the consequentalist approach is that it appears to relate to the world as it is, rather than mystifying it in the name of a series of *oughts*. Its weakness is that it appears to mean we give up our humanity, our spirit as a society, in the face of the determining factors of social processes, and it implies that law, once spoken, should be overruled in favour of economics.

In what follows, elements of the different approaches will be brought together through developing a perspective based on the work of a figure usually thought of as the deontologist *par excellence* of modernity, Immanuel Kant.

Ideas for a Kantian Model of Social Development and Drug Usage

Kant would appear an unusual choice upon which to build a philosophical structure for dealing with our current drug problems. Within the narratives of criminal justice he is best remembered for adherence to the absolute necessity for punishment in response to crime. Yet there are two ways of reading Kant; first, a static model, and secondly, a dynamic model in which Kant's writings should be positioned within his own system of social development. Within, that is, an image of the growth of modernity — the development of the empire.

In this way we may also seek to make sense of what is often perceived as a profound contradiction in Kant. On the one hand Kant demands a critical approach in all things, but, on the other, he demands obedience to laws of state. Thus, Kant can begin the essay 'What is Enlightenment' with the rhetorical call that became a resolute call to critique for modernity:

> "Enlightenment is man's release from his self-incurred tutelage. Tutelage is man's inability to make use of his understanding without direction from another. Self-incurred is this tutelage when its cause lies not in lack of reason but in lack of resolution and courage to use it without direction from another. Supere Aude! "Have the courage to use your own reason!" — That is the motto of enlightenment.
> Laziness and cowardice are the reasons why so great a portion of mankind, after nature has long since discharged them from external direction, nevertheless remains under lifelong tutelage, and why it is so easy for others to set themselves up as their guardians."

Although this appears to imply that man should have no guardian other than his own reason, and in the case of drugs, that the individual should answer to his own rationality, the essay also reinforces the subject's absolute obligations to the sovereign, the legitimate ruler. Thus, Kant has been taken to mean that only moral freedom is important and to be actually conservative when analyzing social institutions or policies. Therefore, his critical philosophy, far from radically subjecting actual social policies to sustained critique and deconstruction, provides tools for formulating and defending existing social obligations. Hereafter following pages, this received wisdom shall be referred to as the static model of Kant.

The Static Model of Kant

This model sees Kant as constructing a demarcated structure of human nature, one in which human beings are eternally divided between their reason and brute desires. Man is halfway between the apes and the angels and Kant is viewed as simply saying it is a basic fact of existence that we will always be torn between these two aspects of our nature. In this model, a powerful state and strict law enforcement is crucial to check the people's brutish desires.

In understanding our reactions to the authority of the criminal law, Kant asks us to use the language of our experience as a guide. We are forced to recognise that there are many concepts which we appear to use in practical life that carry the implication of human freedom and autonomy. Specifically, when we look at a person's actions in the social world, in this world external to ourselves, a world of nature and society, we see links of cause and effect, and have difficulty finding the reflections of our highest aspirations, of our special human qualities. How can we accept ideas of human freedom and dignity? What are we doing when we refer to others and ourselves as individuals? Kant says to call a human being an individual is not to speak in some redundant metaphysical language, which denies scientific advance. Rather, there is a necessity in such use of language for if we abandon this *a priori* and see the "human-being-(non)individual" in the "reality" of an integration of system and impersonal causality, then what possibility is there of a speech-act that refers to, or is conforming to, or allows a demand for, treating human beings as "individuals"?

In many ways Kant can be viewed as responding to two central thinkers; the empiricism of David Hume and the social writings of Rousseau. Kant regarded Humean style empiricism as being correct in many aspects; thus, it was proper to think of a human being as a finite, contingent, complex mind-body, hemmed in on all sides, and interacting with other objective particulars of reality which obeyed the principle of causality. Nevertheless, for Kant this was in a sense an abstract view of the individual. When the actions and choices people make are regarded as events in the spacial-temporal world, then they must be subject to the laws of empirical necessity. When we begin, as independent observers, to explain people's actions, we may trace the commission of crime to factors such as heredity, education and environment. These are, however, so effective in our explanatory scheme as to have made it impossible for them not to have acted in this way, for we realise that the flip side of a law of nature is the obverse of physical necessity, which is the physical impossibility to do other — an inevitability of action. This realization demonstrates that our ascription of freedom to their actions results from a lack of information as to all the conditions, circumstances, factors and degrees of influence that prevent us from a total knowledge of their action — and hence from predicting exactly what they would do in the circumstances.

Kant notes, however, that even in the light of this potentiality, we persist in holding individuals responsible for their actions, and we join in the general social practice of attaching an appropriate blame or reward. In our usage of theoretical reason we adopt a stance which has developed into the various roles of criminologist, sociologist, psychologist and so forth; whilst in our role in civil society where we attribute praise and blame, we consider the situation in the light of 'practical reason'. It is in this light that we hold moral feelings, and legislate laws, which have as their presupposition that people need not breach them. In fact, we are saying that a person should not do certain things, and if they should not have done an action but actually did, then we are saying that it must have been possible for them not to have done it. Yet, we as psychologists, etc., have the potentiality to offer a complete explanation in such a way for there to simply be nothing visible to us that could have enabled the person to have refrained from the action. It is in this quandary that Kant introduces a strange concept peculiar to human action. He calls this "another causality", that of "freedom". A "transcendental object" which transcends experience and sensation-based systems of description. The criminologist who bases his approach upon the foundations of empiricism will never be able to consider the operation of this "causality". However, by the use of transcendental objects we may regard the offence in question (Kant uses an example of lying) as completely undermined in relation to the person's previous condition. It is "as if the offender started off a series of effects completely by himself". Kant goes on to say that when we are faced with a situation where our theoretical reason tells us empirical conditions have determined a person's actions we may still legitimately hold that person responsible and blame him. Thus, we are justified in holding a person responsible for their actions, even as we as (future) criminologists can also say that "before ever they have happened, they are one and all predetermined in the empirical character". Yet, how are we justified in this? Kant states:

> "this blame is founded on a law of reason by which we regard the
> reason as the cause which, independently of all the above mentioned
> empirical conditions, could and should have determined the man's
> actions in another way. We do not indeed regard the causality of
> reason as something that merely accompanies the action, but as

something complete in itself, even if the sensible motives do not favour but even oppose the action; the action is imputed to the man's intelligible character and he is wholly guilty now, in the very moment when he lies; therefore the reason was wholly free, notwithstanding all the empirical conditions of the act, and the deed has to be wholly imputed to this failure of reason."[6]

As well as the closed and determined grip that the empirical observer can hope to identify there is always "another causality" operative which can ensure a different action, and this "another" is of its nature not able to be located in any spacial-temporal causal series. The ability to partake of this other realm of causalities is, moreover, that aspect of man which makes him the fit subject for moral praise and condemnation which accompany participation in the linguistic and practical arrangements of our world. Furthermore, it is upon the supposition of the operation of man's "will" that practical, free and rational life is possible. This rational, free life comes from the interaction of the will with an *a priori* law essential to the operation of morality. Kant held:

"These categories of freedom — for we wish to call them this in contrast to the theoretical concepts which are categories of nature — have a manifest advantage over the latter. The latter categories are only forms of thought, which through universal concepts designate, in an indefinite manner, objects in general for every intuition possible to us. The categories of freedom, on the other hand, are elementary practical concepts which determine the free faculty of choice. Though no intuition exactly corresponding to this determination can be given to us, the free faculty of choice has as its foundation a pure practical law a priori, and this cannot be said for any of the concepts of the theoretical use of our cognitive faculty."[7]

These concepts, which Kant holds as the foundation of practical life, however, present a terrible morass, for they are "beyond the limits" of scientific reason. The result is ambiguous. On the one hand the Kantian philosophy of freedom provides a much needed defence against Humean style scepticism and materialism, of man's special dignity in the universe. On the other it provides a new understanding of the basis of man's dissatisfaction in early modernity, his inability to reconcile his innermost feelings of dignity and autonomy with the reality of the causal chains that determine our interactions with nature and each other.

[6] *Critique of Practical Reason*, A.555, quoted and commented upon in Acton H., *Kant's Moral Philosophy, New Studies in Ethics* (1970) pp. 45–46.
[7] Kant, I., *Critique of Practical Reason*, quoted in Lewis White Beck *A Commentary on Kant's Critique of Practical Reason* (1960) p. 139.

While one consequence of the *Critique of Pure Reason* is that no knowledge of the external world, or any interpretation of human behaviour, can question the freedom and inherent dignity of human beings, various practical and existentialist outcomes appear to follow. For example, man's incapacity to act in a free and human way should no longer be the obstacle to satisfaction in the world; instead satisfaction should be sought in the nomenal and not the phenomenal realm.

Kant construed man's humanity in terms of self-imposed, rather than naturally conditioned, ends and activities. For Kant, the setting up of civil society "was the transition from an uncultured, merely animal condition to the state of humanity, from bondage to instinct to rational control — in a word, from the tutelage of nature to the state of freedom".[8] In the natural state man cannot know freedom; human freedom is precisely the freedom from externally conditioned objects of desire, a state of being which Kant calls the movement from heteronomy to autonomy. The state of autonomy is one of goodness and virtue, independence and self-rule; little is left to say of the state of heteronomy except pleasure. The static model of Kant simply leaves man stranded with this demarcation.

The Dynamic Model of Kant

In two later works, Kant appears to reconcile nature and man's moral life. The subject matter of these essays, *Perpetual Peace*,[9] and *Religion Within the Limits of Reason Alone*,[10] concerns the historical struggles of humanity in the future, a future which transcends the concerns of the nation State and develops the process, already nascent in Kant's time, where the "peoples of the earth have entered in varying degrees into a universal commonwealth".

In *Religion Within the Limits of Reason Alone*, Kant depicts historical development as progress towards the goal of the highest good. Two processes are involved; a social process amongst individuals and states (external to the moral being of the individual), and a process of moral and intellectual development of individuals (internal). Progress at the first level is marked in politics and the development of the external legal system; at the

---

[8] Kant I., *On History* (1963) p. 60.
[9] Kant I., *Perpetual Peace* (1957).
[10] Kant I., *Religion Within the Limits of Reason Alone* (1960).

second, in ethics and internal governance. Two types of social condition appear over time:

> "A juridico-civil (political) condition is the relation of men to each other in which they all alike stand socially under public juridical laws (which are as a whole coercive law). An ethico-civil condition is that in which they are united under non-coercive laws, laws of virtue alone."[11]

The establishment of the juridico-civil condition represents a step forward in moral terms from a political state of nature since there now exist external assurances, in the form of coercive state instruments, that individual members will act lawfully. However, the coercive laws of civil society are, unlike the laws of virtue, based on the principle of strict reciprocity in our treatment of others, *i.e.* that an individual is prepared to grant to others no more than the freedom he/she enjoys. The laws of virtue would require a great deal more, for example, not only forbearance and tolerance, but also sympathy. For Kant "in an already existing political commonwealth all the political citizens, as such, are in an ethical state of nature."[12]

In the ethical state of nature no one accepts a public general authority which has the power to judge "what is each man's duty in every situation"; the individual remains his/her own untutored judge as far as matters of virtue are concerned as the political state does not tell him/her how he/she ought to behave, how he/she ought to interact with his/her fellow citizens, it simply tells him/her how he/she can and must act, how he/she can and must live. Yet an ethical community cannot be founded on coercive laws, such as those found in civil society, since the "very concept involves freedom from coercion". Kant is clear:

> "it would be a contradiction for the political commonwealth to compel its citizens to enter into an ethical commonwealth . . . but every political commonwealth may indeed wish to be possessed of a sovereignty, according to laws of virtue, over the spirits [of its citizens]; for then, when its methods of compulsion do not avail (for the human judge cannot penetrate into the depths of other men) their disposition to virtue would bring about what was required. But woe to the legislator who wishes to establish through force a polity directed to ethical ends! For in doing so he would not merely achieve the very opposite of an ethical polity but undermine the political state and make it insecure."[13]

---

[11] *ibid.*, at p. 87.
[12] *ibid.*
[13] *ibid.*

Historical process will give the resolution of the tension between subject and sovereign; it is not that the inner ethical dispositions are at odds with the operation of a strong sovereignty but that a strong sovereignty was a historical necessity to create a civil society which, over time, dissolved itself into the ethical community. For society to become free it must first exist.

Perpetual Peace was a critique of war. Kant believes three factors will lead mankind into a state of peace. First, the process of natural necessity. History teaches mankind the futility of war, peace, however is not a state of negation of war but a state which builds on past wars. The empirical foundation for peace is the history of war and the issues which were settled (or left unsettled) by force and violence, which have become the material of laws, treaties and constitutions (or understandings). Life teaches the necessity of peace but peace is not easy; it is a stern moral task. Secondly, the principles of moral philosophy. Politics becomes guided not so much by the question "is it feasible?" but "is it right?"; thus a deontological position complements the consequentalist teachings of nature. There are three fundamental criteria to the philosophical position. One is the categorical imperative which enjoins us always to act on the maxim of respect for human beings. In waging war the ruler does not respect this principle, but treats citizens as things to be used. The other is the criterion of publicity which policies must withstand. The third is the combining of these processes in achieving the moral political end. The process is not achievable in a sudden movement but as a gradual movement. Ultimately, the key to perpetual peace, is not the absence of tension, but the presence of justice.

What is the image of legal and personal development? Legal enactment and social control via prohibition is a crude device of society at a non-ethical stage. It is necessary only because knowledge and the ability of the individual to determine himself on laws of practical rationality based on his self knowledge are underdeveloped. Decisions taken in fear of sanctions are not moral but animal. To achieve a free and rational populace, a rational and progressive system of social control is required.

Kant's Image of Personal Development as Part of the Construction of the Rational Self in Modernity

These two later works point to a duality of processes later taken up in the sociology of Durkheim, Weber and Norbert Elias — all see modernity as involving the construction of a rational and self-directing self as the centre of activity. Civilized social life dialectically builds and requires the civilized self. The fully civilized self is not a simple or totally disciplined self (the creature of the Foucaultean nightmare) but a self who takes control and cares for itself and, in so doing, cares for the social body.

What is the role of this self in the construction of modernity? What do we mean here by modernity? The term modernity is a cultural construction used to make sense of the period of dramatic change and social development which has occurred in the West since the eighteenth century — as such it is a meta-historical term depicting an ideal type of a historical epoch. Modernity refers to the period of social life in the West following the enlightenment characterised by various transformations located around the ideas of progress, freedom and the creation of social relations and institutions which will embody the human spirit. The drive of modernity is sustained by the understanding that two processes of construction and potential happiness are at play. First, a social project; it is possible to construct grand societies of cooperation and technological power which create material abundance. Secondly, a personal project; individual human beings will attain happiness within the properly organised whole. Moreover, this will be achieved by allowing individuals to become responsible for their own activities and choices; the free and authentic individual is to be the basic block of modernity. Yet, her social space will be bounded by the rules of the social body — modernity will be the empire of law.

Central to the development of modernity is a knowledge project. The rational organisation of the social is to take place via sound social policy, policy based on secure knowledge rather than the opinions of politics or assumptions derived from metaphysics. Such knowledge enables a state of continual controlled change and development to be sustained, within which individuals overcome coercion and attain a peaceful social life with a high degree of self-control. The developing self-control of individuals is positioned within the rational planning of social relations. Thus, social control and self-control are in a dependent relation.

The Lawyer, Modernity and the Creation of the Empire

Law's empire has not always existed. Before we served this empress there were other sovereigns. Our historians tell us that once, when we spoke Greek (before that a mixture of African and Asian dialects) and confined ourselves to city states, we tried to raise law equal to politics and factionalisation. Outside the walls waited the barbarians; inside the sophists urging us into relativism and reflexive paradoxes. And law lay divided. Antigone recognised both the commands of Creon and the commands of nature. Law offered not the freedom of rights — but double obligation.

Then came God. God seized upon law as if it were her divine will, and man trembled. Whatever the commands of man, it was but a contingency, but a locality — underneath lay the universality of God's dominion. The empress stood and watched over the kingdoms of man. But God died, slowly perishing as the weight of the world, the sight of all that complexity, all that misery became too much for God alone to bear.

Attending upon God's demise stood the jurisprudent. For a while, the foremost of the social scientists, those who took upon themselves the task of reading the will of God as her strength faded and her thoughts became uttered in too low a tone for many to hear. And so it came to pass that the jurisprudent, and in time the lawyer, was to claim the role of the builder of modernity. If social constructionism was to be the task then law was to be the medium. In the Anglo-American territories, the foremost of these truly moderns were Jeremy Bentham and John Austin.

What united Bentham and Austin was their realisation that in dying God had imparted her will into the functionality of the world — knowable in the principle of utility. Here was the formula for constructing modernity. Thus we could give law up to an all-too-human sovereign as a tool, an instrument, but one which the sovereign must use under the guidance of utility. There could be no legal constraints upon the will of the sovereign; the sovereign was to command that which utility demanded; and these commands of the sovereign were to be enforced by sanctions.

Lately, we are told, the sovereign changed. The hierarchical synthesis of Austin weakened. Law took on its own vitality and became a self-regulating system. This autopoietic system was comprised of norms said Hans Kelsen, of primary and secondary rules said H. L. A. Hart, and in time constructed itself into a community of principle claimed Dworkin. Law's empire was constituted.

The Sociologist Arrives

In modernity, the jurisprudent did not control advice. His claims to the central role became usurped. The economist, the sociologist, the social theorist, all claimed rights of audience. Yet, all reinforced the self-understanding — modernity was to be a structure of knowledge and law in right reason; rational administration.

The most confident was the young Marx who loved law above all. Law was to be the people's bible book of freedom. The law was to capture the spirit of social development in its inevitable quest for perfection. Yet law disappointed Marx. It gave itself up to irreason; became abused in the name of class, and a servant of economic determinations. Capitalist modernity would not see fully rational law, the only hope was to abandon modernity and live for the post-modernity of communism.

Weber wavered. Modern law was to be the instrument of the rationalisation of the world — but once rationalised the structure of law and administration would imprison man as if in an iron cage. For if God's will was silent, law could be free from substantive underpinnings — discarding the clothing of "metaphysical dignity" it was free to be formally rational, an instrument of pure domination.

For Durkheim, modernity is distinguished from the pre-modern or traditional primarily in terms of the relative division of labour and the type of social solidarity which ensued. Whereas mechanical solidarity emphasizes the homogeneity of the group, organic solidarity builds upon difference and the capacity of the individual to tolerate diversity and become self-controlling (to create an individual conscience). The fluidity, and yet strength, of organic solidarity derives from the very conditions which destroy the possibility of mechanical solidarity, namely the advanced division of labour and social heterogeneity. Modernity witnesses a process of individualisation, again an interdependency of process is apparent — modern individuals, individuals who are a self and not a status, are not natural but are created in social processes. The dilemma is how to seize these processes creating a moral individualism rather than atomistic individualism. It fell to law to clothe the individual in rights and networks, to open up paths and communication methodologies.

Returning Kant to the Drug Issue

Applying Kant's critique of war makes for interesting results. The argument from nature suggests it is increasingly obvious that the war on drugs cannot be won and the financial and social costs are immense. Moreover, "attempts to enforce the unenforceable weakens respect for the law".[14]

---

[14] Richard Stevenson, quoted in *Police Review*, September 7, 1990.

The argument from moral philosophy stresses the contingent nature of the enemy. Many of the writings of criminology make clear that the figures of the drug barons make symbolic targets for governments and serve as enemies for the country to unite against. Defining the enemy, however, is not a rational process but one strongly influenced by economic interests and power groupings. This links with a second limb; the openness to publicity, or substantive, rational reflexivity in the policy. It is often claimed that the laws against drugs are a coherent and fully rational structure. The body of writings on the subject raise two sets of objections to this assumption. The first concerns the creation of the law and the distinction between lawful and illegal drugs. The second concerns the estimation of harm and the correlation between harm and illegality.

Contrary to official policy, the laws against drugs do not appear to be clearly founded in either pharmacology or any object measure of harmfulness. As David Musto summarised it: "The history of drug laws in the United States shows that the degree to which a drug has been outlawed or curbed has no direct relation to its inherent danger."[15] The researchers are scathing. Weil and Rosen note that tobacco is described, for most people and in most circumstances, as a more pharmacologically dangerous drug than heroin.[16] In the World Health Organisation figures, the threefold increase in lung cancer in western countries between 1955 and 1980 directly correlates to the tripling of tobacco consumption between 1930 and 1955.[17]

Heroin is clearly associated with death, overdose, and the violence of the illegal trade. Yet the violence of heroin is not primarily pharmacological; overdose is either an accident or a kind of suicide. In pure form, the major harmful effect on the body is constipation; it does not break down human tissue. Thus, it differs from tobacco, alcohol, amphetamines, cocaine and many other drugs which cause tissue breakdown.[18] The major risks to health stem from intravenous injection, the sedative effect of the drug and, quite separately, the often desperate lifestyle of the black market trade. The violence empirically correlated with heroin is a product of the social context and networks of supply and usage.

[15] Musto D., *The American Disease: Origins of Narcotic Control* (1987) p. 260.
[16] Weil A. and Rosen W., *Chocolate to Morphine: understanding Mind Active Drugs* (1983): Brecher E. and the Editors of Consumer Reports *Licit and Illicit Drugs* (1972).
[17] Lee P., (ed.) *Tobacco Consumption in Various Countries* (1975): World Health Organization, *(1950–1986)* Annual Reports.
[18] See Weil and Rosen, (1983), *op. cit.*

Other researchers point to the confused semiotics of criminalisation. The legitimate promotion of alcohol and tobacco
signifies to the public that they are not as dangerous as illegal
drugs. But if the criteria for criminalisation of drugs was public
health, then reason suggests a concerted campaign using the
criminal law to fight tobacco use. Others point out that the drugs
presently legalised were once prohibited; in the 1650s the use of
tobacco was prohibited in Bavaria, Saxony and Zurich, and at
about the same time, in Russia, tobacco users were tortured and
executed.[19]

Estimates of consumption claim that cannabis is smoked by an
estimated 50 million North Americans, and tobacco by almost
100 million; in the United Kingdom in 1989, 1.8 million people
are thought to have used cannabis.[20] We can contrast the fact
there are no deaths that are directly attributable to marijuana, as
cannabis is also known, consumption (although it, too, may cause
lung disease), whereas hundreds of thousands of deaths annually
are directly attributed to tobacco.[21] Using the logic of prohibition
in terms of risk to health, the most widely used dangerous drugs
would be alcohol and tobacco.[22] Abuse of alcohol is associated
with violence and violent death, automobile fatalities, deaths at
work, and suicide. Statistics throughout the western world indicate that many of the fatally injured drivers had blood alcohol
levels of well over the legal limit. However, we have a cultural
heritage of managing the consumption of alcohol. We define
"problem drinkers" who create an obvious social harm. In similar
form we have a cultural understanding of tobacco usage which
has become aware, only relatively recently, of the vast health
implications of sustained use. Moreover, tobacco causes relatively strong and quick addiction and escalates consumption to
somewhere between 20 and 60 cigarettes per day. Controlled
tobacco use — one or two cigarettes per day — may involve a
relatively minimal risk to health, but only a small minority of
users can exercise this sort of restraint.

Most people who use marijuana do not become drug dependent, and the drug has less toxic effect than sustained under the
abuse levels for tobacco or alcohol.[23] Normal use is relatively low.

---

[19] Szasz T., *Ceremonial Chemistry* (1974) p. 173.
[20] Health and Welfare in Canada *Licit and Illicit Drugs in Canada* (1989):
National Drugs Intelligence Unit (Scotland Yard) quoted in *Police Review*,
September 7, 1990.
[21] Lee, (1975), *op. cit.*
[22] See Weil and Rosen, (1983), *op. cit.*
[23] Brecher, *et al.*, *op. cit.*, Weil and Rosen, *op. cit.*

The "average" marijuana smoker in North America is said to smoke less than five joints per week and consumption is not correlated with violence or other anti-social behaviours. Thus, criminological writing claims the rhetorical images of illegal drugs are quite different from their pharmalogical representations. We understand now that much of the "scientific evidence" used against many of the illegal drugs were falsehoods or distortions. Marijuana was once thought to be as addictive as heroin, as well as a stepping stone to other drugs. Its image has also been associated with political dissent. Marijuana was, in some senses, the drug of the liberal Left, associated with the campaign against the Vietnam war, and other movements for progressive social change. Alcohol, in contrast, is tied to the more conservative and Christian tradition of western culture.

This is not to deny that all forms of drug abuse, legal and illegal, constitute significant health and social problems. From a self-developmental perspective part of their problem has nothing to do with the issues presented in the past. Instead a danger lies in the degree to which they function as a buffer against the self-realising coherent courses of action. Drug use can be engaged in to avoid dealing with personal difficulties and, over time, this avoidance can make the problem worse. Consequences follow for employment, domestic relationships, family stability and sexual relationships. Intense drug usage over time refocuses the site of personal energy, leading to a deterioration of social webs resulting in personal, familial and occupational neglect.

This perhaps is a reason for the strong correlation between illegal drug usage and underclass membership. For those excluded from participation in traditional and socially rewarded methods of getting high (normally associated with the financial power of consumption) and the achievement of status, drugs offer another route. This correlation provides an easy target for the mobilisation of biases against certain drugs and those who use them. As Newbold classifies the limits of criminalisation:

> "In the case of tobacco, alcohol, and prescribed psychoactives . . . it is their marriage to commerce and respectability that ensures their continued survival. Conversely, the association of illegal drugs with activities and incomes of the less privileged cements their unshakeable stigma. The crux of the matter is not really use or misuse, but power, profit, and conformity. The control of drug use has a clear public health function, but it is one which is overridden by prejudice and dogma."[24]

---

[24] Newbold G., *Crime and Deviance* (1992) p. 132.

The predominance of problematic drug use (defined as abuse of both legal and illegal drugs) with the underclass, the marginalised, causes a practical problem for strategies such as legalisation but resolves a long-standing theoretical one. The practical problem is that while legalisation of drugs would reduce the harmful consequences of the illicit nature of the current trade, without social justice it may condemn vast numbers to dependency upon drugs. While it would decrease many of the problems we now see in the inner cities — the violence of competition for turf and distribution, uncontrolled dosages of drugs, organised crime involvement, the necessity to commit crime to finance drug deals — without strategies to tackle other problems of marginalisation, poverty, and underemployment and frustration, legal drug use may develop into a tactic to pacify the unwanted. The theoretical problem lies in Durkheim's thesis of penal evolution in modernity. It has become usual to claim that Durkheim's law of penal evolution, from repressive law in mechanical solidarity to restitutive law in conditions of organic solidarity, has been empirically disproved: the war on drugs with the severe repressive measures it entails can be seen as convincing counterfactual evidence. However, a neglected feature has been the extent to which Durkheim's formulation depended upon the reality of interdependency. The reality of underclass, marginality, and foreign involvement — groups not tied into systematic interdependency — therefore fits Durkheim's analysis of law in modernity. Conditions of organic solidarity are not something which simply exist in modernity — they have to be achieved.

However, we should not neglect the degree to which drug taking is a furtherance of factors encouraged by modernity and not counter to it. The value structure of modernity is not only the easily identified values in line with what Weber called the protestant ethic but "subterranean values that coexist with other, publically proclaimed, values possessing a more respectable air".[25] These include the search for adventure, excitement, and thrills and exist alongside the conformity-producing values of security, routinisation, and stability.

Moreover, the drug issue provides a unique site for central themes of modernity to intersect — specifically control. Drugs are feared socially, in that they appear to strip subjects of control, and render void crucial aspects of social structure (for example, the image of the crack mother who allows her child to

[25] Sykes G. and Matza D., 'Juvenile Delinquency and Subterranean Values' *American Sociological Review* (1961) pp. 712–719.

be sexually abused by her pusher), they are a social phenomenon beyond the control of the authorities (indeed organised crime may challenge the State's monopoly on violence and revenue raising) and a challenge to certain state and inter-state bureaucracies which claim the scope of control, (*i.e.* the criminal justice system, police and international police and military co-operation). As Bakalar and Grinspoon put it:

> "Users of disapproved drugs become dope fiends because they are possessed by demons the rest of us have cast out. Drugs become a source of fantasies and fears about excessive control (the chemical robot) and loss of control (the wandering intoxicated mind). Unfamiliar drugs in a given culture come to represent the threat of insidious, unknown evil."[26]

For Bentham, in the principle of hedonistic psychology which provides the foundation for deterrence strategies, individuals balance pleasure and pain and opt for the course of action which minimises pain and results in the maximisation of pleasure. But cocaine users, especially crack cocaine addicts, adopt an irrational, anti-utilitarian course of action. They experience a short high followed by a prolonged period of depression. The high acts as a strong motivation to repeat the experience even though the user knows that the depression eventually outweighs its effects. Yet, euphoria is spell-binding. The experiencing of power is an existential phenomenon that the powerless are denied constitutionally so that its attainment, albeit short-lived and false, is valued over the longer term depression. Drugs achieve a "qualitative breakthrough" in the existentialist paradigm.

This suggests, if we are to sustain the rationality of law's empire, that we need to view illegal drugs in a more positive light; to learn about them and learn how to live with them; to search for techniques and methodologies for developing a reasonable relationship with the variety of psychoactive substances over time. In short, to abandon the policy of criminalisation.

Understanding the Continued Criminalisation of Drug Usage: The Autopoiesis of the Criminal Law

According to the previous analysis, the present laws on drug usage are substantively irrational. Criminology has deconstructed

---

[26] Bakalar and Grinspoon, *op. cit.*, pp. 69–70.

any claim for these laws on the basis of rational creation or effective regulation. Instead of the linkage between rationality and knowledge, sociologists have pointed to a variety of causal agents, including moral entrepreneur, racism, rural urban conflict, symbolic reassurance, the role of the Treasury Department and the Bureau of Narcotics.[27] There is very little, if any, rational foundation for their continued existence — their effects are counter productive to the sustained growth of legality and the resource implications in expenditure, wasted on enforcement and lost revenue, are immense. How then do they survive? How has the empress not realised the irrationality of her commands?

A tempting starting point for explanation is that the laws were never meant to work. This is the route taken by followers of Foucault. Just as the fact that the prison has failed in its official aims has not prevented expansion of the gaol programme, so the failure of the drug laws has not affected their existence. For Christina Johns:

"the primary intent of the War on Drugs is not to stop drug trafficking or drug use. The War on Drugs is a tool in a larger war that is about increased authority and social control. . . . [It] . . . has been used as a mechanism for vast expansions of state power and state control. This can be seen domestically in moves to allow warrantless searches, the introduction of illegally seized evidence, asset seizures, random drug testing, the militarization of housing projects, and the incarceration of pregnant women for drug use, among other measures. Internationally, it can be seen in the disdain for international law, increased use of the military in the drug war, assassinations, kidnapping and invasions. . . . [S]uch an effective tool for the expansion of state power . . . is too useful to be given up. . . ."[28]

Johns brings out the paradox in the logic behind continued prison construction and the continuation of the War on Drugs:

[27] A selection. Becker H., *Outsiders: Studies in the Sociology of Deviance* (1963) identifies the crucial part played by the Federal Bureau of Narcotics' search for a new role to play. Musto D., *The American Disease: Origins of Narcotic Control* (1973) points to Southerners' and Westerners' hostility toward blacks and Chinese and the role of the State Department. Duster T., *The Legislation of Morality: Law, Drugs and Moral Judgement* (1970) considers the important role of medical practitioners. Reasons C., 'The Politics of Drugs: An Inquiry in the Sociology of Social Problems' (1974) *Sociology Quarterly* 381–404, considers the role of the Treasury department. Bonnie R. and Whitebread C., *The Marijuana Conviction* (1974) point to prejudice against Mexican-Americans in the federal Bureau of Narcotics.
[28] Johns C., *Power, Ideology and the War on Drugs* (1992) p. 174.

"Prisons have been a failure, so more prisons will be a success; punishment has been a failure so more punishment will be a success; criminalisation and enforcement have been a failure, so more criminalisation and enforcement will be a success."[29]

Yet, the paradox does not bite. Put another way; deligitimation does not follow from the deconstruction. Why? The most obvious answer is the neo-Weberian response of the understanding of law as an autopoietic system. While the drug laws are substantively irrational of course, they are formally rational. Moreover, once in place they create their own self-referring legitimation. Here we face the paradox of illegitimacy-legitimacy. Given that modernity demands that all institutions pass the critique of rationality, the institution of the criminal law on drugs fails; but, once in place it serves as the grounding for its own legitimacy. As a cognitive and decision-making system, the environment in which it must operate does not cause a problem. The activities of production, transportation, supply and consumption can be fitted into the categories of the criminal law without disconcertment or discordance. The failure of the "grand justifications', those of social protection, purposeful rationality, or efficiency, do not touch any of the cognitive or professional concerns of the practice of law *understood* as law. They may impact only on law understood as effectivity, as spread, as purpose, as "the enterprise of subjecting human behaviour to the governance of rules" (Lon Fuller).[30] Internally, this does not matter, since the criminal law is an "endless dance of internal correlations in a closed network of interacting elements, the structure of which is continually being modified . . . by numerous interwoven domains and meta-domains of structural coupling".[31]

Autopoiesis changes our awareness of law as a social system. Instead of the traditional law and society idea of law as an open system responsive to its environment, autopoietic systems are closed to their environments. The empire cannot be attacked from outside. We do not need to overplay this understanding, or see this as a pessimistic conception, as a notion of law which takes it beyond human control. The criminal law is obviously an autopoietic system in terms of its internal development; moveover, its conceptions of truth are defended against its

---

[29] *ibid.*, p. 173.
[30] Fuller L., *The Morality of Law* (1969).
[31] Maturana H., quoted in Teubner G., *Law as an Autopoietic System* (1993) p. 11.

environment. We understand also that it is not an infinitely flexible system of regulation — the interaction between it as a system and its environment is obviously more complex than some open systems models led us to believe. The labelling of events, of individuals, of activities, assumes the imagery of normativisation of social life. Oughts are inscribed into social practice. The law reaches into the structure of a contemporary set of social values and transfigures — that which was legal becomes illegal, that which was normal becomes deviant, that which was deviant becomes normal. Having made the claim of ascription, any dispute must be settled by reference to the law's internal mechanisms. The decision becomes subjected to the criteria of legality, not social values.

Yet for how long can the internal operation of the system (controlled by autopoietic cleansing) ignore the external (un)operationality of the system? Empirically, this can only be a matter of observation and dependent upon the circumstance. But since law is a practical-communicative enterprise, a point can be expected to be reached where cyclic sustainability contributing to legitimacy can be expected to be compromised. This occurred with prohibition; but clearly the current illegal drugs pose a different situation (alcohol being a Christian, all-class drug) with the heavy underclass involvement in trafficking and consumption.

The systems approach alerts us to one thing. The social body is not one system but many. To what system ought the drug problem to be assigned? Why should it be classified as a legal problem? Can it not equally be seen as a social problem? Or a medical problem? Or an educative problem? We have many resources, many systems, many modes of thinking, communicating and expressing our hopes and fears. Why condemn the issue of drugs and their human interactions to the discourse of a strongly repetitive system?

Accepting this framework destroys the grip of the empress. We are not the subjects of law's empire, for law's empire only works in contingent social circumstances. It is not the law which determines the criminality of drugs and drug taking. The ability of the law to function as a hypercyclically closed system should not blind us. Let us control the autopoiesis of law. Reclothe the empress — and let the empire be for the people. Let us step out of the false necessity of this war, rethink the problem of drugs and become . . . "modern".

Chapter Ten

SQUATTING AND THE RECRIMINALISATION OF TRESPASS
by Peter Vincent-Jones

Squatting may be defined as the unlawful occupation of land or buildings for residential purposes, in violation of a greater proprietary interest enjoyed by the State or some other party, and involving the civil wrong of trespass to land.[1] Other forms of trespass with different objectives have been the subject of public debate and government action this century: mass trespasses on mountains and moorland in the 1930s; factory occupations, work-ins and sit-ins in the 1970s; demonstrations and protests in or around public land or buildings in the 1970s and 1980s; and most recently convoys of travellers encroaching on private property in the weeks leading up to the Summer solstice.[2] It is squatting, however, that has been the most persistent focus of government concern. The recent review[2a] of the law is the second (excluding the consultation following the Fagan trespass in Buckingham Palace in 1982) in 20 years, the Law Commission investigation of squatting on residential property begun in 1974 having led to the partial criminalisation of trespass in Part II of the Criminal Law Act 1977.

This chapter focuses on the civil — criminal distinction in respect of squatting trespass: how it emerged historically, how and why it was redefined in the 1970s, and why it became the subject of further attention in 1991. It will be suggested, first, that the law of trespass played a central role in the historical development of capitalism; secondly, that the institution of private property (and the maintenance of exclusive control) depends fundamentally on the ideology and practice of exclusive right; thirdly, that the threat to exclusive right and hence to

---

[1] Whilst strictly within this definition, gypsy trespass is a complex issue, and will not be further considered here. See Holgate G., "The Government's Consultation Paper 'Reform of the Caravan Sites Act 1968': a Solution to Gypsy Site Provision?" (1993) *Conveyancer and Property Lawyer* 39–52 and 111–118: Thomas P., 'Housing Gypsies' (1992) New L.J. 1714–1715.

[2] See Vincent-Jones P., 'The Hippy Convoy and Criminal Trespass' (1986) *Journal of Law and Society* 343–370.

[2a] Home Office (1991) *Squatting: A Home Office Consultation Paper.*

capitalist relations of possession and separation, posed by different kinds of trespass in the 1970s, was resolved at least in part through the partial criminalisation of squatting in the 1977 Act; fourthly, that although proposals for further extension of the criminal law in 1991 lacked coherence, they may nevertheless be understood in the light of the present Government's very different agenda aimed at sustaining the ideology and practice of the market. Finally, it will be argued that no case was made out for further extension of the criminal law in respect of squatting trespass, and that the "squatting problem" can only properly be understood in the broader context of the housing crisis, homelessness, and the general failure of housing policy since the Second World War.

Historical Preconditions of Squatting

Squatting is a social and historical product, presupposing both the development of private property, together with legal forms of action guaranteeing it, and the scarcity of land or buildings relative to demand for them. These conditions were gradually accomplished in the Medieval period, in the transition from feudalism to capitalism, and through the development of the law of trespass.

Rights and Wrongs: the Emergence of Trespass as a Civil Wrong

The law of trespass has a complex history,[3] combining the distinct elements of complaint of wrong (later the law of tort) and the claim of right (law of property). The tortious origins lay in the development of the writ of Trespass in the King's courts during the reign of Henry III. The pre-requisite for the issue of the writ was that a wrong should have been done to the plaintiff, to his body, goods, or land, by force and arms and against the King's peace. Trespass *quare clausum fregit*, alleging *vi et armis* and *contra pacem regis*, would provide a remedy for wrongs to land such as the cutting of timber, the mowing and carrying off of crops, and the trampling of grass, and thus functioned, indirectly, to protect possession. At this historical point there was no clear

---

[3] Holdsworth W., *A History of English Law* (1966): Pollock F. and Maitland F., *History of English Law* (1968): Milsom S., *Historical Foundations of the Common Law* (1969).

distinction between private and public wrongs, the dispute between subjects being a matter of direct concern to the Crown only because of the threat to public order. The corresponding absence of a civil — criminal distinction is evident in that the award of compensation to a successful plaintiff might be accompanied by punishment of the wrongdoer in the form of imprisonment, fine, or outlawry. However, as the Medieval common law gradually began to differentiate civil and criminal aspects of trespass, the former came to dominate the latter. The criminal law developed separate categories of treason, felony and misdemeanour, indictable by the Crown, and took on the function of maintaining public order, through the laws of forcible entry and detainer, requiring that any entry onto land be exercised peaceably without riot or unlawful assembly. As the strict rules requiring force and arms and breach of the peace in trespass actions were relaxed, and punitive sanctions diminished in extent and importance, trespass gradually became a matter of private dispute litigated by the plaintiff seeking redress of a civil wrong.[4]

Just as important as the complaint of wrong in the development of trespass was the demand for the enforcement of proprietary right.[5] From late in the reign of Edward I, in the form of the writ *de ejectione firmae*, trespass could be used by the lessee for a term of years displaced from land, in order to recover damages from the ejector, and ultimately, by the end of the fifteenth century, to recover the land specifically.[6] The scope of the action became enlarged to benefit the freeholder, and later the copyholder, in what became the action of ejectment; by 1601, Coke could pronounce that all titles for land were, for the greatest part, tried by these means. Here, the form of action has evolved in a manner so peculiar that the relationship to trespass *vi et armis* has become virtually obscured. The basis of the action remained the wrongful application of physical force to the plaintiff's land, goods or person, distinguishing it from actions "on the special case" in which the injury was indirect or consequential and no force was used,[7] but the degree of force required was becoming so slight that the merest step on land or wrongful touch would suffice to ground a successful claim.

Today the law may be categorised in terms of a division between pure Trespass *quare clausum fregit* and its historical

---

[4] Milsom, *op. cit.,* p. 256.
[5] *ibid.,* pp. 211–213.
[6] *ibid.,* pp. 127–133: Holdsworth, *op. cit.,* pp. 213–216.
[7] Milsom, *op. cit.,* p. 248. The origins of "the special case" provoked Maitland's famous aphorism that trespass was the 'fertile mother of all actions'.

progeny, ejectment — since 1875, simply the action for recovery of land.[8] The tortious basis of both is unlawful interference with possession of land. What is really being claimed in ejectment, however, is not interference with possession but superior title, only the proprietary basis of the suit has been obscured by a historical accident which continues to leave its mark on the present law.

Trespass, Private Property and Squatting

The modern conception of trespass as unlawful interference with possession of land, embodies exclusive private property right, in contrast to feudal common property which accorded inclusive rights "not to be excluded from" lands and revenues. In the typical English village community in the twelfth century, the free tenants had grazing rights in respect of the fallow field, the meadow and arable fields at certain times of the year, whilst on the wasteland, common rights (for example of pasture, turbary, or estovers of wood) benefited both copyholder and freeholder alike. The free tenant enjoyed *seisin* of both lands and the common rights appurtenant to them, protected in the Royal courts through the Assize of Novel Disseisin, whilst the copyholder was similarly protected (if with less certainty) in the Manorial court according to the custom of the Manor.[9] The thirteenth century saw the beginnings of a conflict between two fundamentally opposing conceptions of property right, one common/inclusive, based on *seisin* and protected by the old Assize, and the other private/exclusive, based on possession and protected through the new writ of Trespass. The displacement of common by private exclusive right helped facilitate the transition from a feudal community producing mainly for its own consumption to a capitalist society organised through exchange and profit, requiring the privatisation of productive resources and separation of labour from the land. The claim of Novel Disseisin would increasingly be met by a counter-claim in Trespass,[10] the mere

---

[8] After this reform in the Judicature Acts 1873 and 1875, the artificiality of the classification of Trespass as personalty was only partly addressed through the assimilation of real property and chattels real in the Law of Property Act 1925.

[9] See Sutherland D., *The Assize of Novel Disseisin* (1973). The copyholder did not enjoy *seisin* but was "seised by rod" to similar effect.

[10] The effectiveness of the Assize was also limited by the Statute of Merton (1236), which provided that the waste could be enclosed so long as "sufficient" common land was left for those entitled to it. See Sutherland, *op. cit.*, p. 50.

continued exercise of common rights constituting interference with the landlord's right to exclude. This struggle over the form of property right continued until the eighteenth century, of which period E.P. Thompson has written:

> "What was often at issue was not property, supported by law, against no property; it was alternative definitions of property rights: for the landowner, enclosure — for the cottager, common rights; for the forest officialdom, preserved grounds for the deer — for the foresters, the right to take turfs."[11]

The historical emergence of squatting was closely connected with these socio-economic and legal developments. In the fourteenth century, cottagers forced onto the unredeemed wastes between townships and parishes by shortage of land had been tolerated to some degree, so long as rights of access to common land remained an integral part of the feudal peasant economy. At this time it was widely held that if a person could build a dwelling on the common and light a fire in it between sunset and sunrise, then he/she could not lawfully be dispossessed; the belief in Radnor in Wales was that a settler was entitled to "as much as he could enclose in the night within the throw of an axe from the dwelling."[12] By the seventeenth century, however, such claims were being definitely discouraged: an Act was passed in the reign of Elizabeth I against "the erecting and maintaining of cottages", and the Act of Settlement of 1662 restricted the freedom of movement of poor non-freeholders who had been wandering the parishes in search of commons on which to build dwellings. In the struggles accompanying the enclosure movement it was the poor squatters who were most vulnerable and whose interests were least represented. According to Christopher Hill:

> "The Midlands uprising of 1607 was caused by Enclosure. Risings in Western England in the late 1620s and early 1630s turned in large part on Royal enclosure and rights of squatters in the forests."[13]

The Digger movement of the seventeenth century was the "culmination of a century of unauthorised encroachments on forests and wastes by squatters and commoners, pushed on by land shortage and pressure of population".[14] By the eighteenth

---

[11] *Whigs and Hunters* (1975) p. 261.
[12] Ward C., 'The Early Squatters', (1980) in Wates N. and Wolmar C., (eds.) *Squatting: the Real Story*.
[13] Quoted in Ward, *op. cit.*, p. 104.
[14] *ibid.*, p. 106.

century, the small farmer, the cottager and the squatter were all losing control of the conditions of their own subsistence. The small farmer might not be able to afford the legal, drainage and fencing charges that must be paid as a contribution to the cost of enclosure, and have to sell out to larger interests. The freehold cottager was similarly squeezed, since the allotment granted by the commissioners in compensation for the loss of common rights was scarcely adequate, whilst the leaseholder gained nothing at all if the value of lost rights was credited to the landlord. The squatter on the wasteland might be permitted to retain an "encroachment", but again essential rights of common were irrevocably lost in the process of reallocation. Squatters were increasingly easily removed from the land through economic compulsion, as well as by eviction with the full authority of the action of ejectment. The dispossession of smallholders and squatters through enclosure was supported by a new ideology of private property, and by the claim that the principle and practice of common right were morally injurious. The commissioners for Windsor forest reported in 1809: "Nothing more favours irregular and lawless habits of life among the inferior classes than the scattered and sequestered habitations of the forest."[15] Traditional use-rights that might have been exercised for hundreds of years, newly incompatible with capitalist requirements of a free and mobile labour force, were now roundly condemned, and squatting acquired fully its modern pejorative meaning of unjustified interference with others' exclusive rights.

In conclusion, the early history of trespass may be understood as a process of decriminalisation. The punitive sanction which originally attached to squatting trespass was formally abolished in 1694, and obsolete in legal practice long before that date. Until 1977, unless squatting involved conspiracy, criminal damage, or trespass on particular property such as railways or certain enclosed gardens in public places, or a particular crime was intended such as theft, the owner out of possession would have to rely solely on the action for recovery in the civil courts. The great achievement of the civil law of trespass, having played an important role in securing the separation of labour from the land, was to guarantee the exclusive ownership and control of this and other productive resources according to capitalist calculation, without the need for overt state involvement through the criminal law.

---

[15] Thompson, *op. cit.*, p. 239.

Post-War Squatting and Recriminalisation

If the immediate function of trespass law is to guarantee private property by protecting possession and enabling those with superior title to recover land from occupiers with lesser interests, the right to exclude embodied in the law of trespass also has an ideological role in legitimating relations of possession and separation under capitalism. The State has tended to become involved in the use of criminal law against trespassers, or has raised the question of the need for specific criminal trespass reforms, whenever these functions have been threatened — as they were by squatting, factory occupations, demonstrations and protests involving trespass in the 1970s.[16]

The Modern Squatting Phenomenon

Medieval squatting had constituted the very locus of conflict between common and private forms of property; what was at issue was the fundamental nature of property right, and the right to exclude triumphed over the right not to be excluded from lands and revenues, at the same moment as the squatter and the cottager were dispossessed of their land and use-rights. Today, by contrast, the law unambiguously upholds the values of private property, and there can be no question, in the squatting act, of a dispute as to the concept of property — even though squatters may explicitly reject dominant legal and social norms. The difference is manifest in the further distinction between traditional squatting as a condition of land occupation, enjoyed for perhaps many years before being subsequently disrupted by the claims of enclosers, and modern squatting as an active and deliberate act of occupation of what is clearly private or state property. If Medieval squatting contested emerging capitalist relations of production, then the modern phenomenon involves an explicit challenge only to the system of distribution of the scarce resource of housing.

---

[16] The implementation of rationalisation programmes during the 1970s recession met resistance through direct action involving trespass on various fronts. In compelling enterprises and landlords to seek redress through the courts, and in placing on the agenda the "problem of reform", squatting and factory occupations momentarily exposed the centrality of exclusive right within capitalist relations, as the last resort of these interests when their powers of economic control were threatened. See Vincent-Jones P., 'Theory and Method Reconsidered: a Marxist Analysis of Trespass Law' (1987) *Economy and Society* 75–119.

Despite some minor occurrences in 1918, squatting assumed significant proportions in its recognisably modern form only after the Second World War. In May 1945, a group calling itself the Vigilantes (the secret committee of ex-servicemen) formed in Brighton with the purpose of installing its members and other demobilised persons and their families in empty holiday homes. The object here, in contrast to Medieval squatting, was the occupation of empty buildings rather than vacant land. The movement spread to disued military encampments, and forced the Government to introduce powers for local authorities to requisition empty property in the private sector for immediate use by the homeless. Many of the service camps squatted in this period became legitimised as public housing stock, or were taken over by the social services to house homeless families, remaining in use until the end of the 1950s.[17]

Whilst it is possible that squatting continued on a small scale during the 1950s and early 1960s, it was not until 1968 that the second major post-war phase began.[18] The London Squatters Campaign, formed in reaction against the harsh conditions endured by homeless families in local authority emergency hostels, successfully squatted four families in empty council houses in Redbridge in 1969. An experiment with "licensing" homes to Lewisham Family Squatting Association was repeated in other boroughs, as councils became aware of the value of this strategy in addressing the problem of homelessness, and in 1970, the Family Squatting Advisory Service was formally established to expedite this process. By the end of 1973, FSAS estimated there were 25,000 licensed "squatters" in 16 London boroughs.[19] A wave of unlicensed occupations began in 1972, however, as the failure of the licensed groups to cope with increasing demand, now from single people as well as families, became apparent. Squatting was becoming a truly national phenomenon. By 1974, there were an estimated 7,000 unlicensed squatters in London, and over 4,000 elsewhere in Britain. Other novel developments during this period included an increasing number of squats in privately owned houses deliberately left empty by speculators; spectacular "propaganda" squats with a political message, such as the occupation of the long empty Centre Point in London; and the occupation of entire streets, such at St Agnes' Place in Kennington, which would otherwise have remained empty pend-

---

[17] Friend A., 'The Post-War Squatters' (1980) in Wates and Wolmar, *op. cit.*
[18] Bailey R., *The Squatters* (1973).
[19] Platt S., 'A Decade of Squatting' (1980) in Wates and Wolmar, *op. cit.*

ing ambitious redevelopment — the resulting communities with their strong local organisation and identity challenging the very conception of housing provision in small exclusive units. By mid-1975, there were 40–50,000 squatters in Britain, the majority concentrated in London, but including significant numbers in Bristol, Portsmouth, Brighton, Swansea, Cambridge, and Leicester.[20]

Available evidence suggests that there is approximately the same number of squatters in Britain today as there was in the 1970s, an estimated 31,000 living in London.[21] According to a recent survey of squatting in London, carried out by the Advisory Service for Squatters in 1991, 74 per cent. of squats were local authority owned, 16 per cent. were owned by housing associations, and less than 1 per cent. were owned by private individuals (the remaining owners being private commercial or government and other public bodies). The survey found that 32.2 per cent. of squatters had children under 16. A number were ex-tenants unable to pay new market rents introduced by the Housing Act 1988, others were ex-mortgagors (victims of repossession). Other squatters included those on low pay, women escaping domestic violence, people declared intentionally homeless by the housing authority, those moving from secure accommodation (owing to overcrowding, racial harassment or health hazards), and students unable to obtain other accommodation.[22]

Media representation

A feature of post-war squatting has been the generally antagonistic role of the media — the vehicle of the ideological defence of private property against the threat of interference. The fact of demobilisation had ensured a measure of public support for those occupying holiday homes and service camps. Detailed and factual newspaper reporting was often accompanied by sympathetic human interest stories and editorials congratulated the squatters in exposing government inefficiency in housing provision. With the occupation of privately owned blocks of flats in 1946, however, the tone began to change: the homeless were being "duped by communists", and *The Mail* and *Express* "gave front

[20] *ibid.*, p. 41.
[21] See Squatters Action For Secure Homes (SQUASH) (1992) *Squatting and Homelessness in the 1990s* p. 3 (London: SQUASH—draft response to Home Office consultation paper on squatting).
[22] *ibid.*, p. 4.

page coverage to unsubstantiated reports of householders afraid to go out shopping for fear of their houses being squatted, and of a rush to buy padlocks throughout suburbia".[23] The same ambivalence in media coverage is evident in the second post-war squatting phase. "Deserving" squatters gained some public sympathy and support: for example, the original Redbridge families, driven out of harshly disciplined hostels and harried by bailiffs without court orders, and the licensed family squatting associations which ensued. On the other hand, no holds were barred in condemnation of the "undeserving," such as the later single squatters, and the hippies who occupied the infamous 144 Piccadilly in 1969. If the early post-war families had been mainly "respectable" families, obvious victims of inadequate council housing provision, then the new wave of squatters at the beginning of the 1970s consisted of a larger proportion of the young, single and unconventional, for whom was reserved an unprecedented degree of unfavourable media reaction.

By 1975, squatting was being portrayed by a vigorous media campaign as a serious danger to society, through the mobilisation of five key representations, all of which were subsequently shown to be either false or substantially without foundation.[24]

First, squatters were an immediate threat to the residential security of ordinary men and women, likely to come home from holiday or shopping to find strangers in their houses. Just as this portrayal was central to the argument for extending the criminal law of trespass in the 1970s, so it has played a prominent role in the Government's case for further criminalisation since 1991. Secondly, squatters were queue-jumpers, taking over houses and flats meant for people on housing waiting lists, who as a consequence would now have to wait longer. Thirdly, squatters were freeloaders and scroungers, flouting society's work ethic and getting something for nothing in return. Fourthly, squatters were wanton destroyers, likely to add insult to injury by pointlessly wrecking homes. Finally, squatters were a threat to dominant social values, undermining respect for property, public order, hard work and just reward.

By portraying an imminent and pervasive threat to ordinary individuals in their own homes, this squatting mythology prepared the way for popular acceptance of the new criminal trespass offences contained in the Criminal Law Act 1977. The passage of the Bill into law, surrounded by intense media

[23] Friend, *op. cit.,* p. 116.
[24] Vincent-Jones, *op. cit.* (1986) pp. 350–353.

attention and public debate, served to celebrate and thereby strengthen the institution of private property in a period of considerable political, economic and industrial instability — this global effectivity being achieved through the centrality of exclusive right and the category of trespass within capitalist relations. The fact that squatting does not appear to have excited the same degree of media attention in 1994 suggests that, whatever the real reasons for its presence on the agenda, the issue is not playing the same ideological role today as in the 1970s.

State Reaction and Legal Reform: From Civil to Criminal Law

The first attempt to apply the criminal law to squatters occurred in 1946, when five communists who had organised the mass occupation of luxury London flats by 1,500 people were arrested and charged with conspiracy and incitement to trespass. The use of the conspiracy charge marked the beginning of a shift from civil to criminal law in the control of squatting. It had been assumed that, in accordance with the general principle that a conspiracy to commit a tort was not a criminal offence, an agreement to commit a civil trespass was not indictable. In *R. v. Bramley*,[25] however, the trial judge instructed the jury that they must convict the communist councillors on such a charge if they thought that the matter had:

> "transcended the sphere where the property owner had ordinary redress in the civil courts . . . and passed into that sphere where it had become a matter of **public concern** of citizens interested in the **maintenance of good order and security**."[26]

The reintroduction of a criminal element on the grounds of public order is reminiscent of the original requirement of *vi et armis* and *contra pacem regis* in the quasi-criminal action of trespass in the Medieval period. Here, however, the State appears to be concerned as much with an ideological (public) threat as with the literal preservation of public order. The case remained of dubious authority until *Kamara v. DPP*[27] in 1974, when the conviction of a group of students who had been charged with conspiracy to

[25] (1946) 11 J.C.L. 36.
[26] *ibid.*, at p. 41: (emphasis added).
[27] [1974] A.C. 104.

trespass on the premises of the Sierra Leone High Commission in London was upheld by the Court of Appeal, on the grounds that such trespass involved "invasion of the domain of the public".[28]

The second attempt at common law to reintroduce a criminal element into trespass in this period occurred in the use of the ancient laws of forcible entry and detainer against squatters. From the fourteenth century, the principal function of these laws had been to preserve the peace. The offences could be committed by "violently entering or keeping possession of lands or tenements with menaces, force and arms", and according to the statutory provisions actual breach of the peace was not necessary: "It is sufficient that there is any kind of violence . . . there must be either such force, or such a show of force, as is calculated to prevent any resistance."[29]

In *R. v. Robinson*[30] in 1971, four convictions under the 1429 Act were upheld by the Court of Appeal, even though no active resistance was offered to the police in the execution of a possession order on the grounds that the mere existence of barricades indicated an intention to use force to deter the true owner from resuming possession. However, the antiquated legal machinery was as much of a hindrance as a help to property owners and local authorities because of the legal protection it afforded squatters against forcible eviction without a court order. It followed from the central concern with public order, that the protection of private property interests was only incidental, so if a trespasser had obtained entry by peaceful means the owner could not enter by force without being liable to criminal prosecution. However, the clear purpose of discouraging public disorder was subverted in the infamous case of *McPhail v. Persons Unknown*[31] in 1973. Here, Lord Denning reasoned that, since possession had not been acquired by the trespassers, but remained with the owner, and since no offence could be committed by an owner entering property in his possession however forcefully, the statute did not apply and the remedy of violent self-help was therefore available to him. In the light of the confusion and controversy surrounding conspiracy to trespass and the laws of forcible entry and detainer, the Law Commission was instructed to consider in what circumstances entering and remaining on property should constitute a criminal offence.

---

[28] *ibid.*, p. 130.
[29] *Halsbury's Laws*, Vol. 10, p. 591.
[30] [1971] 1 Q.B. 156.
[31] [1973] 3 W.L.R. 71.

With regard to statutory reform, Cabinet minutes for 1946 show that a criminal trespass law was briefly considered by the Attlee Government, before the squatting threat receded as rapidly as it had appeared. With the revival of mass squatting and the media hysteria surrounding it in the 1970s, legislation was eventually enacted through the Criminal Law Act 1977. The Act abolished the laws of forcible entry and detainer, limited the scope of conspiracy to criminal acts, and created three new 'squatting' offences. Under section 6, an offence is committed by anyone using, or threatening, violence for securing entry to any premises, where there is someone on the premises opposed to their entry. The offence may be committed by a lawful owner as well as a trespasser, but does not apply to a displaced residential occupier (DRO), who was occupying the premises as a residence immediately prior to the trespass. The section takes the place of the laws of forcible entry, but implicitly reserves for the DRO (supposedly returning from holiday or a shopping expedition) the right of self-help in removing squatters. Under section 7, a trespasser having entered residential premises as such, commits an offence on failing to leave after being required to do so by either a DRO or a protected intending occupier (PIO) — an owner with a freehold or leasehold interest of at least 21 years who requires the premises for occupation as a residence, or a person authorised to occupy premises as a residence by a recognised housing authority. The main target of this section is the squatter supposedly preventing an owner setting up home, or queue-jumping by taking the place of an intending occupier of public or quasi-public housing. Section 10 created the offence of obstructing sheriffs or bailiffs executing process for possession, taking on the function of deterring the defence of squats against eviction previously inadequately performed by the laws of forcible detainer. Under all sections, a police constable in uniform has the power of arrest without warrant, and a person is liable on conviction to six months' imprisonment and/or a fine not exceeding level five on the standard scale.

The extent to which the new offences have been of direct benefit to private owners and public landlords is open to question. There was a spate of convictions under section 10 as soon as the Act came into force, after the mass eviction of large-scale squats in London, since which time the charge does not appear to have been much used. In 1989, 64 persons were charged, and 36 convicted, for using violence for securing entry under section 6,[32]

---

[32] Home Office (1991), *op. cit.*, para. 15.

but these incidents are likely to concern illegal eviction, and have
nothing to do with violence on the part of squatters. As to section
7, only one person was charged and convicted in 1989.[33] It is
unlikely that many of the estimated 50,000 squatters remaining in
Britain have ever intended or needed to displace a residential
occupier, although there is increasing evidence, as will be shown
below, that the powers given to local authorities under the PIO
provisions are being used and abused. The immediate inconvenience caused to property owners, private businesses and public
landlords was dealt with in legal reform, but out of public view
through changes in civil procedure.[34] The significance of the
criminalisation of trespass therefore lay, not so much in any
direct advantage conferred on owners or public landlords, as in
its general symbolic effect in sanctifying private property during a
period of sustained challenge to exclusive rights on industrial,
residential and public fronts. Beneath the appearance of a
universal increase in the security of all householders, the legislative process helped legitimate much more fundamental (and at
this time, contentious) capitalist relations of production, possession and separation.

Squatting, Homelessness, and Housing Policy

The process of criminalisation also served, in making scapegoats
out of squatters, to draw attention away from the problem of
homelessness and the failure of housing policy. One of the
legacies of the 1930s, as Britain entered the Second World War,
was an acute housing shortage, which was then exacerbated by
war-time conditions: many homes were lost through bombing and
evacuation, and the construction of new houses was cut radically
as building resources were concentrated on the war effort. The
problem was compounded at the end of the war by demobilisation, new households having formed at an unprecedented rate
due to a million war-time marriages,[35] and the expansion of public
housing became an integral part of the welfare commitment of
the newly elected Labour Government. Improvement could not
be immediate, however, and the post-war shortage provided the
context for the outbreaks of squatting that took place between
1945 and 1946.

[33] *ibid.*
[34] For the background to the fast route procedures see Vincent-Jones, *op. cit.*,
   (1986) pp. 346–349.
[35] Friend, *op. cit.*, p. 110.

The massive post-war house-building programme meant that the total number of private and council housing starts rose throughout the period, until in 1965, the number of homes exceeded the number of households. From the late 1960s, however, several factors began to cast doubt on the depth of the improvement in the housing situation: the annual number of new housing starts declined steadily following the peak in 1965; the rate of renovation and repair also declined, despite an ageing and deteriorating housing stock; and government spending on housing began to fall consistently, the Conservative administration of 1979 implementing a drastic cut of 49 per cent. in its first four years of office.[36] The housing problem was exacerbated in the early 1970s by the peculiar conditions of the property boom, which doubled the average price of new homes in three years and sent rents soaring at a time when demand was already greatly outstripping supply. Property companies speculated in luxury homes and office blocks or bought land merely as an investment with no intention of developing it; private landlords were encouraged to improve their properties with government grants which would enable them to charge higher rents to richer tenants; and local authorities were squeezed by the rising cost of land acquisition and shrinking budgets. Council houses remained empty for years because of lack of funds for redevelopment, entire neighbourhoods and communities were devastated either by accident or intention, and office blocks and second homes stood empty whilst thousands waited for council accommodation, became homeless or were driven to squatting.[37]

The post-war provision of council housing with rents determined by "pooled historic cost" had succeeded, to an extent, in satisfying working class needs, and enabled some measure of control over housing production.[38] The Labour party, however, increasingly abandoned the commitment to social provision and ownership that had previously distinguished its housing policy from that of the Conservatives: Antony Crosland's 1977 Green Paper sought to encourage "the trend towards owner-occupation which gives people the kind of home they want . . . reducing demands made on the public sector and helping with problems of mobility".[39] The Government was "not opposed to the sales of

---

[36] Wates and Wolmar, *op. cit.*, p. 225.
[37] Cowley J., *Housing for People or Profit* (1979).
[38] Ball M., 'British Housing Policy and the House Building Industry' (1978) *Capital and Class* 78–99.
[39] DOE *Housing Policy: a Consultative Document* (1977) p. 45, Cmnd. 6841.

council homes provided that they can be made without impairing the authority's ability to deal with pressing housing needs".[40] The 1980s saw a further deterioration through a raft of Tory legislation, involving privatisation of public housing through the "right to buy," change of landlord, and "large scale voluntary transfer" (LSVT) schemes. Owner occupation is now the dominant form of tenure, accounting in 1990 for 66 per cent. of total housing stock. The State sector has shrunk to around 23 per cent., with only about 8 per cent. remaining privately rented.[41]

With the retreat of the State, and the increased role of the market, the housing prospects of the poorer members of society have deteriorated: prices have risen exponentially, until very recently, because they are related to market values and the ever-increasing cost of new houses; high interest rates have had to be borne solely by individuals in mortgage repayments; and speculative house building for the upper end of the market has replaced the programmes of the post-war consensus planned according to social need. By 1990, the drawbacks of over-reliance on the market, and of the aggressive policy of encouraging home ownership through council house sales, at the expense of the declining public sector, had become apparent. An ageing housing stock was being allowed to further deteriorate as financially hard-pressed owners delayed essential repairs, and the number of unfit and substandard homes in Britain rose from 900,000 in 1986 to 1.3 million in 1991.[42] Many poorer owner-occupiers, already victims of the recession through unemployment, have been doubly unfortunate in losing their homes and being left with negative equity due to the collapse of the property market. By 1988, the number of homeless households, officially accepted for rehousing in England and Wales, had risen to an estimated 120,000.[43] In addition, an estimated 8,000 are sleeping rough (3,000 in London); 60,000 are in hostels (18,000 in London); 140,000 adults and children, comprising 60,000 homeless families, have been placed in bed and breakfast "hotels" and other temporary accommodation by local authorities; and 30,000 people are in short-life housing, more than half of them in London.[44]

The link between homelessness and squatting is evident in the passage of the Housing (Homeless Persons) Act in the same year

---

[40] *ibid.*, p. 49.
[41] DOE *Housing and Construction Statistics* (1990) Vol. 41, tables 2.22.
[42] *The Times*, February 15, 1993.
[43] SQUASH, *op. cit.*, p. 5.
[44] *ibid.*

as the Criminal Law Act 1977. It should be stressed that the housing shortage is only a necessary, and not a sufficient, condition either of homelessness or of squatting. Other factors may include unemployment, poverty, low incomes, rising expectations, relationship breakdown, the regional mismatching of supply and demand, and social changes in the institution of the family. In addition, some people may squat out of choice rather than necessity, either for economic or cultural reasons. Nevertheless, it appears incontrovertible that the supply of housing has been consistently inadequate to meet demand since the 1970s; that the vast majority of squatters trespass because appropriate housing is not available at a price they can afford; and that if they did not resort to this form of self-help they would otherwise be homeless. It is highly unlikely, given the unsatisfactory, insecure and temporary nature of most squatted accommodation, that many people voluntarily choose squatting as a housing option.

However, the inability of a legal system founded on private property, to allow the social problem of homelessness to compromise the owner's exclusive right, was illustrated in the 1971 case of *Southwark LBC v. Williams*.[45] One question before the Court of Appeal was whether necessity was a good defence to an action under Order 113 — forcing the plaintiffs back to an ordinary possession action on the grounds that the summary procedure should only be used where there was no arguable defence. Whilst recognising the existence of some 400 empty houses in Southwark and the obvious need of the two families involved, Lord Denning rejected the defence of necessity in a classic statement of the inviolability of private property:

> "If homelessness were once admitted as a defence to trespass, no-one's home would be safe. Necessity would open a door which no man could shut. It would not only be those in extreme need who would enter. There would be others who would imagine they were in need, or would invent a need, so as to gain entry. Each man would say his need was greater than the next man's. The plea would be an excuse for all sorts of wrong doing. So the courts must, for the sake of law and order, take a firm stand. They must refuse to permit the plea of necessity to the hungry and the homelessness, and trust that their need will be relieved by the charitable and the good."[46]

Further Criminalisation — 1994

The anti-trespass measures contained in the Criminal Justice and Public Order Act 1994 are the second extension of the criminal

---

[45] [1971] Ch. 734.
[46] [1971] Ch. 734 at p. 744.

law in this area since 1977. In the wake of public disturbances surrounding the so-called "hippy convoy" in the early 1980s, section 39 of the Public Order Act 1986 created a criminal offence of failing to leave land (excluding buildings) after having been directed to do so by a senior police officer, when 12 or more vehicles have been brought onto the land, or there has been damage to property, or threatening, abusive or insulting words or behaviour used against the occupier. Recent Conservative governments appear, therefore, to have been determined to deal with trespass through tougher criminal law on a variety of fronts. This section examines critically the reasoning behind the case for further criminalisation of squatting trespass, as contained in the Government's 1991 consultation paper.

The Government's Proposals: a Private Sector Problem?

The consultation paper argues that the civil law in respect of squatting is inadequate, resulting in expense and inconvenience for owners, and that there are serious deficiencies in the provisions of the Criminal Law Act 1977. There are two problems with section 6: the extent of the self-help remedy available to the displaced residential occupier (DRO) is uncertain; and violence is defined too widely for the DRO, who as a consequence "is prevented from breaking a pane of glass in his own front door to obtain entry . . . this makes squatters almost invulnerable and impairs rights to property".[47]

There are four shortcomings in section 7, which created the offence of failing to leave premises on being required to do so by a PIO or DRO. First, if entry is obtained lawfully, "say by walking into an open door or at the invitation of the owner or one of his household",[48] then no offence can be committed by remaining in defiance of the owner. Secondly, the section does not apply where the owner does not reside in the property, having vacated it with the intention of selling or letting it; although a buyer would immediately become a PIO, and be able to call on the police if the occupiers fail to leave, "if squatters move in, the property will be difficult to sell because they will exclude potential buyers, and may cause damage".[49] Thirdly, the

---

[47] *op. cit.*, para. 26.
[48] *ibid.*
[49] *ibid.*, para. 27.

protection afforded the PIO does not cover intended tenants of private, as opposed to public, landlords, and this omission is unjustifiable because "the government wants to encourage a thriving private rented sector".[50] Finally, the existing requirement that a PIO must have acquired a leasehold or freehold interest for money or money's worth is too narrow: "Why should the protection be denied . . . to a homeless family who have been fortunate enough to inherit a home?"[51] In addition, there is the problem that the Act is confined to residential premises, and so does not catch "shop-squatting" — in which unscrupulous traders move into empty high street properties, frequently steal electricity and sell shoddy goods, and enjoy weeks or months of trading before the commercial owners become aware of the trespass, or can bring civil proceedings.[52]

The Government rejects the solution of extending the criminal law to include unlawful occupation of any property, on the grounds that "this approach reflects an absolute respect for property rights which some might not find acceptable, and would fundamentally alter the present balance of the civil and criminal law".[53] Such a general criminal measure applies in Scotland under section 3 of the Trespass (Scotland) Act 1965.

The first option for reform seriously considered by the Government would extend protection, in certain cases, to the owner who was not living in a home at the time it was squatted. A new offence could be created "where a person who is on residential premises as a trespasser, having entered as such, is required by an authorised person to leave and wilfully fails to do so".[54] The second, and much broader, option would meet the threat posed by squatting on all residential property, including second homes, commercial lettings and tied cottages, which may not be covered by the existing law if temporarily empty. The offence would be triggered by failure to leave, after being formally required to do so. In addition, the Government suggests that section 6 could be amended, so that an "authorised person" would commit no offence in "using reasonable force on his own property in order to gain entry for the purposes of recovering personal property (which he has reasonable grounds to predict may be stolen or damaged)",[55] possibly with the safeguard of having to obtain a court order beforehand.

[50] *ibid.*, para. 48.
[51] *ibid.*
[52] *ibid.*, para. 32.
[53] *ibid.*, para. 63.
[54] *ibid.*, para. 42.
[55] *ibid.*, para. 55.

Rationales: Hardship and Homelessness in the Private Sector

Although the consultation paper is by no means clear in its reasoning, a careful reading reveals two alternative rationales for these proposals. The first centres on homelessness. The paper rejects as "spurious" the connection between squatting and homelessness, denying squatters any motivation other than self-ishness; "they are generally there by their own choice, moved on by no more than self gratification or an unreadiness to respect other people's rights".[56] The paper does however make clear that the Government is indeed concerned with homelessness — of the property owner dispossessed by the squatter — and suggests (in the first option considered above) that the scope of section 7 might be extended on the grounds that other, unidentified, persons are being made homeless by the inability of the recently resident owner, the beneficiary under a will, or the private landlord, to put property on the market for sale or rent.[57] Therefore, it is the threatened homelessness of the *potential occupier in the private sector* that justifies the extension of criminal law protection beyond the existing DRO and public sector PIO. On this analysis, squatters are a *cause* of homelessness, and the proposals make some sense as part of the Government's broader commitment to revitalising the private rented sector and to stimulating the housing market generally.

The second rationale concerns the "degree of hardship" suffered by the owner in having to resort to civil law, and would justify both the reform options discussed above.[58] On this criterion, the intervention of criminal law is clearly justified where the residential occupier is displaced; and just as clearly not justified where "the property has been left derelict and any ensuing trespass will cause little or no harm to the owners", or where "the owner is suffering something more akin to a business or investment loss."[59] The consultation paper acknowledges that "it is the middle range of cases that present difficulties,"[60] and that this would be a difficult statutory test for the criminal law. This rationale might allow greater criminal law protection of absolute private property rights than the first, because of the emphasis on

---

[56] *ibid.*, para. 62.
[57] *ibid.*, paras. 43–45.
[58] *ibid.*, paras. 36–38.
[59] *ibid.*, para. 37.
[60] *ibid.*

the owner's hardship (with its flexible definition), rather than the potential homelessness of the third party to whom he/she might rent or sell.

The proposals, and the reasoning behind them, are open to a number of criticisms. The fundamental problem is that the discussion is focused almost entirely on individuals in the private sector, whereas the vast majority of squatting is in the public or quasi-public sectors. The survey carried out by the Advisory Service for Squatters (discussed above) found that just 0.09 per cent. of squats were owned by private individuals. As Hackney Borough Council comments in its response to the paper: "Such evidence casts doubt on the significance of any changes to the criminal law in favour of the private sector, when the majority of squatters will remain unaffected and the proposals irrelevant to those landlords most affected by squatting — councils".[61]

Few of Britain's estimated 50,000 squatters would be affected by the first reform option, whilst the implications of the second, more general and far-reaching proposal, are not even considered in relation to the public sector. On this evidence, squatters cannot be responsible for the hardship to, or homelessness of, private individuals to any great extent. Moreover, the attempt to encourage the better use of empty housing by targeting squatters appears even less sensible when one notes that there are an estimated 768,000 empty homes in Britain, against a *total* estimated number of 17,000 squatted properties.[62] In the absence of proper consideration of the facts of housing tenure, it must be asked upon what evidence the Government bases its argument for the need for reform. Unfortunately, none of the claims — that "**many people** have argued that the law is inadequate"; "**much concern** has been expressed about the deficiencies of the 1977 Act"; "vulnerable parties **have experienced** considerable emotional and financial distress"; "**there is evidence** that squatting in recently vacated homes causes hardship"; "another **major concern** is the occupation excluding the owner but not making him homeless"; "there are **reported doubts** whether existing remedies give adequate redress"[63] — is substantiated, leaving the impression that there are no sources, and that the Government is in fact merely expressing rhetorically its own preconceived agenda. Many of the criticisms of existing law appear purely

[61] At para. 1.2.
[62] SQUASH, *op. cit.*, p. 3.
[63] Home Office, *op. cit.*, paras. 26, 26, 63, 44, 27, 1, respectively. All emphases added.

theoretical, having no demonstrable basis in reality. So potent is the notion of dispossession by strangers, and so strong the instinct for protection of one's home against intrusion, that the author's imagination seems to have run wild:

> "There are no valid arguments in defence of squatting. It represents the **seizure** of another's property without consent. It can cause **distress** to lawful **occupants** both by the deprivation itself and afterwards when the property is left in a **squalid** state. No matter how compelling the squatters' own circumstances are claimed to be by their apologists, it is wrong that **legitimate occupants should be deprived** of the use of their property".[64]

This portrayal recalls some of the classic representations of squatting in the 1970s, namely the violence of squatters, their destructiveness, and the threat of displacement of *existing occupiers*. The idea that private owners are rendered homeless by squatters (an inversion of the fact that people squat largely because they would otherwise be homeless, due to the failures of a system of private ownership) is without foundation, yet is presented here, as it was in the 1970s, at the centre of the argument for potentially far-reaching reforms. The paper's lack of substance and the poor quality of the Government's reasoning confirms the suspicion, aroused by the announcement of the Home Office review at the time of the 1992 general election campaign, that its impetus was party political, and had little to do with the need to address a real and immediate social problem.

Unfairness in Public Housing Allocation: a Case for Reform?

The question of whether a case can be made for further extending the criminal law of trespass, on a more balanced view and on different grounds, may now be addressed. A written parliamentary answer in 1992[65] stated that of the 216 responses to the consultation paper, the majority were from public bodies and local authorities. Overall, 62 per cent. favoured strengthening the law, 27 per cent. were opposed, and 11 per cent. came to no clear conclusion.

It is clear from the responses from around the country, particularly London where there are many squatters, that there is

---

[64] *ibid.*, para. 1.
[65] *HCD*, June 17, 1992 col. 522–525.

a perceived need for reform, stemming from the inadequacy of civil procedure. Under Orders 113 (RSC) and 24 (CCR), an originating summons (High Court) or application (County Court) may be issued, an affidavit prepared in support, and both documents served on either premises or named persons. In theory, a hearing may take place five days after the commencement of proceedings (even sooner in emergency cases) when an order for possession may be made, specifying a date for the issue of a warrant for possession without further leave of the court. In practice, most evictions by public landlords appear to take between three and five months,[66] although one firm in London claims to be able to evict trespassers in less than three weeks.[67] In addition, there is the problem of cost, estimated by one London borough to be around £800 for each eviction, including loss of rent to its housing revenue account. That this is not just a theoretical problem may be seen in the steady increase in use of the squatters' "fast route" eviction procedure; 9,698 actions were filed against trespassers under Order 24 in 1989; 707 applications were made under Order 113 in 1990.[68]

The only valid argument that emerges from the responses for further extending the criminal law appears to rest on the unfairness of squatting to those accepted by local authorities as homeless under Housing Act 1985 criteria and who are denied access to accommodation occupied by squatters with less deserving or unascertained cases.

Although local authorities may enlist the help of the police in evicting squatters where a prospective tenant has agreed to take on the premises and therefore become a PIO, such tenants may be reluctant to accept the offer of squatted accommodation, due to its frequently poor condition and the difficulty of making viewing arrangements. Hence, in theory, allocation of housing to those most in need is delayed whilst the civil court procedure is followed, and the additional cost is an extra burden on local authorities operating under increasingly stringent financial controls. In practice, however, the evidence suggests that these problems have not been insurmountable in those areas most directly affected. Hackney Council has used section 7 against squatters without recourse to court action, and interpreted the provision in 7(4) that a person may be a PIO of any premises "at

---

[66] Liberty *Response to the Home Office Consultation Paper on Squatting* (1992) p. 6.

[67] Advertisement by Carter Lemon in the *Estates Gazette,* November 30, 1991.

[68] Home Office, *op. cit.,* para. 17.

242 SQUATTING AND THE RECRIMINALISATION OF TRESPASS

any time if at that time" (. . . he has been authorised, etc.) to
allow a considerable period, in one reported case 18 months, to
elapse between the eviction and the PIO moving in. There have
also been cases, involving other authorities, of fictitious PIOs, in
which the identities of supposed prospective tenants have been
fabricated in order to evict squatters more quickly.[69] In another
well documented case, the same PIO was named in at least two
certificates in order to secure the eviction of different squatter
households under the Act.[70]

It may be argued that resort to such abuses and dubious
practices demonstrates a need for reform, and that local authorities should be able to call on the clear support of the criminal
law to facilitate fairer, speedier allocation of public housing in
those cases where possession is required, in order for properties
to be brought up to lettable standard and to allow inspection.
There are several reasons, however, why even a limited extension
of the criminal law should be viewed with caution. First, there
are objections both in principle and in practice. As the Government itself acknowledges, the criminal law needs to maintain
public confidence and respect, and not appear too sectarian. The
criminal courts are not well equipped, by tradition, expertise or
procedure, to resolve private disputes over occupation of property. Using the criminal law, with its "speedy resolution of
disputes . . . where arrests can be made on the spot and any
disputes over title dealt with later after repossession of the
property",[71] may appear superficially attractive, but any advantages have to be weighed against likely problems of public
disorder, difficulties in enforcement by the police, and injustice in
individual cases. The civil liberties organisation, Liberty, argues
that even the existing section 7 is extensively abused, in that it
encourages public landlords to threaten squatters with prosecution when proper grounds do not exist. Where arrests do occur
under the section, there are few prosecutions (only one in 1989)
because:

> "What the authority wants is to regain possession: if this can be done
> by asking occupiers to leave, and then having the occupiers arrested
> by the police if they refuse to do so (by the police forcing entry if
> necessary), then this object is achieved without the necessity of
> prosecution."[72]

[69] SQUASH, op. cit., p. 10.
[70] Liberty, op. cit., p. 9.
[71] Home Office, op. cit., para. 34.
[72] op. cit., p. 8.

Because there is no prosecution, there is no opportunity to establish whether the authority might have exceeded its powers, or the occupier might have had a defence under the section. In other words, section 7 frequently raises questions of rights to possession which need to be properly addressed in a civil court under civil procedure.

Secondly, leading on from these criticisms, it can be argued that more attention should be given to improving civil procedure. Even taking the Government's own narrow definition of economic costs as the key criterion for evaluating its proposals, the reform and wider publicity of civil remedies may ultimately be cheaper than the enforcement of new criminal provisions. Hackney Council suggests the creation of a Property Tribunal specialising in squatting cases, which would be able to deal with cases more quickly and at lower cost, and would be better equipped than the police or the criminal courts to resolve uncertainties over occupiers' legal status. Brent Council's response to the Home Office suggested that, in order to give the courts an incentive to resolve problems of administrative delay, a target time should be set for court officials to deal with squatters' proceedings; if the time were exceeded, the court should pay the local authority a financial penalty commensurate with the amount of lost revenue between the target and actual eviction dates. Yet, the underlying problem here is under-resourcing of the courts, which are consequently unable to provide the fast route legal process theoretically possible under Orders 24 and 113; the only real solution will require more adequate government funding.

In conclusion to the case for reform, it is evident that the consultation paper is a muddled document, and that the resulting proposals lack clarity of purpose and proper justification. With regard to the private sector, there is a certain logic in the argument that owners intending to let or rent should be able to gain vacant possession speedily for this purpose, where it can be shown that the property is not going to remain empty; but the effectiveness of any legal reform would be limited by the fact that there are so few squatters in the private sector, and moreover, the objective could be achieved through the improvement of civil procedure, without the need for further criminalisation with its attendant dangers.

As regards the public sector, an argument for further criminalisation could be made out (but is not in the consultation paper) on the grounds of the unfairness of squatting in delaying allocation of public housing according to accepted criteria. Whilst such a case might be supported by evidence of a need perceived by public landlords most directly affected by squatting, and legal reform would be likely to have some real effect, the benefits might be outweighed by problems of interpretation and implementation; and again, the fundamental weakness of the argument here is that it has not been demonstrated that the objective is not attainable, without the need for further extension of the criminal law, through reform of civil procedure.

If there is no justification for limited criminal reform, there is certainly no warrant for the creation of a general criminal offence of remaining on residential premises when asked to leave by the owner. Such a reform would be particularly open to abuse in the private sector, where it would support exactly that form of absolute private property right (not limited by considerations of hardship and homelessness) which the consultation paper considers not to merit criminal law intervention.

Finally, some concern should be expressed about the possible consequences of any significant decrease in the squatting population, especially in London, brought about through the tightening of eviction procedures, whether civil or criminal. Since approximately one-third of squatters' households contain children, and there are likely to be other households with members vulnerable for other reasons, an increase in evictions is likely to result in an increase in homeless households with statutory priority. Local authorities may therefore incur additional costs for temporary accommodation, unless it is argued that the evicted squatters are 'intentionally homeless' under the Housing Act 1985 section 60, or have no local connection under section 61 (in which case the extra burden will simply be transferred to another authority). Even if the evicted squatters do not qualify for the full Housing Act right to be rehoused, they will still be unofficially homeless and hence contribute to a growing social problem.

The absurd prospect of ex-squatters having to be rehoused by local authorities, in the same or similar property to that from which they were evicted, raises the question of whether reduction of the squatting population through eviction is a sensible policy. There is an established tradition, dating back to the early post-war period, of harnessing the constructive energies of squatters through licensing arrangements, giving a degree of security in properties that would otherwise be unsuitable for letting, and thereby easing local housing shortages. This is the closest equivalent of North American "sweat equity" schemes, in which the time and skills of otherwise homeless people are used to bring semi-derelict buildings up to habitable standard, in return for a secure low-rent (or rent-free) tenancy and grants for materials.[73]

---

[73] SQUASH, *op. cit.*, p. 23.

Introducing such schemes in Britain could be part of a solution to the housing problem, and would have the advantage of appealing to notions of individual responsibility, self-help and citizen empowerment that appear to be forming the political consensus of the 1990s. If it is decided that properties have to remain empty, either temporarily or permanently, then legal complications could be avoided altogether through the taking of preventive measures such as the fitting of proper security screens.

Conclusion

Whilst early squatting was a product of the scarcity of land accompanying the development of private property in the transition from feudalism to capitalism, squatting on the scale seen in Britain since the 1970s has its roots in the failure of post-war housing policy and in the problem of homelessness. Having gradually assumed a civil form in the Medieval period, the law of trespass has come full circle, regaining a criminal dimension in connection with squatting in the late twentieth century.

The explanation of why legislative reform of the criminal law relating to squatting has been placed on the agenda on so many occasions since 1945 lies in three factors: the pressures applied by powerful interest groups and public authorities, inconvenienced by the delay, uncertainty and expense of civil procedure; the political needs of the Government of the day both to satisfy these interests, and to support its programme of policies in related areas; and the ideological need of the capitalist system as a whole, when threatened, symbolically to reinforce the institution of private property. The recent debate on the need for further criminalisation of squatting trespass has taken place in a very different social context to that obtaining in the 1970s.

The Criminal Law Act 1977 was passed in a period of considerable economic and political instability. At this time, capitalism was still vigorously contested by a socialist vision commanding widespread popular support, and existing relations of possession and separation were under challenge both at work and in the home, from factory occupations, student sit-ins, mass squatting, and public protests and demonstrations. In this setting, the further criminalisation of trespass helped guarantee the management and distribution of social resources according to capitalist criteria, and served as an ideological defence of the institution of private property. Media representation of squatting played a crucial role in this process, justifying criminal law reform by reference to the threatened security of ordinary people in their own homes. The commitment to private property and to exclusive right was the basis on which the struggle for hegemony would be won by the New Right in the 1980s, providing the foundation of Thatcherism with its promise of "every man a man of property" (*sic*) in the (private) property owning democracy.

The anti-squatting measures contained in the 1994 Act, however, may be seen against a very different background. The battles of the 1970s have been won by the right; the power of the unions has been significantly eroded, and socialism appears no longer a credible political and economic alternative to capitalism. Successive Conservative governments have ensured the ascendancy of private property at the expense of state property and associated "new property" rights.[74] The fact that the major ideological struggle of the post-war period is over may help explain why the debate over the further criminalisation of squatting is now attracting so little media attention. Having secured the institution of private property in the 1970s and 1980s, the radical Conservative reformers are now addressing the problem of how to release resources to their most efficient uses in an increasing variety of markets, created by privatisation and the dismantling of the old public sector bureaucracies. The consultation paper may be understood in this light, as an attempt to revitalise the flagging housing market through proposals that could theoretically increase the supply of homes for sale or rent. Yet the fact that the proposals have not been properly thought through is evident in the misidentification of private, rather than public, sector squatting as the key problem, and in the failure to recognise distributional unfairness as the only reasonable ground on which an argument (albeit tenuous) might be made for further criminalisation.

In making plain that it is "not concerned with spurious arguments claiming to justify squatting,"[75] the consultation paper implies that there are only two alternatives, condemnation or justification. As has been demonstrated, however, it is not a question of being simply for or against squatting. The squatting phenomenon, properly understood in the light of its historical origins in relation to the development of the law of trespass, must be seen in its economic and social context. Hackney, one of London's most pressed housing authorities, with long experience

---

[74] Reich C., 'The New Property' (1964) Yale L.J. 733–787. Reich's perspective informs the leading modern textbook on land law — see Gray K., *Elements of Land Law* (1993).
[75] Home Office, *op. cit.*, para. 5.

of dealing with homelessness and squatting, made the obvious point in its response to the consultation paper:

"Squatting on this large scale is partly a symptom of the serious shortage of affordable housing. . . . A restoration of investment in rented housing is urgently needed to tackle the fundamental cause of squatting and progress towards a society in which people do not need to squat and where decent, affordable housing is a basic right rather than a privilege".

The main question for the immediate future is whether government policies based on free enterprise and market forces, and committed to the reduction of direct public provision, can succeed in tackling the fundamental problem of the housing shortage. If not, then problems of homelessness and squatting may be expected to continue into this decade and beyond, regardless of reforms in the civil and criminal law of trespass.

INDEX

Aberfan disaster, 112 *et seq.*
Agency
  discourse, concept of, 9–16
  practice, concept of, 9–16
  private, powers of, 21
  regulatory, powers of, 21
Anti-Conscientious Objector League
  emergence in Blackpool, 78
Anton Piller order
  development of, 145
  use of, 129
Auditors
  fraud, responsibilities relating to,
    88
Australia
  dingo baby case, 115–116
  War Crimes Acts, 36–37

Bank of England
  SFO, allegations of fraud reported
    to, 91*n*
Barlow Clowes, 85
Berne Union, 127
Bradford stadium disaster, 114
British Standards Institution
  safety standards of, 155
Buffalo Creek dam disaster, 117
Butler-Sloss Inquiry, 189

Canada
  Deschenes Commission, 37, 44–45
  procedural fairness, 44–46
  war crimes, position on, 37–38
Case-work
  SFO approach to, 100–101
Caution
  non-serious offence resulting in, 20
Channel Islands
  War Crimes Act 1991, application
    of, 29
Civil Service
  objectors, treatment of, 70–71
Civil remedies
  potency of, 146
Clapham rail crash, 114, 115
Cleveland crisis, 187–191

Codes of practice
  consumer protection, 155–156
  trading standards regulation,
    169–170
Common law copyright
  abolition, 133
Compensation
  intellectual property, relating to,
    142–143
Computer fraud, 87*n*
Confidential information
  non-proprietary interest, 132–134
Confiscation order
  court's power to make, 92*n*
Conscientious objection
  anti-objector sentiments, 66
  belief, criminalisation of, 74–75
  cowardice, death sentence for, 68
  desertion, death sentence for, 68
  discrimination against objectors,
    70–71, 78–79
  First World War, 57–71
  generally, 57, 79–81
  informal criminalisation, 69–71
  non-compliance, consequences of,
    67–69, 75–79
  ordinary criminals, objectors
    classified as, 68–69
  political grounds, based on, 62
  religious grounds, based on, 62
  Second World War, 71–79
  state reaction to, 57–81
  substantive law, 60–61
  tribunals, application to, 61–65
Conscription
  conscientious objection. *See*
    Conscientious objection
  female population, of, 73–74
  First World War, 57–71
  Second World War, 71–79
  voluntary enlistment, principle of,
    58–59
Consent
  democratic legitimation through, 25
Consultation
  democratic legitimation through, 25

249

Consumer protection
  code of practice, 155–156
Copyright
  common law, abolition of, 133
  criminal damage of work, 134–136
  statutory criminalisation, 137–138
  theft of work, 134–136
Corporate manslaughter
  Aberfan, 112 *et seq.*
  blaming corporation, 111–118
  Bradford stadium disaster, 114
  Clapham rail crash, 114, 115
  generally, 109–111, 124–125
  Hillsborough disaster, 115
  Kings Cross disaster, 112 *et seq.*
  Marchioness riverboat collision, 112
    et seq.
  meaning, 109
  mechanisms of blame,
    generally, 118
    procedure, 118–121
    recklessness, 121–124
    risk perceptions, 121–124
  Piper Alpha disaster, 114
  Purley rail crash, 115
  Zeebrugge ferry disaster, 109 *et
    seq.*
Counterfeiting
  estimates of losses to, 128
  films, of, 134–135
  meaning, 128n
Court
  confiscation order, power to make,
    92n
  SFO in, 96–98
Cowardice
  death sentence for offence of, 68
Crime
  ambiguity in idea of, 4
  critical scrutiny of references to, 2
  idea of, 1–2
  unitary category, as, 16–21
Criminal damage
  copyright work, of, 134–136
Criminal law
  approach to, 1
  critical scrutiny of references to, 2
  role of, 4
  unitary category, as, 16–21
  weaknesses in treatment of, 2
Criminal Law Revision Committee
    (CLRC)
  sexual offences, review of, 189–190

Criminalisation
  critical scrutiny of references to, 2
  openness, relating to, 21–24
  reconstruction of criminalising
    practices, 26
  resistance, relating to, 21–24
  symbolic aspects of policy, 14–15
  unitary category, as, 16–21
Criminality
  critical scrutiny of references to, 2
  formal, 6
  management of boundaries of, 4–9
  practical, 6
  unitary category, as, 16–21
Cross examination
  live television link, evidence
    obtained by, 43
Crown court
  trial by jury in, 20
Crown Prosecution Service (CPS)
  Code for Crown Prosecutors, 102
  SFO as Crown Prosecutor, 102
Customs and Excise
  fraud investigators, 90n

Decision to prosecute
  SFO, powers of, 101–106
Decriminalisation
  symbolic aspects of policy, 14–15
Delay
  War Crimes Act 1991, effect on,
    39–42
Deschenes Commission
  recommendations, 37, 44–45
Desertion
  death sentence for offence of, 68
Deviance
  sociology of, 1–2
Director of Public Prosecutions (DPP)
  Fraud Investigation Group,
    responsilibty for, 90
  South Coast Shipping, prosecution
    of, 119, 120
Discourse
  concept of, 9–16
  ideologies, relationship with, 10–11
  practice, relationship with, 11
Discrimination
  conscientious objectors, against,
    70–71, 78–79
Dishonesty
  theft case, standard obtaining in,
    89n